Living in Christ

W9-ACE-459

The Church

Christ in the World Today

Second Edition

Martin C. Albl
with Christine Schmertz Navarro
and Joanna Dailey

Saint Mary's Press®

The Subcommittee on the Catechism, United States Conference of Catholic Bishops, has found that this catechetical high school text, copyright 2016, is in conformity with the *Catechism of the Catholic Church* and that it fulfills the requirements of Core Course IV of the *Doctrinal Elements of a Curriculum Framework for the Development of Catechetical Materials for Young People of High School Age.*

Nihil Obstat: Rev. Fr. Timothy J. Hall, STL
               Censor Librorum
               September 30, 2014

Imprimatur: †Most Rev. John M. Quinn, DD
             Bishop of Winona
             September 30, 2014

The nihil obstat and imprimatur are official declarations that a book or pamphlet is free of doctrinal or moral error. No implication is contained therein that those who have granted the nihil obstat or imprimatur agree with the contents, opinions, or statements expressed, nor do they assume any legal responsibility associated with publication.

Printed in the United States of America

1164 (PO6509)

ISBN 978-1-59982-435-2

Contents

Unit 2 ◆ The Church Is One, Holy, Catholic, and Apostolic

Unit 3 ◆ Leadership and Ministry within the Church

Unit 4 ◆ The Church's Mystery and Mission

Unit 5 ◆ The Church and Young People

Introduction

You are about to begin your study of the Church. In many ways, studying this subject will be similar to studying any other subject: you will learn new vocabulary, become familiar with some famous people in the Church, and be introduced to some new concepts and ways of thinking.

But in other ways, this study will be unique, because the subject matter is unique. The Church is unlike any other reality on earth, because she is both within history and beyond it. She is both human and divine. In the Church, we meet God.

This study will engage not only your brain but also your heart and your spirit: in other words, your whole self. You will be challenged mentally to understand teachings about the nature of the Church and to gain a sense of how she has been present in the world throughout history. You also will be challenged to pray more deeply with the Church and to become a more committed and active member of the Church. After all, you are a holistic person, made up of body, mind, and spirit. This study will help you to broaden and deepen all aspects of yourself.

In writing this book, the editors and I have expanded our knowledge about the Church, thought in new ways about the Church, and grown in our own commitment to, and love for, her. I invite you to share in that experience.

Sincerely,
Martin C. Albl

Unit 1

The Church: Christ's Continued Presence and Work in the World

When you hear the word *Church*, what comes to mind? Perhaps you think of a building where Christians worship, or maybe you picture the assembly of people gathered for worship. You may have learned that the Church is sometimes referred to as the Body of Christ or the Bride of Christ. All these associations are correct.

In this course, you will learn about the Church as the continuation of Christ's presence and work in the world. The Father always planned the Church, and his Son, Jesus Christ, instituted the Church through his teachings, sacrificial death, and Resurrection. Christ and his Church are forever united as one. Christ is the Head and we are the members of the one Body of Christ, the Church.

After Jesus' mission was accomplished on earth, the Holy Spirit was poured out on the Church at Pentecost to help the Apostles understand what Christ had taught them. Empowered and guided by the Holy Spirit, Peter, Paul, and the other Apostles embarked on the universal mission of the Church by working to spread the Gospel throughout the Mediterranean world. The early Christians suffered persecution and even martyrdom as a result of their faith, but Christ's love and the Holy Spirit helped them to persevere in sharing and celebrating the truth of Christ. The Holy Spirit gives each of us special gifts, called charisms, that empower us to help build up the Church in every time and place.

The enduring understandings and essential questions
represent core concepts and questions that are explored
throughout this unit. By studying the content of each
chapter, you will gain a more complete understanding
of the following:

Enduring Understandings
1. God calls all people to live in a special relationship
   with him through the Church established by Jesus
   Christ.
2. The Holy Spirit is the principal agent of the Church's
   mission.
3. The Apostles and early disciples began to spread the
   Good News throughout the world.

Essential Questions
1. Why did Jesus Christ establish the Church?
2. What is the mission of the Holy Spirit in the Church
   today?
3. How can we help build the Church?

Chapter

1

The Origin of the Church

Introduction

Where did the Church come from? Who founded it? As we begin our study of the Church, it makes sense to start by considering these basic questions. The Church was always part of the Father's plan. It was instituted by his Son, Jesus Christ, and is given life by the Holy Spirit.

The word *Church* refers to the assembly of people whom God calls together to be in a special relationship with him. The Church was part of God's saving plan from all eternity. It is both the means of our salvation and the goal of God's plan. All people who are saved will be gathered into the perfected Church at the end of time.

God formed a special relationship with Israel, his Chosen People. That relationship foreshadowed his subsequent relationship with the Church. God's covenants with Israel prepared the way for the New Covenant established through Jesus' death and Resurrection.

Jesus' gift of the Eucharist and his saving death on the cross gave birth to the Church. Jesus inaugurated the Church by preaching about the Kingdom of God, healing people in mind and body, and calling people to be part of his family. Jesus also established a structure for the Church, based on the leadership of the Apostles, especially Peter. This structure will last until the Kingdom is fulfilled.

Article 1: The Meaning of Church

Let's begin by clarifying the meaning of the word *church*. In everyday English, we use the word *church* to refer to different realities, such as a building ("the big church downtown"), a parish ("I'm a member of Saint Mary's Church"), a Christian ecclesial community ("the Lutheran Church"), and the Catholic Church. To understand how these meanings of *church* are related, it is helpful to see how the earliest Christians understood and used this word.

The books of the New Testament were originally written in Greek. In these books, the Greek word *ekklesia* corresponds to the English word *church*. *Ekklesia* is related to the Greek verb *ek-ka-lein*, which means "to call out." Thus it refers to the convocation or assembly of people whom God calls together to be in a special relationship with him. The Greek texts of the Old Testament also use the word *ekklesia* to refer to the people of Israel, an assembly chosen by God. The first Christians purposely applied the term *ekklesia* to themselves to show that they were heirs of the assembly of Israel.

In the **Church**, God calls people together from all over the earth. The word *Church* has three meanings for Catholics, all of which involve God's call:

- the entire community of God's People around the world
- the local community, which is known as a **diocese** or an archdiocese, such as the Diocese of Winona or the Archdiocese of Chicago
- the community assembled for **liturgy**, especially the Mass—for example, the people who gather at a parish at 10:00 a.m. on Sunday to celebrate the Eucharist

We cannot separate these meanings from one another. The Church is all the people God gathers in the world, but she exists concretely in local communities and is made real in the assembly that gathers for liturgy, especially to celebrate the Eucharist. As the *Catechism of the*

Church
The term *Church* has three inseparable meanings: (1) the entire People of God throughout the world; (2) the diocese, which is also known as the local Church; (3) the assembly of believers gathered for the celebration of the liturgy, especially the Eucharist. In the Nicene Creed, the Church is recognized as One, Holy, Catholic, and Apostolic—traits that together are referred to as "Marks of the Church."

diocese
Also known as a "particular" or "local" Church, the regional community of believers, who commonly gather in parishes, under the leadership of a bishop. At times, a diocese is determined not on the basis of geography but on the basis of language or rite.

liturgy
The Church's official, public, communal prayer. It is God's work, in which the People of God participate. The Church's most important liturgy is the Eucharist, or the Mass.

Catholic Church (CCC) explains, "She draws her life from the word and the Body of Christ and so herself becomes Christ's Body" (752).

© Paolo Bona / Shutterstock.com

The hierarchy of bishops and cardinals come from a wide range of nationalities, ethnicities, and backgrounds, reflecting the diversity of the Church.

Live It!
Living the Three Meanings of *Church*

You have many opportunities to live out each of the three meanings of the word *Church*:

1. Develop a better sense of the universal nature of the Church. You might learn about Catholic customs in other countries or pray for Catholics in other nations, especially those suffering persecution. You might also have an opportunity to attend World Youth Day.

2. Get involved with your local diocese. Attend diocesan events for teens. If your diocese has a youth board, consider serving as a member.

3. Participate fully in the liturgies at your parish and school. Look for opportunities to serve in particular liturgical ministries, such as singing in the choir or lectoring.

The Father Planned the Church from the Beginning

Calling together human beings is central to the Father's plan of salvation, because he wishes to gather us as his own people in order to save us. Jesus Christ, the only Son of God, who is himself fully God, established the Church when he proclaimed and ushered in the **Kingdom of God**.

Even before the Church was instituted, the Father's eternal plan to call together a holy people had long been taking shape in history. We can see the clearest preparation for the Church in the Father's call to the people of Israel to enter into a covenant relationship with him. God desires that the whole human race, rather than simply one people, may come together as one Church. From all eternity, God planned to form a Church as a way to fulfill that plan.

> **If everyone were to come together as one Church, how might the world be different?**

Article 2: Old Testament Images of the Church

Have you ever wondered why more than half of the Bible is composed of books that were written before the time of Christ? The reason is that the Old Testament has enormous value. Together with the New Testament, it hands on God's Revelation and makes known to us his plan of salvation from the beginning of time. The Old Testament records the history of salvation from Creation through God's covenant with the Israelites.

In describing his Church, Jesus often drew on Old Testament images. For example, the Psalms depict Israel as God's flock of sheep (see 77:21). Jesus likewise referred to his followers as his "little flock" (Luke 12:32). Isaiah also compared Israel to a vineyard (see chapter 5). Accordingly, Jesus called himself the vine and his disciples the branches (see John 15:5).

© Saint Mary's Press / Used with permission of St. Mary's Catholic Church

How does celebrating the Eucharist in our local parish reflect the three meanings of the word *Church*?

Kingdom of God
The culmination or goal of God's plan of salvation, the Kingdom of God is announced by the Gospel and present in Jesus Christ. The Kingdom is the reign or rule of God over the hearts of people and, as a consequence of that, the development of a new social order based on unconditional love. The fullness of God's Kingdom will not be realized until the end of time. Also called the Reign of God or the Kingdom of Heaven.

Fathers of the Church (Church Fathers)
During the early centuries of the Church, those teachers whose writings extended the Tradition of the Apostles and who continue to be important for the Church's teachings.

foreshadow
To represent or prefigure a person before his or her life or an event before it occurs.

Following Christ's example, the early Christians often compared the Church to Israel's Temple. They called themselves "living stones" who form a "spiritual house" (1 Peter 2:5). They described their community as "the temple of God" (1 Corinthians 3:16, 2 Corinthians 6:16) with Christ as the cornerstone (see 1 Peter 2:7, Matthew 21:42).

Another Old Testament image was dear to the **Church Fathers**: the prefiguring of the Church in Noah's ark. Many Fathers of the Church pointed out that the ark saved humankind from the waters of the Flood, whereas the Church saves all of humanity from sin.

God's Covenants with Israel

As these images from the Old Testament begin to show, the community of Israel **foreshadowed** the Church. Just as God chooses to save us as part of the Church, so too did he call Israel as a nation to be his Chosen People as part of his larger plan of salvation.

Pray It!

Praying the Psalms

Jews and Christians continue to share the custom of praying the Psalms. Pray the following passage from Psalm 139, especially at times when you may struggle with your self-worth:

You formed my inmost being;
    you knit me in my mother's womb.
I praise you, because I am wonderfully made;
    wonderful are your works!
    My very self you know.
My bones are not hidden from you,
When I was being made in secret,
    Fashioned in the depths of the earth.
Your eyes saw me unformed;
    in your book all are written down;
    my days were shaped, before one came to be.

(Verses 13–16)

God called Abraham to leave his own country, promising that Abraham would father a great nation, Israel (see Genesis 12:2). Later God made a covenant with Abraham, promising him land for himself and his descendants (see chapter 15). Still later God entered into a covenant with his people through Moses at Mount Sinai. As the people's part of the Sinai Covenant,

© Scala / Art Resource, NY

God gave Israel his Law, summarized in the Ten Commandments. Through these covenants God established a special relationship with Israel as his Holy People.

When the Israelites turned away from God, Moses interceded with God on their behalf. How does this foreshadow Jesus' role as our Savior?

Universal Implications of God's Call to Israel

God's special relationship with Israel was not just about Israel—it had a deeper meaning for the rest of the world as well. The prophets of Israel proclaimed a future when all nations would gather together with Israel in true worship (see Isaiah 2:2–5, Micah 4:1–4). The gathering of the people of Israel foreshadowed the future gathering of all nations into one People of God.

The Israelites, however, were not always faithful to their covenant with God. For example, many Israelites frequently strayed from the one true God to worship false gods. Through the prophets of Israel, God continually called the Israelites to return to their covenant with him. The prophet Jeremiah even spoke of God's plan for a New Covenant between God and his people (see Jeremiah 31:31–34).

The perfect fulfillment of the Sinai Covenant, the Law, is the Son of God, Jesus Christ. As a Jew he was born under the Law of Sinai. But by taking the people's sins upon himself through his self-sacrifice on the cross, he transformed the Law engraved on stone and engraved it upon his own heart. He became the "covenant for the people" (Isaiah 42:6), God's Servant who brings justice. In fulfilling the Law of Sinai, however, Jesus did not abolish it. Instead he revealed its true meaning. Jesus thus initiated the New Covenant at the Last Supper: "This cup is the new covenant in my blood, which will be shed for you" (Luke 22:20).

What are some examples of "false gods" that people worship today?

Article 3: Christ Instituted the Church

When you think of people instituting an organization or corporation, you may think of a ceremony in which men and women dressed in business suits and hard hats use shovels to break ground on a new structure. Jesus did not institute the Church in this way. Let's look more closely at how Jesus did institute the Church.

Primary Sources

Vatican II Teaching on the Church's Relation to the Jewish People

In its *Declaration on the Relation of the Church to Non-Christian Religions (Nostra Aetate, 1965)*, Vatican Council II affirmed that God loves the Jewish people and decries all oppression of Jews. Many Jews have suffered unjust treatment because the sins of the Jews involved in Jesus' death were wrongly extended to include all Jewish people, even those in different times and places.

Nevertheless, God holds the Jews most dear for the sake of their Fathers; He does not repent of the gifts He makes or of the calls He issues—such is the witness of the Apostle. . . . Although the Church is the new people of God, the Jews should not be presented as rejected or accursed by God, as if this followed from the Holy Scriptures. (4)

Jesus Preached the Kingdom of God

At the time appointed by God, Jesus Christ, the Eternal Word of the Father, became man and lived among us on earth. He took on human nature without losing his divine nature. The mystery of the union of the divine and human natures in one Divine Person is called the **Incarnation**.

During his earthly ministry, Jesus inaugurated the Church through his preaching: "This is the time of fulfillment. The kingdom of God is at hand" (Mark 1:15; see also CCC, 763). Jesus drew on the hope announced by Isaiah and the other Old Testament prophets, who looked forward to a coming age when God's will would be done on earth: "Then the eyes of the blind shall see, / and the ears of the deaf be opened" (Isaiah 35:5).

Jesus' message was intended for all people. Yet in a special way, Jesus directed his message to the poor and proclaimed that all nations will be judged on how well they take care of people who are hungry and thirsty (see Matthew 25:31–46). Jesus also directed his message toward sinners, calling them to repentance and assuring them of the Father's great mercy. Jesus' message often took the form of parables, which challenged listeners to make the radical choice to truly follow him.

Jesus' listeners learned about the Kingdom from his actions as well as from his words. His miracles, including his healing of the sick, were signs that the Kingdom had already begun on earth.

Incarnation
From the Latin, meaning "to become flesh," referring to the mystery of Jesus Christ, the Divine Son of God, becoming man. In the Incarnation, Jesus Christ became truly man while remaining truly God.

During his earthly ministry, Jesus preached the Kingdom of God. How does the Gospel message continue to be taught today?

Jesus Sent Disciples

To help Jesus establish the Kingdom of God, the Father gathered people to become his first followers. Jesus sent out these disciples to preach the Kingdom and to make disciples of the nations, calling all people to join Christ's Church. This group of followers, his disciples,

grace
The free and undeserved gift that God gives us to empower us to respond to his call and to live as his adopted sons and daughters. Grace restores our loving communion with the Holy Trinity, lost through sin.

bishop
One who has received the fullness of the Sacrament of Holy Orders and is a successor to the Apostles.

became the Church—Jesus' true family, and the seeds of the Kingdom on earth. The Church is thus a sign, as well as the actual beginning, of that perfect peace and happiness that all of us desire: the Reign of God mysteriously present in the world.

Jesus Gave Himself Fully for the Church

Jesus established the Church primarily through the saving gift of himself, which was fulfilled on the cross. He anticipated this gift when he instituted the Eucharist. At the Last Supper, when he said, "This is my body" (Luke 22:19), he expressed his complete self-giving in handing over his life for the sake of humanity. By participating in the Eucharist today, in a mystical way we share in Christ's sacrifice and also in the **grace** that his sacrifice gives the Church. The Sacrament of the Eucharist also deepens the unity of the People of God and enables us to share in the divine life.

Jesus Created the Structure of the Church

Have you ever wondered why the Church is governed by the Pope and **bishops**? Jesus set up this structure himself. He appointed the Twelve Apostles as the leaders of the

Did You Know?

Whom Does Jesus Call?

© Erich Lessing / Art Resource, NY

When Jesus gathered followers to help him proclaim and establish the Kingdom, he did not call the most talented and powerful. Rather, he chose ordinary fishermen (see Mark 1:16–20) and even a tax collector (see 2:13–17)—a person despised by most Israelites. Jesus' choices are consistent with Saint Paul's reminder that "God chose the weak of the world to shame the strong" (1 Corinthians 1:27). God's call comes to everyone, even (or perhaps especially) to those who think they may not be worthy.

community gathered around him (see Mark 3:14–19), and he gave Peter a special role as the head of the Church (see Matthew 16:18–19, Luke 22:31).

To build the Church and to proclaim the faith, Christ sent out his Apostles into the world and gave them a share in his own mission. To them, and to those who have succeeded them, he granted the power and authority to act in his place. The bishops are the Apostles' successors, and the Pope, the Bishop of Rome, is the successor of Peter. In their authoritative roles as leaders, together the Pope and bishops form the hierarchy of the Church. The structure and hierarchy of the Church

Faith in Action
Saint Stephen: The First Martyr

© Zvonimir Atletic / Shutterstock.com

Good King Wenceslas looked out
On the feast of Stephen,
When the snow lay round about,
Deep and crisp and even.

This familiar Christmas carol refers to the feast of the first martyr of the Church, Saint Stephen the Deacon. Because he was the first to lose his life for Christ, he was given the feast day of December 26, the first day after the birth of Jesus. This carol tells us that King Wenceslas (a historical tenth-century duke of Bohemia) was looking out his castle window on December 26.

Because Stephen stood up for the truth, he was stoned to death. Indeed, a young man named Saul (who later converted and became the great Apostle Paul) watched over the cloaks of those who stoned this first martyr of the Church (see Acts of the Apostles 7:58).

The acts of the Apostles says clearly that Saint Stephen died as Christ died. Stephen's last words, addressed to Jesus, echoed Jesus' own words to the Father: "Lord Jesus, receive my spirit" (Acts 7:59; see Luke 23:46). Stephen also echoed Jesus' prayer for forgiveness for his persecutors: "Lord, do not hold this sin against them" (Acts 7:60; see Luke 23:34). As the first martyr, Saint Stephen was the model for every other Christian martyr to follow. His death reminds us that although we should never seek martyrdom for its own sake, it is sometimes asked of those who have pledged to follow Christ.

established by Christ continues to this day and will remain until the Kingdom is fully established at the end of time.

Jesus' choice of Twelve Apostles mirrored the Twelve Tribes of Israel, God's Chosen People. This aspect of Jesus' inauguration of the Church recalls the Jewish hope that someday the Twelve Tribes, scattered in exile, will be gathered together again.

Chapter Review

1. What are three meanings of the word *Church* in Christian usage?

2. What is the Church's role in the Father's plan to save us?

3. Why was God's covenant with Israel significant for the rest of the world?

4. How is Jesus the perfect fulfillment of the Sinai Covenant?

5. How did Jesus establish the Church through his preaching?

6. How is Jesus' self-giving on the cross related to his establishment of the Church?

The Holy Spirit and the Church

Introduction

In this chapter, we will study the Holy Spirit's action in the Church. First we will learn about the Holy Spirit, the Third Divine Person of the Holy Trinity. Although we can trace the workings of the Holy Spirit throughout Sacred Scripture, the Holy Spirit was not fully revealed until Pentecost, after Jesus died, rose from the dead, and ascended into Heaven. The Holy Spirit and Christ are inseparable in their mission.

In the Acts of the Apostles, the account of Pentecost takes us back to the day when Christ poured out the Holy Spirit upon the Church. We celebrate Pentecost every year to commemorate this Revelation of the Church, of the Holy Spirit, and of the Trinity.

The Holy Spirit animates, sanctifies, and builds the Church. Saint Paul described a new kind of life according to the Holy Spirit: a life that is full of love and joy instead of selfishness, conflict, and a blind focus on short-term pleasure. The Holy Spirit's role in this new life includes teaching us to pray.

The Holy Spirit confers special graces on the Church. These special graces are known as charisms. Charisms include extraordinary gifts, such as speaking in tongues and miraculous healing, but also more ordinary gifts, such as teaching and being a leader.

Article 4: Introducing the Holy Spirit

Trinity
From the Latin *trinus*, meaning "threefold," referring to the central mystery of the Christian faith that God exists as a communion of three distinct and interrelated Divine Persons: Father, Son, and Holy Spirit. The doctrine of the Trinity is a mystery that is inaccessible to human reason alone and is known through Divine Revelation only.

As you have become familiar with the Old Testament and the Gospels, you have come to know the Father, the Son, and the Holy Spirit, the Third Divine Person in the **Trinity**. The Holy Spirit first appears in the Book of Genesis. The first account of Creation tells us that the Holy Spirit was present in the form of a mighty wind that swept over the waters (see 1:2). Throughout the Old Testament, we see that the Holy Spirit was present and participated with the Father and the Son in the work of salvation. However, we witness the Holy Spirit's greatest participation in the work of salvation when we read the New Testament, beginning with accounts of the Incarnation (see Luke 1:27–35). The Holy Spirit was fully revealed at **Pentecost**, when he descended upon the Apostles, with Mary present among them (see Acts 2:1–4).

The Holy Spirit and Christ

Although the Holy Spirit and Jesus Christ have shared a common mission since the beginning of time, the Holy Spirit was fully revealed to us when he was poured out on the Church by Jesus at Pentecost. During his earthly ministry, Jesus referred to the Holy Spirit in his conversations with his Apostles and in some public settings, but he did not fully reveal the Holy Spirit to us until after his death, Resurrection, and Ascension.

The mission of Jesus and the mission of the Holy Spirit are united and inseparable. Whenever God sends his Son, he also sends his Spirit. Yet the missions of Jesus and the Holy Spirit are also distinct. Jesus' mission as the incarnate Son of God was to save us by reconciling us with God. The Holy Spirit's mission is to continually sanctify, or make holy, the Church.

Two symbols of the Holy Spirit are a dove and fire. What might these symbolize about the Holy Spirit?

© Zvonimir Atletic / Shutterstock.com

The Holy Spirit's Mission

Although Revelation and salvation are the common work of the three Divine Persons, the Holy Spirit is the principal agent of the Church's mission. Over time the Holy Spirit has revealed the mission of Christ. The Church continues Christ's path. Because Christ shared the Good News with the poor, the Church must also do so. Following Christ means sharing in his poverty, obedience, service, and self-sacrifice, and even in his willingness to sacrifice his life.

Where does the Holy Spirit lead the Church? Through the power of the Holy Spirit, the Church carries out her mission to bring all people into union with the Trinity. Because we live in harmony with one another only when we are in union with God, the Church is also a means to create unity among human beings. This unity has begun, but it will not be complete until sometime in the future. The Church is a sign and instrument of the full realization of this unity: that final and eternal

Pentecost
The fiftieth day following Easter, which commemorates the descent of the Holy Spirit on the early Apostles and disciples.

Live It!
Being Open to the Spirit

How can you be more open to the activity of the Holy Spirit in your own life? Consider the following suggestions:

- Make time for quiet reflection and prayer. If you are constantly busy, you may have a hard time hearing the voice of the Holy Spirit within you. Many people find it helpful to set aside a specific prayer time in the morning. Spending an hour in Eucharistic Adoration on a weekly basis is another great way to hear the Holy Spirit.
- Join or form a prayer group or Bible study group. Many groups read and discuss the readings for the upcoming Sunday Mass. The Holy Spirit often guides participants into a deeper understanding of the Scriptures.
- Discover or develop particular gifts that the Holy Spirit has shared with you. Volunteer opportunities often provide a chance to discover or develop talents and abilities. A trusted adult can also help you to discern your own particular gifts.

Gentile
A non-Jewish person. In Sacred Scripture, the Gentiles were the uncircumcised, those who did not honor the God of the Torah. Saint Paul and other evangelists reached out to the Gentiles, baptizing them into the family of God.

Communion
Refers to receiving the Body and Blood of Christ. In general, your companionship and union with Jesus and other baptized Christians in the Church. This union has its origin and high point in the celebration of the Eucharist. In this sense, the deepest vocation of the Church is Communion.

perfection in which people will truly be one in union with the Trinity.

An important step in this mission occurred when the Holy Spirit revealed the Church to the world at Pentecost. The Holy Spirit inspired the Apostles and other disciples to share the Good News with Jews and **Gentiles**.

Where do you see the Holy Spirit at work in the Church?

Article 5: Pentecost: The Church Revealed to the World

Whenever we pick up a newspaper, watch the news on television, or surf the Internet, we cannot avoid reports of violent conflicts. However, God made human beings to live in harmony with him and with one another. The Church, revealed on Pentecost, is a means to achieve this harmony, which we also call **communion**.

The Day of Pentecost

After Jesus' Ascension his followers gathered in Jerusalem (see Acts 1:15) at the time of the Feast of Weeks, a Jewish festival. The Feast of Weeks was also known as Pentecost, from the Greek for "fiftieth," because the festival is celebrated fifty days after Passover.

The account in the Acts of the Apostles tells us that "a noise like a strong, driving wind" suddenly filled the house where Jesus' Apostles were gathered. "Tongues as of fire" rested on each of them, and they were filled with the Holy Spirit (2:2,3). The Apostles began to preach in different languages. As they went out into the city, around them gathered a crowd of Jews from Egypt, Rome, modern-day Turkey and Iraq, Palestine, and many other places, all of whom were in Jerusalem for the Pentecost festival. Miraculously, each person heard the message of the Apostles in her or his own language. This multilingual chorus caused some bystanders to think the Apostles were drunk (see Acts 2:13). Peter, the Apostles' leader, proclaimed to the crowd that these events were fulfilling Old Testament prophecies (see 2:14–32), especially the prophet Joel's words:

> "It will come to pass in the last days," God says,
> "that I will pour out a portion of my spirit upon all flesh.
> Your sons and your daughters shall prophesy,
> your young men shall see visions,
> your old men shall dream dreams."
>
> (Acts 2:17; see also Joel 3:1)

Peter explained that the glorified Jesus himself was pouring the Holy Spirit upon the Apostles and enabling them to speak in such a miraculous way that they could be understood by all who heard them (see Acts 2:33). Peter instructed his listeners to repent and be baptized so that their sins would be forgiven and so that they too would receive the Holy Spirit. Three thousand people were baptized that day (see 2:37–41).

Do you remember the account of the Tower of Babel, described in the Book of Genesis (see 11:1–9)? At one time the whole world spoke one language. Genesis tells us that some people wished to build a tower up to the sky, in order to "make a name" for themselves (11:4). To confound their plans, God scattered these people throughout the earth, confusing their languages so they could no longer communicate. At Pentecost, however, we see a great contrast: the Holy Spirit enabled people who spoke many different languages to hear the same message. At the Tower of Babel, God put up barriers to understanding; at Pentecost he broke them down.

In the account of the Tower of Babel, God confused the speech of humanity. Why does he reverse this in the preaching of the Apostles at Pentecost?

How does the Pentecost account in the Acts of the Apostles help us to understand more about the Church?

© Elena Schweitzer / Shutterstock

Article 6: The Meaning of Pentecost

We sometimes call Pentecost the birthday of the Church. This can be misleading though, because we don't mean that the Church began on Pentecost. Remember that the Father planned the Church from all eternity, and his Son instituted the Church before the Holy Spirit descended on the Apostles. The Church was born primarily from Christ's total self-giving for our salvation, anticipated when he instituted the Eucharist, and fulfilled in his death on the cross.

At Pentecost the Holy Spirit broke through into our world in a new way. How did the action of the Holy Spirit make the Blessed Trinity known to us?

A child's day of birth can help us to understand something important about the revelation of the Church at Pentecost. When a child is born, we see the baby with our eyes for the first time, but the child has been prepared for several months within her or his mother. In a similar yet greater way, the outpouring of the Holy Spirit at Pentecost revealed the Church to the world for the first time. The Church was not a new entity, however, as she had been in God's plan long before the world was created.

© Prado, M–adrid, Spain / Bridgeman Images

On Pentecost, God as the Trinity was fully revealed for the first time. Jews who followed Jesus at the time of Pentecost already worshipped God the Father—the God of Abraham, Isaac, and Jacob. They also believed that Jesus was the Divine Son of God the Father. The action of the Holy Spirit at Pentecost made these Jewish followers aware of their encounter with the Third Divine Person of the Trinity: the Holy Spirit. For the first time in salvation history, God fully revealed himself as the Blessed Trinity. This mystery of the Trinity—one God in three Divine Persons, Father, Son, and Holy Spirit—is the central mystery of our faith. God alone can make this mystery known to us.

The Age of the Church

In God's plan of salvation, Pentecost marked the beginning of the Church's mission on earth, when the Apostles were able to begin their work of **evangelization** and to baptize in Jesus' name. Christ was no longer present on earth in the same way as before his death and Resurrection. By sending us his Holy Spirit, Christ now lives and acts in the world through his Church. In this way, Jesus has fulfilled his promise to his disciples: "Behold, I am with you always, until the end of the age" (Matthew 28:20).

The Church celebrates Pentecost fifty days after Easter. During the Easter season, we celebrate the life, death, Resurrection, and Ascension of Jesus and the

evangelization, evangelist
The proclamation of the Good News of Jesus Christ through words and witness. An evangelist is one who actively works to spread the Gospel message of salvation.

Pray It!

"Come, Holy Spirit"

The chant "Come, Holy Spirit" (in the original Latin, *"Veni, Sancte Spiritus"*) dates from the Middle Ages. Use this prayer now to ask for guidance from the Holy Spirit:

Come, Holy Spirit, come!
And from your celestial home
   Shed a ray of light divine!
Come, Father of the poor!
Come, source of all our store!
   Come, within our bosoms shine.
You, of comforters the best;
You, the soul's most welcome guest;
   Sweet refreshment here below;
In our labor, rest most sweet;
Grateful coolness in the heat;
   Solace in the midst of woe.
O most blessed Light divine,
Shine within these hearts of yours,
   And our inmost being fill!
Where you are not, we have naught,

Nothing good in deed or thought,
   Nothing free from taint of ill.
Heal our wounds, our strength renew;
On our dryness pour your dew;
   Wash the stains of guilt away:
Bend the stubborn heart and will;
Melt the frozen, warm the chill;
   Guide the steps that go astray.
On the faithful, who adore
And confess you, evermore
   In your sevenfold gift descend;
Give them virtue's sure reward;
Give them your salvation, Lord;
   Give them joys that never end.
Amen.
   Alleluia.

(Pentecost Sequence, *Lectionary for Mass*)

animate
To give life to.

sanctify
To make holy; sanctification is the process of responding to God's grace and becoming closer to God.

redemption he won for us. Pentecost marks the end of the Easter season in the liturgical year. You may have noticed that the priest celebrating the Mass on Pentecost wears red vestments. Can you guess why? Red symbolizes the transforming power of the Holy Spirit. A second special component of the Pentecost liturgy is the singing or recitation of *"Veni, Sancte Spiritus,"* or "Come, Holy Spirit," a Latin sequence that dates from the twelfth century. (See the "Come, Holy Spirit" sidebar for the text of this sequence.)

What is an example of the transforming power of the Holy Spirit from your own life?

Article 7: The Holy Spirit Builds, Animates, and Sanctifies the Church

We hear phrases such as "school spirit" or the "spirit of teamwork." These phrases refer to a kind of energy or atmosphere within a group that we can't see but that we know is real and active. When this energy brings people together, strengthens their relationships, and deepens their ability to share in a common mission for the sake of others, it gives us a glimpse of the Holy Spirit's way of working in the world.

The Holy Spirit, given to the Church's members by Christ, builds, **animates**, and **sanctifies** the Church. These three elements of the Holy Spirit's mission are evidence of the Holy Spirit's energy.

The Holy Spirit Builds the Church

At Pentecost the Holy Spirit's power to build the Church was made known. Once the Apostles received the Holy Spirit, more than three thousand people were baptized.

After Jesus told his followers they would receive the Holy Spirit, he also told them what to do next: "You will be my witnesses in Jerusalem, throughout Judea and Samaria, and to the ends of the earth" (Acts 1:8). The

mission of the Church is to bring people into communion with the Trinity. The Holy Spirit builds individuals'
faith lives, builds community, and builds the Church by
calling new members.

The Holy Spirit Animates the Church

The Holy Spirit animates or gives life to the Church.
Saint Augustine of Hippo said that what the soul is to the
human body, so the Holy Spirit is to the **Body of Christ**,
the Church. Before his Ascension, Jesus told his disciples,
"You will receive power when the holy Spirit comes upon
you" (Acts 1:8). At Pentecost, tongues of fire, symbolizing
the transforming energy of the Holy Spirit, rested on the
disciples. This power took a group of followers who had
been huddling behind closed doors out of fear (see John
20:19) and converted them into bold missionaries who
went into the world to proclaim their faith in the Risen
Christ.

The Holy Spirit Sanctifies the Church

The Church is sanctified or made holy by the Holy
Spirit. The Holy Spirit works to increase the holiness of
the Church and her members through the Sacraments,
through the **virtues** by which we live a moral life, and
by the many gifts the Holy Spirit gives to each person.
Church members first receive the Holy Spirit through
Baptism, the first Sacrament of Christian Initiation. Baptism brings each person into the Body of Christ. Saint
Paul wrote, "For in one Spirit we were all baptized into
one body" (1 Corinthians 12:13).

> **What are some things you can do to strengthen
> your commitment to do good?**

Article 8: Images of the Holy Spirit

We know that the Holy Spirit works in the world to bring
us together, to strengthen our relationships, and to unite
us in a common mission. But because we cannot experience the Holy Spirit with our five senses, it can be helpful

Body of Christ
A term that
when capitalized
designates Jesus'
Body in the
Eucharist, or the
entire Church,
which is also
referred to as the
Mystical Body of
Christ.

virtue
A habitual and firm
disposition to do
good.

Sacred Tradition

Tradition comes from the Latin *tradere*, meaning "to hand on." Sacred Tradition refers to the process of passing on the Gospel message. It began with the oral communication of the Gospel by the Apostles, was written down in Sacred Scripture, and is interpreted by the Magisterium under the guidance of the Holy Spirit.

to look at some images or symbols that describe the work of the Holy Spirit in Sacred Scripture and **Sacred Tradition**. Important images of the Holy Spirit include wind, fire, and a dove.

Breath and Wind

In Greek, the language of the New Testament, the word for Spirit is *pneuma*. This word can also mean "wind" or "breath." In Hebrew, the primary language of the Old Testament, the word *ruach* has these same meanings.

The Scripture writers took full advantage of this range of meaning. In the Gospel of John, we read that Jesus breathed on his disciples and said, "Receive the holy Spirit" (20:22). This recalls God's action in Genesis 2:7: "The Lord God formed the man out of the dust of the ground and blew into his nostrils the breath of life, and the man became a living being." And as we have already seen, the Acts of the Apostles tells us that there was "a noise like a strong driving wind" when the Holy Spirit came upon the disciples at Pentecost (2:2).

As Jesus said, "The wind blows where it wills, and you can hear the sound it makes, but you do not know where it comes from or where it goes; so it is with everyone who is born of the Spirit" (John 3:8).

© Fiber Art by Linda S. Schmidt /
www.ShortAttentionSpanQuilting.com / Used with permission

Fire

Just as the Holy Spirit often appears as wind or breath throughout Sacred Scripture, we also glimpse the Holy Spirit in examples of fire in both the Old and New Testaments. You may recall the burning bush from which God spoke to Moses in the Book of Exodus (see 3:2). Later the Book of Exodus tells us the Lord led the Israelites through the wilderness, showing them the way by sending a pillar of flame during the night and a pillar of cloud during the day (perhaps another example of the Holy Spirit as wind) (see 13:21). If we return to the Pentecost account, we read that the Holy Spirit appeared to the disciples in the form of "tongues as of fire, which parted and came to rest on each one of them" (Acts 2:3).

The Dove

In addition to images involving wind and fire, Sacred Scripture often portrays the Holy Spirit as a dove, an image frequently echoed in Christian art. When Jesus was baptized, Luke tells us, "the holy Spirit descended upon him in bodily form like a dove" (3:22). In his poem "God's Grandeur," the Jesuit poet Gerard Manley Hopkins (1844–1889) followed Luke's example by using the image of the dove to describe the Holy Spirit (called the Holy Ghost here):

© Robert Young / Shutterstock.com

> And though the last lights off the black West went
> Oh, morning, at the brown brink eastward, springs—
> Because the Holy Ghost over the bent
> World broods with warm breast and with ah!
> bright wings.

What other images have you encountered that describe the work of the Holy Spirit in the world?

Article 9: Life According to the Holy Spirit

Sometimes people go through dramatic changes in their lives. Let's say Lauren, who has always been somewhat rude and inconsiderate, suddenly becomes much nicer and thoughtful. You might think to yourself, "It's like Lauren is a different or new person!" The Gifts of the Holy Spirit bring about this kind of startling change in a person's life.

Life When We Ignore the Holy Spirit

We may know about the transforming power of the Holy Spirit, but we have the free will to ignore him or, as Saint Paul said, to live "according to the flesh" (Romans 8:4). The Apostle Paul contrasted a life lived according to the flesh with a holy life lived according to the power of the Holy Spirit. The person who lives according to the flesh focuses on immediate gratification of his or her own needs. As a result, this person's life will be filled, as Paul said, with hatred, jealousy, lack of self-control, and selfishness. According to Paul, someone who focuses only on immediate gratification and pleasure may well abuse alcohol and be sexually promiscuous (see Galatians 5:19–21). The person who ignores the Holy Spirit is so focused on meeting his or her own immediate desires that he or she has no time to consider other people.

Life When We Live in the Holy Spirit

Saint Paul contrasted this selfish life with a life "according to the Spirit" (Romans 8:4). He spoke of the fruits of the Spirit: "love, joy, peace, patience, kindness, generosity, faithfulness, gentleness, self-control" (Galatians 5:22–23). Those who live according to the Spirit focus not on themselves but rather on the needs and well-being of others.

The Holy Spirit helps teach us how to pray. The next time you pray, begin by asking the Holy Spirit to guide you.

© Bill Wittman / www.wpwittman.com

Saint Paul said, "The love of God has been poured out into our hearts through the holy Spirit that has been given to us" (Romans 5:5). This life in the Holy Spirit is a kind of sneak preview of our life in Heaven, where we will share in the perfect love and happiness of the Trinity. Think of people who are filled with the Spirit— they radiate calm and joy even during tough times.

The Holy Spirit allows us to deepen our relationship with himself, the Father, and the Son, showing us that we are "children of God" (Romans 8:16), and thus we can cry out, "Abba, Father" (8:15, Galatians 4:6).

The Teaching of the Holy Spirit

The Holy Spirit has an important teaching role in the Church. Jesus told his disciples that the Holy Spirit "will teach you everything and remind you of all that [I] told you. . . . When he comes, the Spirit of truth, he will guide you to all truth" (John 14:26,16:13). The Holy Spirit helps us to understand the truths of faith.

The Holy Spirit especially teaches us to pray. Do you ever feel that you would like to pray, or even that you should pray, but you don't know what to say? Ask the Holy Spirit for help. The Apostle Paul tells us, "The Spirit too comes to the aid of our weakness; for we do not know how to pray as we ought, but the Spirit itself intercedes with inexpressible groanings" (Romans 8:26). When we don't know how to pray, it's good to know that we can call on the Holy Spirit, the "master of prayer," to help us (CCC, 741).

The Holy Spirit, as the master of prayer, not only intercedes for us but also instructs us in our prayer life, inspiring us to express new forms of the five basic types of prayer: blessing, **petition**, **intercessions**, thanksgiving, and praise. The Holy Spirit has been teaching people to pray for thousands of years. The Holy Spirit operates through Sacred Tradition, the living transmission of God's truth to us. The Holy Spirit is like a well of living water within the heart of a person who prays, but the Holy Spirit also points the praying person to the source of the living water, Jesus Christ. From the medieval Gregorian chants to the latest praise and worship songs, from the Eucharistic Prayers of the Mass to our own spontaneous prayers before we fall asleep at night, the Holy Spirit is endlessly creative in our prayer lives.

What kind of prayer have you found particularly powerful or meaningful?

petition
A prayer form in which one asks God for help and forgiveness.

intercession
A prayer on behalf of another person or group.

charism
A special grace of the Holy Spirit given to an individual Christian or community, commonly for the benefit and building up of the entire Church.

Article 10: Charisms: The Holy Spirit's Special Graces for the Church

The Holy Spirit gives various special graces, called **charisms**, to the members of the Church for the benefit of the whole Church and, through the Church, the whole world. As Saint Paul wrote, "To each individual the manifestation of the Spirit is given for some benefit" (1 Corinthians 12:7).

Saint Paul's Description of the Charisms

Saint Paul listed several examples of charisms in his First Letter to the Corinthians: the expression of knowledge and wisdom, faith, healing abilities, the ability to do great deeds, prophecy, "discernment of spirits," and the ability to speak in tongues (12:8–10).

Did You Know?

Gifts of the Holy Spirit

© Zvonimir Atletic

The Gifts of the Holy Spirit are different than the charisms given by the Holy Spirit. These gifts help us to deepen our faith and grow closer to God. The essential meaning of each gift is given below, yet, because each of us receives these gifts in our own individual way, they may have a slightly different effect for each of us:

Wisdom This gift enables us to see the world, and our own situation, as God sees it. We can see the Holy Spirit at work, and we can see where our decisions can contribute to God's designs.

Understanding This gifts helps us to find the meaning of God's truth and its significance for our own lives. This gifts helps us to root our lives in truth and honesty.

Right Judgment (Counsel) This gift helps us to know the difference between right and wrong, and between something good and something better. It helps us to know and live God's loving will for us.

Courage (Fortitude) This gift helps us to live out the saying "When the going gets tough, the tough get going." Every life has its challenges and obstacles. This gift of the Holy Spirit helps us to face them, go through them, and keep on track towards God.

Knowledge This gift, closely related to the gifts of wisdom and understanding, helps us to understand the meaning of God's Revelation, particularly the Good News of Jesus Christ. Through the gift of knowledge, we strive to learn more about God by studying Scripture Sacred Tradition.

Reverence (Piety) This gift gives us a deep sense of respect for God, honoring him with humility, trust, and love. This gift also helps us to love and respect the Church as the Body of Christ on earth.

Wonder and Awe (Fear of the Lord) This gift makes us aware of God's greatness, love, and power, sometimes to the point of being overwhelmed. This awareness may fill us with joy or bring us to our knees when we recognize that God himself is with us and in us.

These charisms should not be confused, however, with the Gifts of the Holy Spirit. These are seven dispositions or tendencies, not specific skills. The seven Gifts of the Holy Spirit, based on Isaiah 11:2, are Wisdom, Understanding, Right Judgment (Counsel), Courage (Fortitude), Knowledge, Reverence (Piety), and Wonder and Awe (Fear of the Lord).

Ordinary and Extraordinary Charisms

There are ordinary charisms and extraordinary charisms, and both kinds are important. Ordinary charisms are those simple and humble graces that build up the Church, contribute to human good, and respond to the needs of the world. These charisms are spiritual graces. Often they build on natural talents. On any given day, you can see ordinary charisms at work all around you. A teacher may be graced with wisdom to touch the hearts of students in a deep way. A nurse or doctor may be graced with compassion. A friend may be graced with a special concern for immigrants and may use a talent for learning languages to help these newcomers.

Some of the Holy Spirit's special graces are extraordinary, involving spiritual powers beyond normal human abilities. A person's extraordinary charism of healing, for example, might be visible to others through a miraculous cure that has no scientific explanation. Some people have the charism of prophecy, or the charism of speaking in tongues and interpreting those who speak in tongues. Speaking in tongues is the special graces of praying in a spiritual language; no one else can understand it except someone with the charism of interpreting tongues (see 1 Corinthians 14:2,14).

Charisms of Leadership

Sometimes we describe political leaders or other leaders as charismatic, meaning they possess a certain power of personality or speaking ability that draws people to them. The Church too has charisms of leadership, but these are special graces of the Holy Spirit that enable a leader to provide benefit to the whole Church. In his discussion

infallibility
The gift given by the Holy Spirit to the Church whereby the pastors of the Church, the Pope and the bishops in union with him, can definitively proclaim a doctrine of faith and morals without error.

of charisms, Saint Paul wrote that God has designated believers to be, for example, Apostles, prophets, teachers, administrators, and assistants (see 1 Corinthians 12:28).

Founders of religious orders or congregations often have specific charisms that their followers also pursue. Saint Benedict of Nursia's charism of combining work and prayer has inspired the spiritual life of vowed Benedictines and their associates for centuries. Saint Francis of Assisi's charism of embracing a life of poverty and simplicity has similarly inspired thousands to follow in his footsteps.

As leaders and teachers of the Church, the Pope and the bishops in union with him have the charism of

Faith in Action
Sisters of the Holy Spirit and Mary Immaculate

© Used with permission of Healy-Murphy Center

In 1893, the order of the Sisters of the Holy Spirit and Mary Immaculate was established in Texas. This was the first community of religious women established in that state. One Sunday Margaret Mary Healy-Murphy heard the priest read a letter from the bishops of the United States asking people to reach out to African American people who did not have many opportunities for an education.

With the help of the Holy Spirit, she discerned that the Holy Spirit was calling her to serve and educate African American children who were poor. She built a church and a small schoolhouse, naming them for Saint Peter Claver, the Jesuit saint known for helping slaves in Colombia. When she had trouble recruiting volunteers, she established a religious community with the help of the local bishop. She gathered a group of young women who dedicated their lives to serving those living in poverty.

After Saint Peter Claver Academy closed in 1971, the sisters established the Healy-Murphy Center, an alternative school for young people at risk, such as teenage mothers and those who have not been successful in traditional high school settings. The sisters also opened day care centers for the teens' children. In addition to their work at the Healy-Murphy Center, the Sisters of the Holy Spirit and Mary Immaculate now minister in seven dioceses in Texas, five in Louisiana, two in Mississippi, and one in Mexico. (From the website for the Healy-Murphy Center)

infallibility, so that the Church may always avoid error in her teaching on faith and morals. Infallibility extends to all of Divine Revelation. The Pope, as supreme pastor see the gift of and teacher, uses this gift when he defines a **doctrine** as infallible. The most recent infallible teaching was Pope Pius XII's proclamation of the **Assumption of the Blessed Virgin Mary** in 1950. Another example of the Church's infallibility occurs when the bishops, together with the Pope, agree on a teaching that all Catholics must believe because it has been divinely revealed. We see this kind of agreement especially in an **Ecumenical Council**.

doctrine
An official, authoritative teaching of the Church based on the Revelation of God.

The Church Needs All Charisms

The Holy Spirit gives special graces to every member of the Church, no matter how humble, because each person can help to build up the Church. Some have a musical charism. Others have the charism of leadership or coaching, and yet others have the charism of patient listening and the ability to give wise advice. As a young person, you may already know some

Each of us has gifts we can contribute to the building up of the Church. These gifts may be obvious, such as musical abilities, or subtle, such as being a good listener. What gifts do you possess that you can share with the Church?

© Diane White Rosier / iStockphoto.com

Primary Sources

A Challenge from Pope Benedict XVI to Youth

How can you embrace the power of the Holy Spirit to know how best to serve the world? Pope Benedict XVI delivered this challenge to young people like you at the 2008 World Youth Day in Sydney, Australia:

> Dear young people, let me now ask you a question. Are you living your lives in a way that opens up space for the Spirit in the midst of a world that wants to forget God, or even rejects him in the name of a falsely-conceived freedom? How are you using the gifts you have been given, the "power" which the Holy Spirit is even now prepared to release within you? What legacy will you leave to young people yet to come? What difference will you make?

Assumption of the Blessed Virgin Mary
The dogma that recognizes that the body of the Blessed Virgin Mary was taken directly to Heaven after her life on earth had ended.

Ecumenical Council
A gathering of the Church's bishops from around the world convened by the Pope or approved by him to address pressing issues in the Church.

of your particular charisms. You will discover more as you grow up.

Chapter Review

1. What does it mean to say that the works of Jesus and the Holy Spirit are inseparable?

2. Where does the Holy Spirit lead the Church?

3. Describe the events of Pentecost.

4. What did Peter say would happen to those people who repented and were baptized on the day of Pentecost?

5. Why is it appropriate to say that the Church was revealed rather than born on Pentecost?

6. Why was Pentecost the Revelation of the Holy Trinity as well as the Church?

7. What are the three important elements of the Holy Spirit's mission with regard to the Church?

8. Describe three images we often associate with the Holy Spirit.

9. How did the Holy Spirit transform Jesus' disciples?

10. Contrast a life lived ignoring the Holy Spirit with one lived in the Holy Spirit.

11. How does the Holy Spirit help us to pray?

12. What is the subtle difference between a charism and a gift of the Holy Spirit?

13. Describe two examples of founders of religious orders whose charisms are still followed by members of those orders today.

The Work of the Early Church

Chapter 3

Introduction

Sent by Jesus and empowered by the Holy Spirit, the Apostles participated in the universal mission of the Church by spreading the Gospel throughout the Mediterranean world. Before he died, Jesus commissioned his Apostles to share in his mission of preaching the Good News and healing. After his Ascension he sent the Holy Spirit to be with them and guide them. Christ's love and the presence of the Holy Spirit gave the Apostles and other disciples the motivation and energy to share the truth of Christ with those they encountered.

Saint Paul, sometimes called the Apostle to the Gentiles, preached to both Jews and Gentiles in ways both groups could understand. Paul preached to Jews by focusing on the Old Testament and its prophecies of a Messiah. He similarly spoke to Gentiles in terms they were accustomed to. For example, he quoted from Greek poets when he shared the Good News of Jesus Christ with Greek communities.

Still, neither the Jews in Jerusalem nor the Romans always welcomed the Gospel message, and their hostility led to the persecution of Christians and even martyrdom. The early martyrs inspired others to be strong in their faith. But persecution and suffering are not unique to the early Church in the Roman Empire. Sacred Scripture and Sacred Tradition reveal that there will be a final trial or tribulation at the end of the world.

Article 11: The Church Continues Christ's Mission

When we first receive good news—we pass a difficult test, we hear that a sick friend is getting better—our first inclination is to share that news. In a similar but even greater way, the early Apostles were motivated to share the Good News about Jesus with everyone. This is how the early Church continued Christ's mission.

The Mission of the Apostles

In the early Church, the mission of the Apostles actually began during their time with Jesus, before his death, Resurrection, and Ascension. Jesus proclaimed the Good News and healed people, and he sent the Apostles out to do the same (see Matthew 10:5–15). After his Resurrection, Christ made it clear that the Apostles' mission was universal, meaning it was for everyone:

> Go, therefore, and make disciples of all nations, baptizing them in the name of the Father, and of the Son, and of the holy Spirit, teaching them to observe all that I have commanded you. (Matthew 28:19–20)

Jesus gave the Apostles an important charge when he commissioned them to "make disciples of all nations." It is no wonder then that the Church spread rapidly in communities throughout the Mediterranean.

Primary Sources

Pope Saint John Paul II on Mission

In his encyclical *Redemptoris Missio*, Pope Saint John Paul II tells the Church about her own mission:

Today, as never before, the Church has the opportunity of bringing the Gospel, by witness and word, to all people and nations. I see the dawning of a new missionary age, which will become a radiant day bearing an abundant harvest, if all Christians, and missionaries and young churches in particular, respond with generosity and holiness to the calls and challenges of our time. (92)

The Spread of Christianity

The Acts of the Apostles tells us that within a few years of Jesus' death and Resurrection, the Apostles and disciples had proclaimed the faith from Jerusalem to Samaria, Damascus, Phoenicia, and Antioch (see chapters 8–11). Saint Paul traveled to various cities in Asia Minor and Greece and had made plans to travel as far as Spain before he was executed in Rome. Other historical evidence shows that the Church also spread south into Egypt and farther into eastern Syria just a few years after Jesus' Ascension.

Why did the Apostles and early disciples travel so far and work so hard to spread the Good News? The universal love of God, who desires that all be saved, motivated and energized them to travel throughout the known world to share the truth of the Gospel with all who would listen. Saint Paul said, "The love of Christ impels us" (2 Corinthians 5:14). The Church needed to be missionary so she could share the truth that many people already longed for.

The Holy Spirit and the Apostles' Mission

In the Acts of the Apostles, we find accounts of Pentecost and how the Holy Spirit was involved in every aspect of the missionary spread of Christianity. The Holy Spirit came to repentant sinners who were baptized and helped the Church to make decisions, such as assigning Paul and Barnabas to a certain task (see 13:2), ruling on what laws Gentile converts to Jesus must follow (see 15:28), and guiding Paul and Timothy to preach only in certain areas (see 16:6–7).

Yet the Holy Spirit was not working alone. The Church's mission is **Trinitarian**. This means that the work of the Church is the work of the three Divine Persons in the Trinity—the Father, the Son, and the Holy Spirit. According to the Father's eternal plan, the Church continues the mission of the Son with the help of the Holy Spirit. The ultimate purpose of the Apostles' mission

Trinitarian
Of or relating to the Trinity or the doctrine of the Trinity.

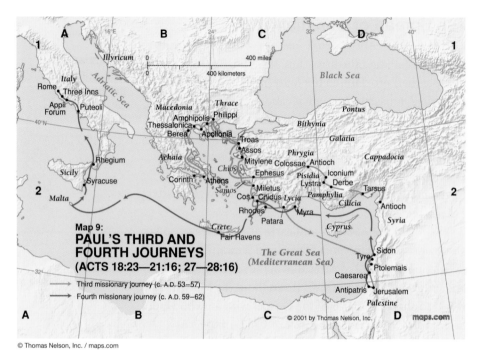

Map 9:
PAUL'S THIRD AND FOURTH JOURNEYS
(ACTS 18:23—21:16; 27—28:16)

⎯⎯ Third missionary journey (c. A.D. 53–57)
⟶ Fourth missionary journey (c. A.D. 59–62)

© 2001 by Thomas Nelson, Inc.

© Thomas Nelson, Inc. / maps.com

By modern standards Paul did not travel very far, but through these journeys Paul established and supported numerous churches that led to the spread of Christianity throughout the known world.

was to cooperate with the Holy Trinity's plan by inviting people to share in the communion between the Father and the Son in the Holy Spirit.

> **What helps you to feel connected with the Church?**
> **How is this an example of the Holy Spirit at work?**

Article 12: How Did the Early Church Spread the Gospel?

How do you learn best? A good teacher knows that all students do not learn in the same way. Some students learn best by reading silently, others by listening to a lecture, still others by discussing the content. Like any good teacher, the Church recognizes that she must adapt her way of spreading the Gospel to reach diverse audiences and the great variety of learners, or disciples, on earth. In fact, in the New Testament, the Greek word for *disciple* is *mathetes*, which literally means "learner."

Saint Paul Preached to Both Jews and Gentiles

Although he was called to be the Apostle to the Gentiles at his **conversion**, Saint Paul preached to Gentiles and Jews alike. In his missionary work, Paul always tried to communicate the Gospel to his audience in a way they would best understand. Paul himself was comfortable in the cultural worlds of both Jews and Gentiles. Though he was a devout Jew who belonged to the party of the Pharisees, Paul was born and raised in the **Hellenistic** city of Tarsus in modern-day Turkey and wrote in an excellent Greek style.

When preaching to a Jewish audience, Paul focused primarily on the Old Testament. He reminded his fellow Jews that the Hebrew Scriptures prophesy about a Messiah, and he connected these prophecies to the life, death, and Resurrection of Jesus (see Acts 13:16–43). But when Paul spoke to a Gentile audience, he changed his approach. When he preached to Greeks in Athens, for example, he began by relating the Good News in a context more familiar to the Greeks. He said that among the many altars the Greeks had set up to worship various gods, such as Zeus and Apollo, he had noticed one altar dedicated to an "unknown God." This unknown God,

conversion
A change of heart, turning away from sin and toward God.

Hellenistic
Of or relating to Greek history, culture, or art after Alexander the Great.

Live It!
How Do You Preach the Gospel?

There is no single way to spread the Gospel today. The Holy Spirit gifts some people with the skills and personality to speak boldly and publicly about their faith, while other people witness to the truth and power of their faith through simple, humble lives of serving others.

Many types of witnesses have allowed Christ to transform their lives. Once that true inward transformation has begun, the outward effects cannot be hidden, whether proclaimed from the rooftops or quietly lived out among friends and family. What special gifts and skills do you have? How can you use them to spread the Gospel?

© Victoria & Albert Museum, London / Art Resource, NY

Today the Good News of Jesus Christ continues to be shared through preaching, much like Paul did on his journeys. Think about preachers you have heard. What makes someone an effective preacher?

Paul proclaimed, was the one true God who had created all things. Paul then quoted from Greek poets to further support his points, knowing that the Athenians weren't familiar with the Old Testament (see Acts 17:16–34).

Paul summed up his own methods in this way, referring to the Gentiles when he spoke of those outside the law: "To the Jews I became like a Jew to win over Jews. . . . To those outside the law I became like one outside the law . . . to win over those outside the law" (1 Corinthians 9:20–21).

Paul Used Familiar Imagery to Reach His Audience

Jesus, who preached in rural Galilee, used images familiar to his audience, such as a farmer sowing seed and fishermen using nets. Following Christ's example, Paul used images suitable to his audiences. For example, when he spoke to audiences in large urban areas, he taught with images that included athletes competing in a stadium (see 1 Corinthians 9:24), military armor and weapons (see Ephesians 6:10–17), musical instruments such as gongs and cymbals (see 1 Corinthians 13:1), and temples (see 1 Corinthians 6:19).

Paul's ways of presenting the faith changed with his audience, but he never changed the truths of the faith. Effective evangelization includes a presentation that is appropriate for those who are learning or listening, but it does not distort the message.

How Did Christianity Spread So Quickly?

The Apostles and disciples spread the Christian message in the regions surrounding the Mediterranean as far east as Armenia, southwest into northern Africa and modern-day Ethiopia, and through much of what we know today as Europe. In addition to preaching in ways people could understand, what other factors explain this remarkable spread of Christianity? Certainly, expanding the Church's mission to reach out to Gentiles increased the Apostles' potential audience for evangelization. Paul's ability to speak Greek allowed him to explain important Christian truths to people from Greco-Roman cultures so they could understand the faith. This outreach also attracted more intellectual and well-educated believers in addition to those who were perhaps less educated. We begin to see how the Church was able to spread the Good News to people from a range of religious and socioeconomic backgrounds.

Faith in Action
Saint Francis Xavier: Patron of Foreign Missions

© Bartolemé Estebán Murillo (Spanish, 1618-1682), Saint Francis Xavier, c. 1670, Oil on canvas, 85 5/16 x 63 7/8 in. (216.7 x 162.3 cm), The Ella Gallup Sumner and Mary Catlin Sumner Collection Fund, 1937.3, Wadsworth Atheneum Museum of Art, Hartford, CT

Saint Francis Xavier was born to a noble family of the Kingdom of Navarre, in modern-day Spain. Giving up a promising career as a professor of philosophy, he joined Saint Ignatius of Loyola to become one of the original members of the Society of Jesus, or the Jesuits.

Leaving Europe in 1541, Francis spent the rest of his life as a missionary in Mozambique, India, southeastern Asia, and Japan. He baptized and taught the basics of the faith to thousands of people. He even hoped to evangelize China, but he died on an island just off the mainland.

Francis preferred to live and work among the poor, often ministering to the sick in addition to his preaching. Like Saint Paul, he changed his methods of presenting the faith to suit his audience. He taught people at their level of understanding—for example, he taught catechism to children using rhyming verses set to popular tunes. He also became welcome in the courts of rulers and engaged in theological and philosophical discussions with those more educated. His ministry was accompanied at times by miraculous signs, including the gift of healing.

What about the Roman Empire? The Roman Empire's persecution of early Christians is well known, but we must remember that certain strengths of the Roman Empire also greatly helped the Church to carry out her mission. The empire was large and unified and had a good road system for travel. It also provided a certain level of protection from bandits and other threats. Missionaries were able to take the Good News throughout lands controlled by the empire, including southern Europe, parts of the Balkans, the eastern Mediterranean, and northern Africa. Later centuries brought Christianity to northern Europe and the British Isles along with Roman conquerors. By the fourth century, according

© Tom Fakler / Shutterstock.com

to scholars' estimates, approximately 10 percent of the people in the Roman Empire were Christian. Later in the same century, the Emperor Constantine issued the Edict of Milan, which finally granted tolerant support of Christianity throughout the empire, ending centuries of official persecution. But even persecution and martyrdom played a role in helping to spread the Good News.

What factors in our society today make it easy to witness to the Good News of Christ? What factors make it difficult?

Article 13: Persecution and Martyrdom

Let's face it. Being a serious disciple of Christ is not always easy and often not popular. Refusing to attend parties where underage drinking is going on, for example, can alienate you from some of your peers. Resisting the temptation to have sexual relations before Marriage can potentially clash with friends' values. Living out your faith as a teen might at times lead to suffering, mockery, and loss of popularity. Yet the Church calls all of us to be witnesses to the truth of Christ, both in our words and in our deeds, whether this is popular or not.

Persecution of the Church by Jewish and Roman Authorities

Early Christians witnessed to the truth of Christ, and some suffered persecution from both Jewish leaders and Roman authorities. Jewish leaders did not accept Jesus as the Messiah. They considered claims of Jesus' divinity to be blasphemous, because they believed that only God could be fully divine. Because of this charge of **blasphemy**, Paul, a devout Pharisee, sought to destroy the Church (see Galatians 1:13) before his conversion to Christianity.

Roman authorities persecuted the Church because early Christians often refused to offer sacrifices to the emperor, a religious duty required of everyone who lived in the Roman Empire. Christians regarded this requirement as idolatry. Roman authorities, however, interpreted their refusal as disloyalty to the

blasphemy
Speaking, acting, or thinking about God, Jesus Christ, the Virgin Mary, or the saints in a way that is irreverent, mocking, or offensive. Blasphemy is a sin against the Second Commandment.

This stained-glass image depicts the martyrdom of Saint Polycarp of Smyrna. Take a moment and read his prayer. Why do you think he is giving thanks to God for being martyred?

Pray It!

© The Crosiers / Gene Plaisted, OSC

A Martyr's Prayer

Around the year 150, when he was eighty-six years old, Bishop Polycarp of Smyrna was burned at the stake for refusing to deny his Christian beliefs and worship the Roman Emperor. The following excerpt is from his beautiful prayer before he was executed. Pray it whenever you need reassurance that God's grace is at work in your own life:

> I bless you for having judged me worthy from this day and this hour to be counted among your martyrs. . . . You have kept your promise, God of faithfulness and truth. For this reason and for everything, I praise you, I bless you, I glorify you through the eternal and heavenly High Priest, Jesus Christ, your beloved Son. Through him, who is with you and the Holy Spirit, may glory be given to you, now and in the ages to come. Amen.[1] (Catechism of the Catholic Church [CCC], 2474)

© Scala / Art Resource, NY

Early Christians often faced persecution and death for practicing and sharing their faith. What obstacles do you face in practicing your faith and sharing it with others?

martyr
A person who suffers death because of his or her beliefs. The Church has canonized many Christian martyrs as saints.

emperor, a crime punishable by death. Despite the threats of execution, many Christians still refused to compromise their faith in Christ, some suffering the ultimate consequence.

Martyrs of the Early Church

The highest form of Christian witness is giving up one's life for the sake of Christ. The Greek word *martys* reveals this connection: it literally means "witness" and is also the basis for our English word ***martyr***.

In chapter 1, "The Origin of the Church," you read about Saint Stephen the Deacon, the first martyr of the Christian faith. After Jesus' Ascension the Jewish leaders in Jerusalem put Stephen on trial for blasphemy (see Acts 6:8–7:60). At the trial an enraged crowd dragged him out of the city and stoned him to death. Saint Stephen witnessed to his faith to the end, saying as he died: "Lord Jesus, receive my spirit. . . . Lord, do not hold this sin against them" (7:59–60).

After Stephen's death a general persecution of the Jerusalem Church broke out, causing many Christians to flee (see Acts 8:1). Later King Herod had James, one of the Twelve, killed, and he also had Peter arrested (see

12:1–3). Eventually both Peter and Paul were martyred in Rome for their faith.

We may find it hard to believe this today, but the followers of Jesus often accepted their suffering with joy. Saint Ignatius of Antioch, awaiting his execution in Rome, wrote: "It is better for me to die [in order to unite myself] to Christ Jesus than to reign over the ends of the earth. . . . My birth is approaching"[2] (*CCC*, 2474). The early Christian martyrs were honored to die for Christ. They knew that by sharing in his suffering and death, they would also share in his glorious Resurrection.

Far from destroying the Church, persecution produced brave martyrs whose examples encouraged other Christians to remain steadfast in their faith. As

Did You Know?

The Church's Role within History

© Noradoa / Shutterstock

We can see the mysterious aspects of the Church only with the eyes of faith. We cannot fully comprehend these mysteries, but the Church's accomplishments throughout history are visible signs of this divine reality of salvation. Consider these examples:

- Like Jesus the healer, the Church has always been active in health care. The early Church played a central role in developing hospitals. Today there are 624 Catholic hospitals in the United States alone.
- Monasteries played a major role in preserving knowledge throughout the late ancient and medieval periods, studying and copying not only Scripture and Church writers but also works of classical philosophy and literature.
- In the Middle Ages, the Church was a great patron of the arts. Pope Julius II, for example, commissioned Michelangelo's great paintings in the Sistine Chapel.

These are only a few of the outward manifestations of the hidden sources of healing, knowledge, and creativity that lie within the mystery of the Church.

Tertullian, a Church Father, wrote, "The blood of martyrs is the seed of Christians"[3] (*CCC*, 852).

The Church's Final Trial

Both Sacred Scripture and Sacred Tradition teach us that in the last days of the world, before Christ's Second Coming, the Church will undergo a final persecution (see Matthew 24:3–28). No one, however, knows the precise events and timing of the end times except the Father. Even the Son himself does not know the exact date and hour (see Mark 13:32). One scriptural prediction tells us that the antichrist, a false messiah, will set himself up in the place of God and will deceive many (see 2 Thessalonians 2:3–12).

What might an antichrist really be like? We see previews of the antichrist's deception when any *earthly* power tries to claim the *ultimate* power and authority of God. Examples include the Nazi party's claim that the "master race" in Germany was the key to history's meaning, and the Marxist claim that a proper economic system can eventually lead to a Heaven on earth.

We must resist these human claims to have ultimate answers. We know that God alone has the answers, and we also know that God's love is more than enough to support us, even during times of suffering and persecution.

Chapter Review

1. Why did the Apostles and early disciples travel so far and work so hard to spread the Good News?

2. What are three ways the Holy Spirit was involved in the missionary spread of Christianity?

3. Explain how Paul's preaching to the Jews differed from his preaching to the Gentiles.

4. Explain how Paul made his message more understandable to an urban audience.

5. Why did Jewish leaders persecute the early Christians? Why did the Roman Empire do so?

6. Identify some early martyrs of the Church, and describe their attitude toward martyrdom.

The Church Is One, Holy, Catholic, and Apostolic

In the Nicene Creed, we state: "I believe in one, holy, catholic and apostolic Church" (*Roman Missal*, page 527). This statement professes the four Marks of the Church. *Marks* is another word for "essential features." It is important to remember that the Church has no independent claim to these features of identity. It is Christ who, through the Holy Spirit, "makes his Church one, holy, catholic, and apostolic" (*Catechism of the Catholic Church [CCC],* 811). In this unit, we will look at each of these marks in turn.

First, the Church is One. The unity of the Divine Persons in the Trinity sets the example for our unity as the People of God. We are all different, but we are united by God's love, our profession of faith, our worship, and Apostolic Succession. Our unity is not something we create of ourselves, however. We, the Church, are one because our founder (Christ) makes us one as his Body, and this Body of Christ shares one soul, the Holy Spirit, who dwells in each of us.

Second, the Church is Holy. She is holy because God created her. She is holy because Christ loved her, joined her to himself as one Body, and gifted her with the Holy Spirit, who continues to dwell within her. The Church depends entirely on God's grace, which prepares us to respond to his invitation to grow in holiness. In God's grace, the Church is the holy People of God, and its members may truly be called saints (see Acts 9:13 and 1 Corinthians 6:1, 16:1). The saints canonized by the Church serve as models of holiness for us—especially Mary, who responded perfectly to the Father's will.

Third, the Church is Catholic. The Church is catholic because Christ is present in her, as the Head with the Body, creating one full and whole Body. In this Body can be found the fullness of faith, the fullness of sacramental life, and the fullness of apostolic ordained ministry This may seem obvious, but the Catholic Church is universal (the definition of *catholic*). She is in relationship with every person, Christian and non-Christian. She calls all people to unity in the People of God, even as she embraces our differences.

Finally, the Church is Apostolic because she is founded on the Apostles. Jesus gave his Apostles the authority and power to continue his mission. Through the power of the Holy Spirit, the Church faithfully keeps and hands on the teaching of the Apostles. Today the Pope and the bishops are direct successors to the Apostles, in communion with Christ. They form the Magisterium, the living teaching office of the Church, entrusted with faithfully interpreting the Gospel message today.

The enduring understandings and essential questions represent core concepts and questions that are explored throughout this unit. By studying the content of each chapter, you will gain a more complete understanding of the following.

Enduring Understandings

1. The Church is One: united in charity, in the profession of faith, in the common celebration of worship and Sacraments, and in Apostolic Succession.
2. The Church is Holy: Although Church members may sin, the Church as the Body of Christ is sinless.
3. The Church is Catholic: It exists for all people and is the means of salvation for all people.
4. The Church is Apostolic: Christ calls all Church members to proclaim and live the Gospel of salvation.

Essential Questions

1. How does diversity relate to unity in the life of the Church?
2. What contributes to the holiness of the Church?
3. How can the Church live out catholicity?
4. How can we carry on the apostolic mission of the Church in our own lives?

Chapter 4

The Church Is One

Introduction

The first Mark of the Church is that the Church is One. She is One because her example and source of unity are the three Divine Persons in the Trinity: the Father, the Son, and the Holy Spirit. But unity does not mean uniformity, for the Church is diverse in many ways. The unity of the Church is sustained by God's love and is demonstrated by several bonds, including our profession of one faith, our common worship, and Apostolic Succession.

Unity among Christians has been threatened over time by heresies, schism, and other breaks. The results of these breaks can be seen today in the different Churches and ecclesial communities that exist. Ecumenism—the movement to restore unity among Christians and, ultimately, among all humans through the world—is an effort to bind the wounds caused by these breaks.

Article 14: The First Mark of the Church

What do you think of when you hear talk about oneness or unity? Do you think of a married couple, two people who have become one through the Sacrament of Marriage? Perhaps you think of a community in which all members work together harmoniously toward shared goals.

Both images are a good start to understanding the first **Mark of the Church**: the Church is One. The New Testament makes this perfectly clear: there is only one Church, one Body of Christ, and it is characterized by oneness or unity. Saint Paul wrote, "For in one Spirit we were all baptized into one body, whether Jews or Greeks, slaves or free persons, and we were all given to drink of one Spirit" (1 Corinthians 12:13). Paul also spoke of "one body and one Spirit . . . one Lord, one faith, one baptism; one God and Father of all" (Ephesians 4:4–6). This teaching has been affirmed many times throughout the Church's history.

Christ gave the Church the gift of unity, a gift she cannot lose. For the unity to grow and deepen, however, members of the Church need to pray for and work to keep the unity and make it increasingly perfect. Before his death Jesus prayed that his community of followers would be one, just as he is one with the Father (see John 17:21). The Holy Spirit also calls us to this work, animates us in carrying it out, and lives within each member of the Church.

Marks of the Church
The four essential features or characteristics of the Church: One, Holy, Catholic (universal), and Apostolic.

The Source of the Church's Unity

The ultimate example and source of the Church's unity is the eternal unity of the three Divine Persons of the Trinity: the Father, the Son, and the Holy Spirit. The Trinity brings the people of the universal Church into unity with the Trinity and with one another.

The Church is One because of her founder, Jesus Christ. Through his Passion, death, Resurrection, and

© Bildarchiv Preussischer Kulturbesitz / Art Resource, NY

How is the Holy Trinity the source of the Church's unity?

Ascension, Jesus reconciled all people with God. In this way, he restored our unity and made it possible for us to be reconciled to one another and to form one People, one Body.

The Church is also One because the Holy Spirit, the soul of the Church, lives within each member of the Church and draws us together in communion with one another and with Christ.

Diversity within the Church's Unity

Unity should not be confused with uniformity. When we proclaim that the Church of Christ is One, we don't mean that all Church members strive to be the same; rather, we celebrate the great diversity that exists within the one Church.

In his First Letter to the Corinthians, Saint Paul noted this diversity within unity:

> There are different kinds of spiritual gifts but the same Spirit; there are different forms of service but the same Lord; there are different workings but the same God who produces all of them in everyone. (12:4–6)

Vatican Council II

The Ecumenical or general Council of the Roman Catholic Church that Pope Saint John XXIII convened as Pope in 1962 and that continued under Pope Venerable Paul VI until 1965.

People are diverse, and so are the gifts God has given us. The Holy Spirit gives each of us our own gifts. All of our gifts are needed to increase the unity of the Body of Christ (see 1 Corinthians 12:14–31).

The Church gathers people from various cultures and nations. This reality is captured in the **Vatican Council II** document titled the *Dogmatic Constitution on the Church* (*Lumen Gentium*, 1964):

> Though there are many nations there is but one people of God, which takes its citizens from every race, making them citizens of a kingdom which is of a heavenly rather than of an earthly nature. (13)

The Church draws her members from all over the world. If we think about all the cultures that make up the Church, each person contributing his or her unique gifts and callings, we can begin to imagine the great diversity in the Church.

The Pope as a Symbol of Unity

As the successor to Saint Peter, whom Jesus called to lead his Church, the Pope is the visible principle and foundation of the unity of the whole Church. As the shepherd of

Faith in Action
The Taizé Community

© TONY GENTILE / Reuters / Landov

The Taizé community began as an ecumenical monastic community in Taizé, France. It was originally founded by Br. Roger Schutz-Marsauche to shelter refugees fleeing the German occupiers of France during World War II. In 1949, after the war, the seven brothers of the community committed themselves to vows of celibacy and community life.

The aim of the community has always been to be a sign of unity and reconciliation among divided Christians and throughout the world. The brothers come from both Catholic and Protestant backgrounds. Many live as witnesses of peace in small communities around the world. They choose to live among the poorest of the poor, vulnerable, and oppressed.

The monastery of Taizé has become a magnet for young people. Its ecumenical style of worship, as well as the simple but compelling music that has sprung from the heart of that worship, has drawn thousands of young people to days of retreat and spiritual renewal. Church leaders of many Christian faiths have also visited Taizé and have commended this simple but powerful witness of unity. As Pope, Saint John Paul II visited in 1986 and said: "One passes through Taizé as one passes close to a spring of water. The traveler stops, quenches his thirst and continues on his way."

In 2010, on the fifth anniversary of Brother Roger's death, Pope Benedict XVI wrote, "May his witness to an ecumenism of holiness inspire us in our march towards unity." Today the community of Taizé and all who are drawn to its ideals continue that witness.

Vicar of Christ
A title for the Pope, indentifying his role as Christ's human representative on earth.

creed
Based on the Latin *credo*, meaning, "I believe," a creed is an official presentation of the faith, usually prepared and presented by a council of the Church and used in the Church's liturgy. Two creeds occupy a special place in the Church's life: the Apostles' Creed and the Nicene Creed.

the whole Church, he is the "visible sign and guarantor of unity" (*Ut Unum Sint: On Commitment to Ecumenism,* 88). As the **Vicar of Christ**, the Pope is the visible representative of Christ on earth. As Pope, Saint John Paul II called on non-Catholic Christians to work with Catholics to develop ways to express this universal role of the Pope in a way that would be acceptable to all Christians.

How does the Pope lead the Church? The Pope does not lead by domination and power. Rather, he leads as the *servus servorum Dei,* the "servant of the servants of God." This term has been used for centuries and continues to be used today. For example, Pope Benedict XVI used this term immediately after his election in 2005 when he delivered his first message, "Striving to Be the *Servus Servorum Dei.*" This term also emphasizes the Pope's role as a symbol of unity, describing the Pope's calling to serve *all* who serve God.

Sin as a Threat to Unity

Sin and its aftermath threaten Christ's gift of Church unity. The Apostles could see this challenge in the early Church, and they warned all Christians to do their part to maintain and perfect the gift of unity. Despite those warnings, over the centuries, disagreements among Christians have arisen as a result of sin, contrary to God's will for the Church to be one. Today we continue to experience the challenge that sin presents to Christian unity. We are called to do our part in praying and working for the unity of all Christians and all humanity. Later in this chapter, we will look more closely at efforts to restore and strengthen Christian unity.

> **Think of an example where you see sin threatening the unity of the Church. How can we work as Christians to overcome this challenge?**

Article 15: Bonds of Unity

How does the Church retain her unity? Church members are connected by both visible and invisible bonds of unity. The greatest bond of unity is God's love, which binds us together in an invisible way. Several visible characteristics of the Church also bind her in unity: our profession of one faith, our common celebration of divine worship, the martyrdom of faithful Christians, and the recognition of the ordained leaders of the Church, who are successors of the Apostles.

Unity of Faith

People all over the world profess the one faith by praying the Apostles' Creed and the **Nicene Creed**. Both **creeds** have special places in the Church's life.

The Apostles' Creed is a statement of Christian faith that was developed from the baptismal creed of the ancient Church of Rome. We often pray it during Lent and the Easter season:

> I believe in God,
> the Father almighty,
> Creator of heaven and earth,
> and in Jesus Christ, his only Son, our Lord,
> who was conceived by the Holy Spirit,
> born of the Virgin Mary,
> suffered under Pontius Pilate,
> was crucified, died and was buried;
> he descended into hell;
> on the third day he rose again from the dead;
> he ascended into heaven,
> and is seated at the right hand of God the Father almighty;
> from there he will come to judge the living and the dead.
>
> I believe in the Holy Spirit,
> the holy catholic Church,
> the communion of saints,
> the forgiveness of sins,
> the resurrection of the body,
> and life everlasting. Amen.

(Roman Missal, page 528)

Nicene Creed
The formal statement or profession of Christian belief originally formulated at the Council of Nicaea in 325 and amplified at the Council of Constantinople in 381.

The Nicene Creed was developed at the Church's first two Ecumenical Councils, the Council of Nicaea (AD 325) and the Council of Constantinople (AD 381). You may recognize it as the creed we pray most often at Sunday Mass:

> I believe in one God,
> the Father almighty,
> maker of heaven and earth,
> of all things visible and invisible.
>
> I believe in one Lord Jesus Christ,
> the Only Begotten Son of God,
> born of the Father before all ages.
> God from God, Light from Light,
> true God from true God,
> begotten, not made, consubstantial with the Father;
> through him all things were made.
> For us men and for our salvation
> he came down from heaven,
> and by the Holy Spirit was incarnate of the Virgin Mary,
> and became man.
>
> For our sake he was crucified under Pontius Pilate,
> he suffered death and was buried,
> and rose again on the third day
> in accordance with the Scriptures.
> He ascended into heaven
> and is seated at the right hand of the Father.
> He will come again in glory
> to judge the living and the dead
> and his kingdom will have no end.
>
> I believe in the Holy Spirit, the Lord, the giver of life,
> who proceeds from the Father and the Son,
> who with the Father and the Son is adored and glorified,
> who has spoken through the prophets.
>
> I believe in one, holy, catholic and apostolic Church.
> I confess one Baptism for the forgiveness of sins
> and I look forward to the resurrection of the dead
> and the life of the world to come. Amen.

(*Roman Missal*, page 527)

The Nicene Creed summarizes truths about the Father ("I believe in one God, the Father almighty . . ."), the Son ("I believe in one Lord Jesus Christ . . ."), the Holy Spirit ("I believe in the Holy Spirit, the Lord, the giver of life . . ."), as well as belief in the Church ("I believe in one, holy, catholic and apostolic Church") and other essential beliefs. If you look again at the Apostles' Creed, you'll see that it professes the same beliefs, just in slightly different words.

When you recite the Nicene Creed this Sunday, imagine scores of people around the world joining with you and all those assembled with you in professing one faith. This is a visible (and audible) sign of unity that affirms the basic beliefs we share. When we profess what we believe, we also commit ourselves to what we believe.

Although both the Nicene and Apostles' Creeds summarize the key points of the faith, our profession of faith goes far beyond them. Think of the size of the *Catechism of the Catholic Church* (*CCC*) and the Bible as closer to the amount of knowledge we should have about our faith as Catholics. Learning about the faith through Catholic education, a parish religious education program or ministry, and personal study are all ways for us to understand, articulate, and share the faith.

Primary Sources

Young People in Prayer

The Taizé community in France welcomes thousands of young people each year to pray and sing together. Here, a brother from the community reflects on these young people:

> We brothers are often impressed by the ability of the young people to remain in our church, sometimes for hours on end, in silence or supported by meditative singing.
>
> What enables the young people to become truly open to an inner dialogue in prayer? How do we manage to let them discover that, even without knowing how to pray, even without knowing what to ask for or what to expect, God has already placed in us the longing for a communion?
>
> ("Young Adults and Prayer at Taizé")

Apostolic Succession
The uninterrupted passing on of apostolic preaching and authority from the Apostles directly to all bishops. It is accomplished through the laying on of hands when a bishop is ordained in the Sacrament of Holy Orders as instituted by Christ. The office of bishop is permanent, because at ordination a bishop is marked with an indelible, sacred character.

Unity of Worship

In addition to our profession of faith, we are also united through our participation in divine worship and the Sacraments. The Seven Sacraments, especially the Eucharist, create bonds of unity within the Church. The Eucharist is both a sign of the unity of the Church and a means to bring about that unity. The Sacrament of the Eucharist therefore is the totality and summary of our faith. Saint Paul taught, "Because the loaf of bread is one, we, though many, are one body, for we all partake of the one loaf" (1 Corinthians 10:17). Our Eucharistic celebrations always include the same essential elements: proclaiming the Word of God, giving thanks to God for all his benefits, consecrating the bread and wine, and receiving the Body and Blood of Christ.

People of every race, nationality, culture, and age belong to the Church. The liturgy, especially Sunday Mass, is a good place to witness the unity and diversity of the Church. The Diocese of Oakland, California, for example, has offered Masses in at least twelve languages, including Portuguese, Korean, Latin, and American Sign Language. The essential elements of the Mass are the same across the world, but aspects of the Church's liturgy can be adapted to fit the culture of the people in the assembly—such as the liturgical music or the art and architecture of church buildings. Yet the unity and integrity of the Church's worship is guaranteed because the ritual has been passed down from the Apostles through the bishops.

WEEKEND MASS SCHEDULE

Saturday:	12:30 p.m. (Korean), 5:30 p.m. (English)
Sunday:	9:00 a.m., 11:00 a.m., 7:00 p.m.

DAILY MASSES

Monday–Friday:	5:30 p.m.

Sacrament of Reconciliation: (Confessions)
Monday–Friday: 4:30–5:00 p.m.
Wednesday: 8:30–9:30 p.m.
Saturday: 4:00–5:15 p.m. and by appt.

Sacrament of Baptism of Infants:
Held on the fourth Sunday of every month, in English at 1:00 p.m. and in Spanish at 2:00 p.m. Scheduling is done at the Baptism class.

Baptism Class: (a prerequisite to have your child baptized)
Classes in English and Spanish meet on the second Monday of each month at 7:30 p.m. in the Catholic Center. Attendance at a Baptism class is required for parents and godparents.

Unity of the Apostolic Succession

We are united by recognizing the authority of the same Church leaders: the bishops in union with the Pope. The bishops and the Pope have received their authority by means of

Apostolic Succession through the **Sacrament of Holy Orders**. The bishops, as successors of the Apostles, and the Pope, as the successor of Peter, provide us with a concrete guarantee that we are still following the same faith and sacramental worship that was passed down from Jesus and the Apostles.

© Marzolino / Shutterstock

© neneo / Shutterstock.com

"The Roman Pontiff, as the successor of Peter, is the perpetual and visible principle and foundation of unity of both the bishops and of the faithful" (*Lumen Gentium*, 23). Pope Francis is the 266th Roman Pontiff.

The Unity of the Martyrs

Speaking about Catholics and other Christians who have given their lives as martyrs, Pope Saint John Paul II said, "I now add that this communion is already perfect in what we all consider the highest point of the life of grace, *martyria* unto death, the truest communion possible with Christ who shed his Blood" (*Ut Unum Sint: On Commitment to Ecumenism*, 84).

Holy Orders, Sacrament of
The Sacrament by which baptized men are ordained for permanent ministry in the Church as bishops, priests, or deacons.

The Catholic Church is not the only Christian Church to recognize the sacrifice of martyrs. The Church of England makes its own tribute to men and women it considers to be Christian martyrs. In London the figures of ten twentieth-century martyrs are carved into the stone above Westminster Abbey's west door. These martyrs represent a range of Christian Churches, for example, Dietrich Bonhoeffer (a Lutheran pastor), Dr. Martin Luther King Jr. (a Baptist minister), Oscar Romero (a Catholic archbishop), the Grand Duchess Elizabeth of Russia (a member of the

© Tutti Frutti / Shutterstock

Orthodox Church), and Lucian Tapiedi (a member of the Anglican Church).

How can martyrs be an example of faith for you today?

Article 16: Divisions That Wound Christian Unity

The Church is united by bonds of professed faith, worship, Apostolic Succession, and reverence for martyrs who were willing to die for Christ. Although the Apostles urged the early Christians to preserve the gift of unity they had received, we know that they and later Christians found it challenging to unite as one. Divisions among Christians are a result of our sinful nature; they do not reflect God's will for us. **Heresy** and **schism** have been principal causes of divisions within the Church.

Heresy

heresy
The conscious and deliberate rejection by a baptized person of a truth of faith that must be believed.

schism
A major break that causes division. A schism in the Church is caused by the refusal to submit to the Pope or to be in communion with the Church's members.

In our society today, we value diversity of opinion, and we may even become nervous when one group insists that it alone possesses the truth. Considering different opinions can be beneficial in certain circumstances, but disagreements and misunderstandings about key areas of theology or religious practice have led to confusion and division among Christians.

Heresy results when a person or group consciously and deliberately rejects a **dogma** of the Church. The word *heresy* comes from *haeresis*, a Greek word meaning "party" or "faction," reflecting the fact that heresies have often led to the establishment of opposing groups within the Church, especially in her early centuries. Early Church heresies included Gnosticism, Arianism, Nestorianism, Monophysitism, and Appolinarianism. Some of these heresies questioned Christ's divine and human natures, Mary's role as the Mother of God, and the fact that Christ made salvation possible for all, not just a privileged few.

Schisms

A Christian community in schism with the Catholic Church is one that does not recognize the supreme authority of the Pope or otherwise is not in communion with the Church. Schisms sometimes occurred when a community did not accept the teachings of a Council. The Assyrian Church of the East, for example, did not accept the outcome of the Council of Ephesus, and the Oriental Orthodox Churches rejected the definitions from the Council of Chalcedon.

In its later centuries, the Roman Empire was divided into East and West. Constantine's successors ruled the Greek-speaking Eastern half, the Byzantine Empire, from its capitol, Constantinople. Other emperors ruled the Latin-speaking West from Rome. The distance and difficult travel conditions between the Churches in the East and the West made communication difficult, a situation that fostered disagreements for many centuries after the decline of the Roman Empire in the West, in the late fifth century.

Then in 1054 when he was Pope, Saint Leo IX sent a delegation from Rome to the Orthodox Patriarch Michael of Constantinople (in present-day Turkey). After a series of disagreements, the Roman delegation **excommunicated** the patriarch, and the patriarch in turn excommunicated the delegation. This is why the current schism between Eastern Orthodox Christianity and the Catholic Church is often dated to 1054. However, later events, including the destruction of Constantinople in 1204 by European crusaders, eventually led to a complete break in relations between the Eastern Orthodox Church and the Roman Church.

You may be familiar with the Russian Orthodox Church, the Greek Orthodox Church, or others. In 2004,

dogma
Teachings recognized as central to Church teaching, defined by the Magisterium and considered definitive and authoritative.

excommunication
A severe penalty that results from grave sin against Church law. The penalty is either imposed by a Church official or happens automatically as a result of the offense. An excommunicated person is not permitted to celebrate or receive the Sacraments.

the Center for the Study of Global Christianity estimated that there were approximately 216,574,000 Orthodox Christians worldwide.

Despite ongoing differences, the Catholic Church considers herself to be almost in full communion with the Orthodox Church. In 1984, Pope Saint John Paul II and Moran Mar Ignatius Zakka II, then the patriarch of Antioch and all the East and supreme head of the Universal Syrian Orthodox Church, declared that the past schism between their Churches was due to differences in terminology and culture, rather than any true differences in belief. The Churches pledged to continue to work toward full communion.

© Robert Harding World Imagery / Alamy

The Catholic Church shares a special relationship with the Eastern Orthodox churches in part because they have maintained Apostolic Succession and celebrate true Sacraments.

The Protestant Reformation

The Protestant Reformation in the early sixteenth century also divided Christians. Various conflicts arose that led some Christians to break away from the Catholic Church and form new ecclesial communities. These communities became known as Protestants, from the infinitive *to protest*. The term *Protestant* today describes the Christians that descended from this movement. A key figure in the Protestant Reformation was Martin Luther, a German monk, priest, and Scripture scholar. One of the Church practices Luther criticized was the selling of **indulgences**. When Luther could not resolve his conflict with the Church, he was excommunicated. People who then followed Luther in forming a new ecclesial community became known as Lutherans.

Theological principles that were central to the Protestant Reformation were *sola scriptura* and *sola gratia,* ideas that contradict the truth of Catholic teaching. The first phrase, *sola scriptura*, means that "Scripture alone," rather than Sacred Scripture and Tradition, should be the basis for Church teaching. The second phrase, *sola gratia,* means that salvation comes through God's grace alone, not through any human effort. This solitary focus on grace contradicts the truth that although God's grace is our ultimate source of salvation, we can either cooperate with his grace through good works, or we can deny God's grace.

Not long after the start of the Protestant Reformation and Luther's break with the Church, other Christian ecclesial communities were established in northern Europe. For example, in 1530 King Henry VIII of England broke with the Catholic Church following a dispute with the Pope over his right to divorce and remarry. Henry VIII established the Church of England and declared himself the head of that Church. Around the same time, another group that broke away from the Catholic Church was the Calvinists, who followed the teachings of John Calvin. In later centuries, ecclesial communities such as Presbyterians, Baptists, Methodists, and Episcopalians evolved from congregations that had split from the Catholic Church in the early sixteenth century.

The Counter-Reformation (or Catholic Reformation), most notably the Council of Trent (1545–1563), addressed the issues at the heart of the division created by the Protestant Reformation. Although the Council made many positive changes to correct abuses, it was unable to restore unity among Christians.

Do you have a friend or relative who belongs to a Protestant church? What do his or her worship and beliefs have in common with your own?

indulgence
The means by which the Church takes away the punishment that a person would receive in Purgatory.

Martin Luther is known for his posting of the *Ninety-five Theses on the Power and Efficacy of Indulgences.* Martin Luther did not intend to cause a split in the Church; instead he hoped the Church would discuss and resolve the points he was raising.

© traveler1116 / iStockphoto

Article 17: Ecumenism

We have examined some reasons for divisions that prevent the perfect Christian unity that Christ called for. But we must also recognize that all who are baptized in Christ and brought up in the faith of Christ are Christians and are brothers and sisters with one another and with the Church.

Catholics and Other Christians

All Catholics are Christians—but not all Christians are Catholic. We share many elements of holiness and truth with non-Catholic Christians, such as the Bible; the life of grace; faith, hope, and love; the Gifts of the Holy Spirit; and many visible elements of worship. Christ works through other Churches and ecclesial communities as a means of salvation. Yet the salvation that is possible through these Christian communities ultimately depends on the fullness of the heritage of faith that Jesus entrusted to the Catholic Church.

Did You Know?

Sharing the Eucharist

© Robert Harding Picture Library / Superstock

To Christians who are not Catholic, it may seem as if the Catholic Church is arrogant and intolerant in not sharing the Eucharist with them. To help us understand why that is not the case, let's look more closely at the Church's reasoning.

The Eucharist is a sign of the oneness of the faith, liturgy, and leadership of the Church. Unfortunately, however, Christians currently are not fully united. Many Christians belong to congregations that are outside the Apostolic Succession. Though those congregations share many beliefs and practices with us, they do not share them fully. It would be dishonest to celebrate a sign of unity together before the Church is actually united or before a member of another Christian community comes into full communion with the Catholic Church.

If you have friends who would like to become Catholic, suggest that they talk with your school's campus minister or with a priest or staff member at a nearby Catholic parish.

Non-Catholic Churches and Ecclesial Communities

Although the Eastern Orthodox Church is not in full communion with the Catholic Church, these two Churches are especially close because both have maintained Apostolic Succession. The Orthodox Church also celebrates true Sacraments, especially Holy Orders and the Eucharist. One major cause of continuing division, however, is that the Eastern Orthodox Church does not acknowledge the Pope's authority over the whole Church.

The Catholic Church recognizes that all those "who believe in Christ and have been properly baptized are put in some, though imperfect, communion with the Catholic Church" (*Decree on Ecumenism [Unitatis Redintegratio, 1964]*, 3). All who are baptized are made part of the "crucified and glorified Christ" (22). For this reason, all who are baptized can rightly be called brothers and sisters in Christ. However, some ecclesial communities, such as those that originated in the Protestant Reformation, do not receive apostolic authority from the Apostles and their successors, the bishops, through the Apostolic Succession. Those ecclesial communities that lack Apostolic Succession do not have the fullness of the Sacraments or of salvation. The Church continues to engage in dialogue with other Christian ecclesial communities to work toward Christian unity.

ecumenism
The movement to restore unity among all Christians, the unity to which the Church is called by the Holy Spirit.

Pope Francis has often met with leaders of the Eastern Orthodox Church to deepen the relationship between the two Churches.

© Milos Bicanski / Stringer / Getty Images

The Ecumenical Movement

The ecumenical movement, or **ecumenism**, is an effort by Christians from different Churches and ecclesial communities to be more open to one another and to work to restore unity among all Christians. The movement has focused on two immediate goals: (1) to achieve better mutual understanding and (2) to cooperate in various endeavors (for example, assisting people who are poor, or producing new Bible translations). As Pope, Saint John Paul II made clear that the ultimate goal of the ecumenical movement is to return all Christians to visible unity and full communion. The Catholic Church is committed to the ecumenical movement; many Vatican Council II documents address this issue, especially the important *Decree on Ecumenism.*

Although we can deepen our understanding of non-Catholic communities in conversation with Christian friends, an essential part of the movement is dialogue between official representatives of the Catholic Church and of other communities. The Catholic Church has participated in a number of exchanges that have yielded concrete results. For example, in 1965 Pope Venerable Paul VI (1897–1978) and Athenagoras I, patriarch of Constantinople, issued a joint Catholic–Orthodox declaration in which they apologized to one another for the offensive actions surrounding the 1054 schism, nullified (or lifted) the excommunications that were part of that schism, and stated that they deplored the other events surrounding the schism that led to their break in communion.

Live It!
Dialogue with Non-Catholics

Because our world is diverse, you probably have frequent interactions with non-Catholic Christians, as well as members of non-Christian faiths and those who do not profess any faith. Follow these two practical guidelines whenever you find yourself discussing religious topics with those who are not Catholic:

- Develop a solid understanding of your own faith. If others challenge your beliefs, be ready to explain them in a clear and calm way (see 1 Peter 3:15–16).
- Be open to learning about other faiths. The Church affirms that the Holy Spirit works through Christians who are not Catholic, and she rejects nothing of what is true and holy in non-Christian religions.

We can be open to learning from other faith traditions, while at the same time being ready to share the truth of our Catholic faith.

Essential Elements of the Movement toward Unity

The commitment to the ecumenical movement involves several essential elements for all Church members—including you (see *CCC*, 821):

- growth in holiness through a constant renewal of the Church
- conversion of heart
- prayer for unity, including joining together in prayer with other Christians
- deeper knowledge of one another and our traditions
- formation for ecumenical dialogue for all the faithful, especially priests
- ecumenical dialogue and meetings among **theologians** and other Christians
- collaboration between Catholics and other Christians in various areas of service to all of humanity

> **What is one concrete thing you can do today to help promote Christian unity?**

theologian
One who engages in the academic discipline of theology, or "the study of God," in an effort to understand, interpret, and order our experience of God and Christian faith.

Pray It!

Praying for Christian Unity

The following prayer is taken from "Resources for the Week of Prayer for Christian Unity, and Throughout the Year 2009," prepared jointly by the Pontifical Council for Promoting Christian Unity (a department at the Vatican) and the Commission on Faith and Order (part of the World Council of Churches). This week is observed every January 18 through 25.

Lord our God, we thank you for the wisdom we gain from your scriptures. Grant us the courage to open our hearts and our minds to neighbors of other Christian confessions and of other faiths; the grace to overcome barriers of indifference, prejudice or hate; and a vision of the last days, when Christians might walk together towards that final feast, when tears and dissension will be overcome through love. Amen. (Prayer for Day 7)

Article 18: The Church of Christ

Jesus Christ established the Church, sometimes referred to as the Church of Christ, and he appointed Saint Peter and the Apostles to lead her. The Church of Christ—which we profess to be One, Holy, Catholic, and Apostolic—exists in the Catholic Church. Only the Catholic Church has sustained the apostolic structure and succession of leadership that Christ established. The Kingdom of God is already present in the Catholic Church and will be perfected at the end of time. When the Kingdom of God is perfected, the just will reign with God in Heaven for eternity, their souls united with their glorified, resurrected bodies. God will be all in all, because all of creation will be in perfect and direct relationship with its Creator.

Achieving Christian unity is a work of the whole Church—but unity cannot come from human effort alone. Through prayer and other actions, we participate in the Trinity's work to reconcile all Christians.

Chapter Review

1. What is the example for, and source of, the Church's unity?

2. What is the difference between unity and uniformity?

3. What are the visible bonds of unity in the Church?

4. Why does the Catholic Church not allow all Christians to receive the Eucharist?

5. What were the final events that led to the schism between the Roman Catholic Church and the Eastern Orthodox Church?

6. Explain the two theological principles that were at the heart of the Protestant Reformation.

7. What elements of holiness and truth are shared among Catholics and other Christians?

8. What is the ecumenical movement, and what is the Catholic Church's approach toward it?

Introduction

The second Mark of the Church is that she is Holy. How is the Church holy? Why is she different from other organizations that do good things? This chapter will answer those questions.

Unlike any other organization, the Church is made up of a human element and a divine element. The divine element can be seen with the eyes of faith. The eyes of faith tell us that the Church is holy because she was created by the most holy God, who has given her the gifts to be an instrument of salvation, and because the Holy Spirit dwells in her. The holiness of the Church on earth is real yet imperfect because her members cannot be perfectly holy in this life, even though we take steps toward holiness.

The Church depends completely on the free gift of God's grace to be holy. Through this grace we are prepared to respond to God's invitation of love and are able to grow in holiness. As individual members of the Church, we need to cooperate with God's grace.

When we speak of the Communion of Saints, we mean the visible things that help us to grow in holiness. The Communion of Saints also refers to our communion with other holy people, both those who are living and those who are dead on this earth but alive in Christ. All of humankind experiences three stages of sanctification: life on earth, Purgatory, and Heaven.

The Church recognizes the power of the Holy Spirit as she identifies certain people as saints to serve as models of holiness for us. We also pray to ask them to intercede with God on behalf of ourselves or others. Mary, who by God's grace is perfectly holy, is the model toward which all other Church members strive. She responded perfectly to the Father by agreeing to be the Mother of the Father's only Son, Jesus. After her earthly life, Mary was assumed into Heaven and became Queen over all things. Because she is so close to God, we often ask Mary for her intercession.

Article 19: The Church's Holiness

We know we live in a world of both good and evil. How can we say the Church is holy if she is obviously part of this sinful world?

The Church Is Both Human and Divine

Let's explore a truth about the Church that helps us to understand her holiness. She is one but is made up of two elements, one human and one divine. We see the human, visible reality of the Church in the people gathered for the Eucharist; the church buildings; the Pope, bishops, and priests; young people praying on retreats and serving others; the Bible; and so on.

But the Church is more than what we can see. She has an invisible dimension as a bearer of divine life, a mystery we can see only with the eyes of faith. This mystery builds on the visible reality. Through the action of the Holy Spirit, the aspects of the Church that we can see put us in touch with her divine dimension.

The Holy Spirit assures us that the Church is always carrying out Christ's mission, despite the sins and failures of the members. Through us God is doing what we could never do on our own. Our work is participation in the real, but unseen, divine life of the Trinity. The earthly structure of the Church exists for the sole purpose of sanctifying the members—that is, making us holy.

When we understand the true nature of the Church as both human and divine, we see that she is not limited to her visible aspects, and we recognize the source of her holiness. The Church is holy because the most holy

vocation
A call from God to all members of the Church to embrace a life of holiness. Specifically, it refers to a call to live the holy life as an ordained minister, as a vowed religious (sister or brother), or in a Christian marriage. Single life that involves a personal consecration or commitment to a permanent, celibate gift of self to God and one's neighbor is also a vocational state.

consecrated life
A state of life recognized by the Church in which a person publicly professes vows of poverty, chastity, and obedience.

God created her. Christ, her Bridegroom, loves her and gave up his life for her to make her holy (see Ephesians 5:25–26). Christ also joins himself to her as his Body and gave her his Holy Spirit. The Spirit of holiness gives the Church her life.

The Church Has God's Holy Gifts

The Church is holy because she is united with Christ, and he has given her the means of salvation. In other words, God has given her the gifts that enable her to sanctify, such as Sacred Scripture, the Sacraments, models of holiness, the leadership of the Apostles and their successors, and everything else that we require for salvation. The Church is his instrument of salvation.

Our Call to Holiness as Members of the Church

The holiness of the Church on earth is real but imperfect. Christ calls all members of the Church to perfect holiness, but this perfection always lies in the future. We cannot fully achieve this perfection in the present. Perfect holiness will be achieved in Heaven, the state of supreme and definitive happiness with the most Holy Trinity and the Communion of Saints. This supreme, definitive happiness is the ultimate fulfillment of all our human longing.

Love is at the heart of holiness. Encounters with human and divine love can give us glimpses into what eternal communion with God might be like. Love is the means by which the Church sanctifies her members. We encounter the love of God in Sacred Scripture, in the Sacraments, in personal prayer, in relationships with loved ones, and in learning about the faith. Saint Thérèse of Lisieux (1873–1897) described love as the principal **vocation**, or calling, of each person. The more specific vocations, such as priesthood, **consecrated life**, or Marriage, are different ways to live out the calling to love.

Holiness and Sinners

Despite the holiness of the Church, her members include sinners. In fact, all of the members of the Body, including her leaders, are sinners. Because the Church sanctifies, it is natural that she embrace sinners. Her holiness lies in the truth that with Christ and in Christ she is fully focused on saving people from sin. The presence of sinners in the Church does not detract from her holiness.

Do you remember Jesus' Parable of the Weeds among the Wheat (see Matthew 13:24–30)? An enemy plants weeds in the same place where the farmer sowed his wheat. Although the farmer's slaves ask him if they should pull the weeds out, the farmer says to wait until harvest to separate the wheat and the weeds. His concern is that if the slaves pull out the weeds, they might pull out some of the wheat as well. Each of us is a mix of wheat and weeds within. As the *Catechism of the Catholic Church* (*CCC*) explains: "In everyone, the weeds of sin

Live It!
The Desire to Be Holy

We have all felt the pressure to go along with the crowd and accept the standards of our culture. Many worldly promises are ultimately false and hollow; only holiness brings true and lasting happiness.

Here are a few practical steps that can help you to develop an increasingly holy life:

- **Take time for prayer, reflection, and worship.** It is difficult to grow in holiness when we are caught up in the "busyness" of the world, causing us to lose the big picture of life's true meaning.
- **Choose your friends wisely.** If we choose friends who are serious about living a holy life, their example will rub off. A true friend will challenge us to become even more holy.
- **Fill your heart and mind with holy things.** We live what is in our hearts and imagination. So if we deliberately choose to read holy literature, watch inspiring movies, or listen to spiritual songs, our hearts will become holier, and our actions will reflect that inner change.

One way we can grow in holiness is through reading and praying with Scripture. What opportunities for growing in holiness are available to you in your school or parish?

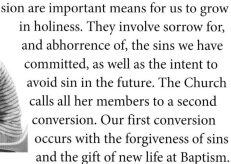

will still be mixed with the good wheat of the Gospel until the end of time.[1] Hence the Church gathers sinners already caught up in Christ's salvation but still on the way to holiness" (827).

Affirming the Church's holiness and her role in sanctifying people does not mean that members of the Church do not need to constantly do penance and seek purification and renewal. Repentance and conversion are important means for us to grow in holiness. They involve sorrow for, and abhorrence of, the sins we have committed, as well as the intent to avoid sin in the future. The Church calls all her members to a second conversion. Our first conversion occurs with the forgiveness of sins and the gift of new life at Baptism.

© Christopher Futcher / iStockphoto.com

Did You Know?

Pope Saint John Paul II and the Purification of Memories

© Massimo Sambucetti / Associated Press

How does it feel to own up to something you have done wrong? It can be difficult and humbling, but it is important. The Church is holy, but she realizes that her members have sinned in the past and wants them to honestly face those sins. During his papacy at the beginning of the third millennium of the Church, Saint John Paul II called for a purification of memories, a process in which both Catholics and non-Catholics would together study their shared past, honestly admit wrongs, and ask one another for forgiveness. At a Day of Pardon Mass in the year 2000, the Pope asked for God's forgiveness for these wrongs over the last two thousand years:

- sins that have led to division in the Body of Christ
- sins against the people of Israel
- sins that have violated the rights of ethnic groups or not respected their cultures and religious traditions
- sins against the dignity of women

This second one is a lifelong effort for us to hear Christ's call to conversion and become increasingly holy.

What does *conversion* mean to you?

Article 20: The Church Makes Us Holy through God's Grace

You probably know the spiritual song "Amazing Grace." Have you ever stopped to consider how truly amazing grace is?

Each of us, each member of the Church, is called to be holy. Jesus said, "Be perfect, just as your heavenly Father is perfect" (Matthew 5:48). To grow in holiness, we must make conscious choices to respond to the Holy Spirit through praying, reading Sacred Scripture, and receiving the Sacraments, the Eucharist in particular. But we must remember that the holiness of the Church and of each member is the result of God's grace, not of our human efforts. Grace is the free and undeserved gift of God's loving presence in our lives. It enables us to respond to his call to be his adopted sons and daughters. Grace enables us to participate in the life of the Trinity.

Grace is supernatural. In other words, it transcends the power of human intellect and will. Because it is supernatural, it can be known by faith only. We cannot rely on our feelings or experiences to recognize God's grace. We can, however, see the results or fruits of God's grace at work in ourselves and in the lives of holy people.

It's All about Grace

The Holy Spirit always makes the first move in our lives. If the Holy Spirit did not prepare us beforehand to receive and cooperate with his grace, we would never choose on our own to seek him and his holiness.

You have learned that when the Father created us, he placed in our hearts the desire and longing for him alone. The gift of grace, a response to this longing, enables us to cooperate with the Holy Spirit in order to grow in

sanctifying grace
The grace that heals our human nature wounded by sin and restores us to friendship with God by giving us a share in the divine life of the Trinity. It is a supernatural gift of God, infused into our souls by the Holy Spirit, that continues the work of making us holy.

actual grace
God's interventions and support for us in the everyday moments of our lives. Actual graces are important for conversion and for continuing growth in holiness.

sacramental graces
The gifts proper to each of the Seven Sacraments.

holiness and to avoid things that separate us from God. Yet we are given freedom along with grace, so how we respond to the gift of grace is up to us. When we freely choose to cooperate with grace, we are at our best, perfecting our God-given potential to form loving relationships with God and others. Grace brings with it the gifts we need to work with the Holy Spirit and to help sanctify others and build up the Church.

Types of Grace

The Holy Spirit gives the Church specific types of grace:

- sanctifying grace
- habitual grace
- actual grace
- sacramental grace
- special graces (charisms)

Sanctifying grace is God's free and generous gift, sometimes called the state of grace. It brings about a change in us that orients us to God and helps us to respond to his call. The Holy Spirit infuses our souls with sanctifying grace to free us from sin and to make us holy. Through Baptism we receive sanctifying grace and a share in the divine life. Sanctifying grace is a habitual grace, meaning that it is a stable and supernatural disposition, always with us, helping us to live according to God's will.

Sanctifying grace therefore differs from another kind of grace called **actual grace**. Actual grace is the name for God's interventions that can come at the beginning of the conversion process and during the everyday moments of our lives.

We also receive **sacramental graces**, gifts that come from the particular Sacraments. Grace comes to us through the Sacraments because Christ instituted them and works through them. Each Sacrament gives us grace in a unique way. For example, the Sacrament of Matrimony gives couples the grace to love each other with the love with which Christ loved his Church, perfecting their human love and strengthening their unity. The grace of the Sacrament of Penance and Reconciliation enables us to have a peaceful conscience and increases our spiritual strength to resist temptation.

The charisms discussed in chapter 2, "The Holy Spirit and the Church," are also special graces of the Holy Spirit. All graces are at the service of love and the building up of the Church. Graces of state accompany us in our specific vocations to live a Christian life and to minister within the Church. For example, the Holy Spirit gifts parents as they do their best to raise their children, and the Holy Spirit inspires a hospital chaplain to know what to say or how to pray when ministering to someone who is dying.

Faith in Action
Saint Aloysius Gonzaga: A Patron Saint for Teens

© Zvonimir Atletic / Shutterstock.com

Saint Aloysius Gonzaga (1568–1591) was born to a wealthy Italian family. His father, a cavalry commander, wanted him to enter a military career as well. But at a young age, Aloysius recognized that God was calling him to a religious life instead. Due to ill health for much of his childhood, he spent much time praying and reading about the lives of the saints. At age nine he even made a vow of perpetual chastity.

Inspired by the saints and his love of prayer, the eighteen-year-old Aloysius gave up a life of luxury and comfort to join the Society of Jesus, also known as the Jesuits. While Aloysius was in Rome studying for his ordination, a great plague broke out. Despite his own poor health, he volunteered at a hospital for the plague victims, soon catching the disease himself. He died at the age of twenty-three.

In the centuries since his canonization, Aloysius has been declared a patron saint of students and of all Christian young people. Gonzaga University, the Jesuit university in Spokane, Washington, was named after Saint Aloysius Gonzaga at its founding in 1887.

God's grace will not automatically make us holy without our cooperation. We must make a real effort to work with God and to fight the temptation to do things that separate us from him, such as going along when our friends are doing things we know are wrong. It is a struggle to work toward holiness, but the end result—true peace and joy and everlasting life—makes our struggle infinitely valuable.

> **Think of a time when you made a choice that separated you from God. How did you make this choice? How did you feel afterward?**

Article 21: The Communion of Saints

We most often profess the Nicene Creed at Sunday Mass but, particularly during Lent and Easter time, the Apostles' Creed may be used. In this creed, we profess our belief in the Communion of Saints. This term refers to the Church, a communion of holy people, those living and those who are dead but alive with God.

There is a second, closely related, meaning of *Communion of Saints*. The English *saint* can translate two Latin terms: *sancti* ("holy people") and *sancta* ("holy things"). The holy things are primarily the Sacraments,

especially the Eucharist. When we profess belief in the Communion of Saints, we do recognize our relationships with all faithful people living now and in the past, but that is not all. We are also saying that "holy things," especially the Eucharist, bind us to one another and unite us to God. When we participate in the Sacraments, particularly the

Eucharist, we are nourished with the Body and Blood of Christ, and we become the Body of Christ for the world.

Love, by its very nature, brings us into communion in the Body of Christ. Saint Paul wrote in his Letter to the Romans, "None of us lives for oneself, and no one dies for oneself" (14:7). Every act of love, no matter how small, builds the communion.

Humankind's Three Stages of Sanctification

The Church is a Communion of Saints that exists in one of three stages of sanctification:

- the faithful, followers of Jesus, here on earth
- the faithful who have died and are being purified and made holy in **Purgatory** to join God in Heaven
- the faithful who have already attained the perfect holiness and glory of Heaven, seeing God as he is

The communion that Christ has given the Church through the Body of Christ enables the boundaries between the living and the dead to be surpassed by life in the Holy Spirit. The living and the dead benefit each other spiritually through their prayers. As we draw closer to the saints in Heaven through our veneration of them, we also draw closer to Christ.

We pray for those who have passed away from this life. Our prayers help them as they are purified of the effects of earthly sin in their journey through Purgatory to the fullness of the heavenly life. We especially remember the faithful departed by offering the Eucharistic sacrifice of the Mass for them.

> **How do those who have died benefit from your prayers? How do you benefit from theirs?**

Purgatory
A state of final purification or cleansing, which one may need to enter following death and before entering Heaven.

Article 22: The Saints: Models and Intercessors

Because the Church is holy, all of us in the Church are saints or holy people. So why does the Church give only certain people the official title Saint?

The Church recognizes the work of the Holy Spirit in certain people and holds them up as examples to the rest of us. These deceased people lived a life of extraordinary holiness or died for their faith. The holiness of the Church shines more clearly in their lives. Those whom the Church has recognized as saints inspire us to grow in holiness and nourish our hope in God on earth and in eternal life.

Saints Are the Face of Christ in the World

Cardinal José Saraiva Martins, CMF, who once led the Congregation for the Causes of Saints at the Vatican, summarized why saints are so important in the Church:

> To understand the Church, we need to be acquainted with the saints who are her most eloquent sign, her sweetest fruit. To contemplate the face of Christ in the changing, diversified situations of the modern world, we must look at the saints who are "the living reflection of the face of Christ," as the Pope reminds us. The Church must proclaim the saints and she must do so in the name of that proclamation of holiness that fills her and makes her, precisely, a means of sanctification in the world. ("Reflection by Cardinal José Saraiva Martins," 2)

Pray It!

Praying with the Communion of Saints

Many wonderful prayers come directly from the saints. It is good to keep these prayers nearby for different situations you may face. Like everyone, you may sometimes find yourself at a loss for words and ready for an established prayer that you know is appropriate. Here is a short prayer from Saint Catherine of Siena (1347–1380), a Doctor of the Church. You can easily memorize it to use when you are short on time or patience:

Lord, take me from myself and give me to yourself.

As we learn about saints or read their writings, we see holiness in action in real life. Those saints whose lives share common elements with our own may particularly inspire us.

Saints Are Models of Holiness

As models of holiness, saints encourage others. Throughout history saints have been sources of renewal for the Church in difficult times. In the fourth century, for example, Saint Athanasius championed the orthodox Christian faith when many were led astray by the Arian heresy. Martyrs such as Saint Maximilian Kolbe (1894–1941), who took the place of another man about to be executed in a concentration camp in World War II, are great examples to us of people who were not afraid to lay down their lives for Christ's sake.

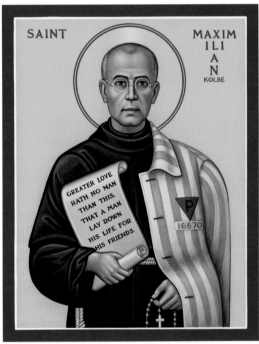

© Monastery Icons

Saints Intercede for Us

Because saints are so closely united to Christ in his heavenly glory, they can intercede with (or pray to) God on our behalf in a special way.

Members of other Christian churches sometimes ask why we honor or venerate the saints and ask for their prayers. Maybe you have wondered this yourself. It is important to realize that the saints do not take the place of God for us. We do not pray to them. Nor does our honoring the saints suggest that we cannot pray directly to God or that we need the saints as intermediaries. We simply ask the saints to pray for us just as we might ask

Notice the concentration camp uniform draped over the shoulder of Saint Maximilian, recalling his loving sacrifice. Many people are inspired to live holier lives because of his example. Who are the saints that inspire you to live a holy life?

any friend to pray for us when we are going through a difficult time.

We also associate some saints with particular needs. If you have ever searched your room for something lost, you know that you wouldn't mind some help. You can pray for the intercession of Saint Anthony of Padua for help in finding lost items. Pray for the intercession of Saint Blasé when you have a sore throat. Pray for the intercession of Saint Teresa of Ávila for help with headaches.

Learning about the saints can be very inspiring. Come February, everyone is talking about Saint Valentine, whose feast day is February 14. It may not surprise you to learn that he is the patron saint of engaged couples and happy marriages. Did you know, however, that he was a Roman priest martyred in the third century? Sources tell us that he was arrested for marrying Christian couples, which was then a crime in the Roman Empire.

We Honor the Saints through the Liturgy and the Liturgical Year

Next time you participate in the Mass, notice the strong connection between the saints in Heaven and the saints on earth in our Eucharistic prayers. We pray for our past loved ones: "Remember . . . our brothers and sisters who have fallen asleep in the hope of the resurrection, and all who have died in your mercy: welcome them into the light of your face" (*Roman Missal*, page 649). We join our prayers and worship with the prayers and worship of those in Heaven: "And so, with the Angels and all the Saints, we declare your glory" (page 645).

The Church honors Mary, especially, because of her link to the saving role of her Son. We celebrate Mary's role on special days of the liturgical calendar, such as the Feast of the Assumption, on August 15. The Church honors other saints on fixed days of the year. Honoring the saints with the whole Church reminds us of the Paschal Mystery visible in their lives, exposes us to holy people, and unites us with the liturgy of Heaven, which is constant praise of God, as revealed in the Book of Revelation.

The examples of the saints inspire us, teach us, and help us to see what it means to live like Christ. At Confirmation most of us choose a saint's name as a Confirmation name because we feel drawn to the saint for some reason. You can get to know a saint well by reading about him or her, especially one who particularly inspires you.

> **Have you chosen a Confirmation name based on the example of a saint? Who is the saint, and why is he or she meaningful to you?**

Article 23: Mary: Perfect Model of Holiness

Marie, Mariam, Maureen, Moira, Mariah, Molly, Maria, Moya, Maryam, Maura, Mary. Do you have any friends with these names? Ask them if they know why their parents chose their name. Parents have named their children after the Virgin Mary for centuries, as a way to honor her special role in the Church. Perhaps this is true for your friends.

Mary's Holiness and Role in the Church

The Church honors Mary above all other saints. Mary is the holiest human being who ever lived. She was perfectly holy, born completely free of **Original Sin** and

Original Sin
From the Latin *origo*, meaning "beginning" or "birth." The term has two meanings: (1) the sin of the first human beings, who disobeyed God's command by choosing to follow their own will and thus lost their original holiness and became subject to death, (2) the fallen state of human nature that affects every person born into the world, except Jesus and Mary.

Primary Sources

Heavenly Intercession

During their lifetimes, many saints have had a strong sense that they would still be able to help those on earth through their heavenly intercession after death. Saint Thérèse of Lisieux hoped to make a difference after her death: "I want to spend my heaven in doing good on earth." Saint Dominic shared the same thought with his brothers on his deathbed: "Do not weep, for I shall be more useful to you after my death and I shall help you then more effectively than during my life."

fiat
Latin for "let it be done."

remaining pure from all personal sin throughout her life. We strive to become like Mary, so we ask her to help us become holier. The destiny of the Church is to be "holy and without blemish" (Ephesians 5:27). Mary has already reached that perfection—she is the masterpiece of the mission of the Son and the Holy Spirit. Mary's life is therefore a model toward which all members of the Church strive.

The Holy Spirit has always worked through Mary to bring people into communion with Christ. Grace alone, through Jesus, saves us. God willed that a human should take a real and active role in accomplishing his divine plan. He chose Mary from among the descendants of Eve to be the Mother of Jesus. The Holy Spirit worked in Mary's life to prepare for the coming of the Son of God, Jesus Christ. Through the Holy Spirit's divine intervention, the Father gave the world Emmanuel, God-with-us.

© Prado, Madrid, Spain / Bridgeman Images

Notice the scene on the far left of the picture. What is the connection between the Annunciation and the Fall?

Mary's Yes

Mary, the ever-virgin, modeled the perfect response to God by saying yes to him. When the angel Gabriel announced that Mary, though still a virgin, would give birth to Jesus, she cooperated freely and fully with the Father's plan, saying: "Behold, I am the handmaid of the Lord. May it be done to me according to your word" (Luke 1:38). Mary, by her **fiat**, by her acceptance of Gabriel's message, by her yes cooperated in a very real way in the Father's plan of salvation through Jesus.

In part because of Mary's yes, the Church draws a parallel between Mary and Eve, calling Mary the New Eve. Just as Eve's disobedience signaled humanity's fall into sin, Mary's obedience and cooperation with God's will revealed humanity's release from sin. Saint Irenaeus (130–202) wrote, "The knot of Eve's disobedience was untied by Mary's obedience: what the virgin Eve bound through her disbelief, Mary loosened by her faith." Saint Jerome taught, "Death through Eve; life through Mary." Through her obedience, Mary "became the new Eve, mother of the living" (*CCC*, 511).

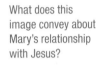

Theotokos
A Greek title for Mary meaning "God bearer."

Mary Is *Theotokos*

The Greek word **Theotokos** means "God-bearer." The Church uses this term for Mary because she is the Mother of Jesus Christ, the Eternal Son of God who became man and who is himself God. For Mary to play such an important role, some preparation was needed.

The Holy Spirit prepared Mary to be the Mother of God. In order for her to carry the Son of God within her and then be a mother to him, she needed to be sinless and humble, full of grace. She was thus prepared in her own mother's womb to be the holy Mother of God. She was free of Original Sin and was redeemed at the moment of her conception. She is the first and best fruit of Jesus' coming to redeem us.

It was through Mary that the amazing work of the Holy Spirit in Christ and the Church first began to be seen. She introduced the Father's Son to us for the first time. The Son of God was revealed first to humble people and Gentiles, and they were the first to accept him.

Mary said yes throughout her life, notably as she stood by her Son, sharing in his suffering on the cross. When Mary's earthly life was over,

What does this image convey about Mary's relationship with Jesus?

© Roca/Shutterstock.com

she was taken up, body and soul, into Heaven, where she already shares in the glory of her Son's Resurrection. We call this wonder the Assumption of Mary. The Lord glorified his mother by making her Queen over all things.

In her lifelong obedience and openness to the Father's will, through her Son's work of salvation, and according to the guidance of the Holy Spirit, Mary is the Church's model of faith and love, the first to collaborate with Christ in his mission. Mary foreshadows the destiny of all the members of the Body of Christ. We all hope to be resurrected on the last day, perfected through God's grace, and accepted into the heavenly Jerusalem, where there is no sadness or death.

Mary, Holy Mother of the Church and Intercessor

Because of her unique, active role in the Father's plan of salvation through his Son, Mary can be called our Mother in the order of grace. Mary is thus the Mother of the Church because she actively participates in the divine plan of giving birth to believers.

We know we can pray for Mary's intercession. After Jesus' Ascension, she prayed with his other followers for the outpouring of the Holy Spirit. Through her intercession we receive gifts that help us to move spiritually toward eternal salvation. Because of her assistance, we call her our Advocate, Helper, and Benefactress.

Chapter Review

1. How is the Church both visible and invisible?

2. How is the Church holy even though her members are sinful?

3. How is our holiness the result of God's grace?

4. What is sanctifying grace?

5. Explain the Communion of Saints as the communion of holy things.

6. Explain the Communion of Saints as the communion of holy people.

7. How do the saints model holiness for us?

8. How do the saints intercede for us?

9. Why is Mary a perfect model of holiness for us as members of the Church?

10. What is the Assumption of Mary?

The Church Is Catholic

Introduction

You may be tempted to say: "Of course the Catholic Church is Catholic. That is why it is called the Catholic Church." As easy as that might sound, in this case we are saying that the third Mark of the Church is *Catholic,* meaning "universal."

The One, Holy, Catholic, and Apostolic Church is universally present in the worldwide Church, in each particular church or diocese, and in each assembly gathered to celebrate the Eucharist. The Church in each case has the fullness of Christ and the full means of redemption when she is in communion with the other bishops and the Pope.

Because the Church calls all people to unity in the People of God, she is in relationship with every person, Christian and non-Christian. She has a special bond with Judaism, and she shares a lesser bond with Islam. The Church is also in relationship with people who follow Hinduism, Buddhism, and other traditions.

The universal Church is universal, yet diverse, because instead of trying to erase differences, she embraces them. The communion between the Roman Catholic Church and the Eastern Catholic Churches, who have different rites and practices, is an example of uniting diversity into a common effort. The Church can also take different cultural traditions throughout the world and integrate them into her worship. Her catholicity is expressed in a variety of popular devotions and prayer forms that reflect the variety of cultures throughout the world.

Article 24: The Meaning of the Word *Catholic*

The general term *catholic* comes from the Greek word *katholikos,* which means "universal." The Church is **Catholic**, or universal, in two senses. First, she is Catholic because Christ is present in her. She possesses the fullness of Christ and has received from him the fullness of the means of salvation. Second, Christ has sent her on a mission to gather all the people of the world into the People of God. Therefore, whereas the Church is One because of her indivisibility, the Church is Catholic (or universal) because she possesses the total means of salvation for all people.

To help you distinguish between the two senses of "Catholic," you might think of the first meaning as "The Church has it all," because she has the fullness (or "all") of Christ and of the means of salvation. You might think of the second meaning as "The Church calls to all," because she invites all humanity to the People of God.

The Church Has It All

The Church is Catholic because Christ is fully present in her and because he has given the Church the full means of salvation. The means of salvation are divine gifts freely given to the Church through the Holy Spirit. These include the fullness of the faith, the fullness of the Seven Sacraments, and the fullness of the ordained **ministry** passed down from the Apostles.

The Church Calls to All

The Church is also Catholic in the sense that Jesus Christ has sent her out on a mission to the whole human race. Jesus commanded his Apostles, "Go, therefore, and make disciples of all nations" (Matthew 28:19).

Because all human beings share the same Divine Creator and the same destiny with God, the Church's purpose is to gather all people from all times together as one. The Church is already a sign of this unity because she has unified people from all over the world in a

Catholic
Along with One, Holy, and Apostolic, *Catholic* is one of the four Marks of the Church. *Catholic* means "universal." The Church is Catholic in two senses. She is Catholic because Christ is present in her and has given her the fullness of the means of salvation and also because she reaches throughout the world to all people.

ministry
Based on a word for "service," a way of caring for and serving others and helping the Church to fulfill her mission. Ministry refers to the work of sanctification performed by those in Holy Orders through the preaching of God's Word and the celebration of the Sacraments. It also refers to the work of the laity in living out their baptismal call to mission through lay ministries, such as that of lector or catechist.

common faith. However, the perfect union of all people with one another and with God will not take place until the end of time.

A Church Father Explains the Word *Catholic*

Saint Cyril of Jerusalem, a Church Father, explained the connection between the Church and wholeness or totality (emphasis added):

> It is called Catholic then because it extends over all the world . . . and because it teaches *universally and completely* one and all the doctrines which ought to come to men's knowledge . . . and because it brings into subjection to godliness the *whole race of mankind* . . . and because it universally treats and heals the *whole class* of sins . . . and possesses it itself *every* form of virtue. (*Catechetical Lectures* 18.23)

How might you summarize in your own words Saint Cyril's explanation of the word *Catholic*?

Article 25: Catholicity: The Fullness of Christ in the Church

The word *Church* refers to the convocation or assembly of people whom God calls together to be in a special relationship with him. The full definition of the word *Church* that you learned in chapter 1, "The Origin of the Church," includes three distinct references. The first refers to the entire community of God's People around the world. The second refers to the local community, or diocese. The third refers to the community assembled for liturgy, especially the Mass. In each of these three references, the Church is fully Catholic, in that she has the fullness of Christ and the means of salvation.

Which of these three references first comes to mind when you hear the word *Church*? It seems logical that the first reference would be the fullest manifestation of the Church. But the Church is indivisible, as is Christ. The Diocese of Winona in Minnesota, for example, is called a particular church. Each particular church, in union with Rome, has the full means of salvation within it.

When you gather with others in your community for the Mass, you hear the Gospel of Christ preached, and an ordained priest presides over the mystery of the Lord's Supper. When this happens, Christ is present, and through Christ the One, Holy, Catholic, and Apostolic Church is also present. That same Church is present at every Mass said throughout the world, no matter how small or poor the local community is.

It would be a mistake, however, to see the Church as simply the sum total of all of the dioceses worldwide, like a federation with its global headquarters in Rome. The Church is fully present throughout the world, but she is also fully present in given locations, which differ from one another.

Catholicity and the Roman Catholic Church

Particular churches are fully Catholic when they are in communion with the Church of Rome. Why is the Roman diocese so important?

In the early centuries of Christianity, Christians struggled with many misleading beliefs. For guidance they turned to, and relied on, the apostolic churches: those established under the authority of the Apostles.

Primary Sources

Saint Thomas Aquinas and the Word *Catholic*

The thirteenth-century theologian Saint Thomas Aquinas had this to say about the third mark of the Church:

> The Church is Catholic, i.e., universal, first in respect to place, because it is everywhere in the world. . . . Second, the Church is universal with respect to the state of men, because no one is rejected, whether master or slave, male or female. . . . Thirdly, it is universal with respect to time. . . this Church began from the time of Abel, and will last to the end of the world. ("Exposition of the Apostles' Creed," in Avery Dulles, *The Catholicity of the Church*, page 181)

College of Bishops
The assembly of bishops, headed by the Pope, that holds the teaching authority and responsibility in the Church.

They did so because these churches had preserved the full and authentic apostolic teaching.

The Church of Rome had special authority among these apostolic churches because two great Apostles, Peter and Paul, had proclaimed the Gospel and were martyred in Rome. The Bishop of Rome is the successor of Peter, who was the leader among the Apostles. In the second century, Saint Irenaeus wrote this about the Roman Church: "It is a matter of necessity that every Church should agree with this Church, on account of its preeminent authority." When churches are in communion with Rome, they possess the fullness, or catholicity, of the apostolic faith as it is preserved in the Roman Church.

© Ugorenkov Aleksandr / Shutterstock.com

Pictured is Vatican Square, in front of Saint Peter's Basilica. The Vatican is the seat of the Bishop of Rome, the Pope.

Churches in full communion with the Church of Rome recognize the authority of the Pope as the visible foundation for the unity of the **College of Bishops** and of all members of the Church. Because the Pope is pastor of the whole Church, those in communion with the Pope share the fullness of Christ because they are united with the earthly, visible leader of the universal church.

The Fullness of the Sacraments

The Church retains the fullness of the Sacraments by celebrating all Seven Sacraments that Christ instituted. Though many Christian ecclesial communities recognize only Baptism and the Eucharist as Sacraments, the Catholic Church, along with the Orthodox Church, celebrates seven.

The Seven Sacraments express fullness in the sense that they touch the totality of a person's life, from Baptism at the beginning to Anointing of the Sick at the end. The Sacraments of Christian Initiation—Baptism, the Eucharist, and Confirmation—lay the foundation of Christian life. The Sacraments of Healing—Penance and Reconciliation and Anointing of the Sick—show us Christ's will that the Church continue his work of comprehensive, total healing, both physical and spiritual. The Sacraments at the Service of Communion—Matrimony and Holy Orders—reflect the different aspects of the Church's universal mission to and in the world.

© The Crosiers / Gene Plaisted, OSC

Which of the Sacraments have you already received? How are they important to your faith life?

Article 26: The Church's Relationship with All People

In chapter 4, "The Church Is One," we looked at the relationship between the Church and other Christian ecclesial communities, including the ecumenical movement that seeks to unify all Christians. Now let's turn to the Church's relationship with the more than four billion people belonging to non-Christian religions, such as Islam, Hinduism, and Buddhism, as well as those who are not affiliated with any religion.

Recall that the catholicity of the Church can be seen as the Church calls all of humanity to unity in the People of God. Just as the Church participates in dialogues with non-Catholic Christian communities, she is also open to dialogue with people of non-Christian religions. The Church recognizes that non-Christian religions seek God and that goodness and truth can be found in them. She considers this goodness and truth to be a preparation for the Gospel. She has a duty to proclaim clearly that Christ is the way, the truth, and the life (see John 14:6).

In dialogue with people of different religions, the Catholic Church witnesses to her own faith while acknowledging and encouraging the spiritual and moral truths found in their religions. Note, however, that the Church does not support any religious groups that lead people astray or distort the image of God found in all people.

The Church is in relationship with all people of non-Christian religions, but she is more closely connected to Jews and Muslims. Like Christians, Jews and Muslims acknowledge belief in one God.

The Church's Relationship with Jews

The Church has a unique relationship with the Jewish people and religion. Many links bind us together. Jesus himself was Jewish; God revealed himself to the Jewish

Did You Know?

Gathering for a World Day of Prayer for Peace

REUTERS / Vincenzo Pinto / LANDOV

During his papacy, Pope Saint John Paul II organized a World Day of Prayer for Peace in Assisi, Italy, on January 24, 2002, partly in response to the terrorist attacks of September 11, 2001. This was the second time the Pope had assembled representatives from different Christian communities and world religions to pray for peace and to discourage the use of religion as a motive for modern-day conflict.

At this event the Pope welcomed representatives from many world religions, Christian and non-Christian. The delegates included patriarchs from Eastern Catholic and Orthodox Churches, the archbishop of Canterbury of the Anglican Church, the secretary general of the Ecumenical Council of Churches, and representatives of other Christian communities. The Pope also greeted distinguished members of world Judaism; representatives of world Islam; Buddhist representatives; Hindu representatives; representatives of African Traditional Religion; Sikh delegates; and Confucian, Zoroastrian, and Jain delegates, among others.

people through the old covenants, and the Jewish faith is a response to his Revelation. God gifted the Jews with the promises, the Law, and the covenants, and he called them to be his People. These gifts can never be revoked: "The gifts and the call of God are irrevocable" (Romans 11:29).

© ChameleonsEye / Shutterstock.com

This young man is celebrating his Bar Mitzvah at the Western Wall in Jerusalem. Jesus was raised in the Jewish tradition and participated in many of the Jewish rituals that continue today.

Although Christians are a people of the New Covenant, we should not assume that God has rejected or cursed the Jews and their covenant with God. On the contrary, the Jewish people remain dear to God, "since God does not take back the gifts he bestowed or the choice he made" (*Declaration on the Relation of the Church to Non-Christian Religions* [*Nostra Aetate*, 1965], 4; see Romans 11:28–29). The Catholic Church especially warns us not to blame Jewish people for the death of Christ, as some Christians have unfortunately done through the centuries. Although Jewish leaders were involved in Jesus' death, in no way can we blame the Jewish people as a whole, either in ancient times or today, for his death.

The Church's Relationship with Muslims

God's plan of salvation also includes Islam. Muslims acknowledge the one Creator, trace their faith back to Abraham, and worship the one God by praying, giving alms, and fasting (see *Relation of the Church to Non-Christian Religions*, 3). Though Muslims do not accept the divinity of Jesus, they do recognize him as a great prophet. They also honor Mary and believe that she gave birth to Jesus

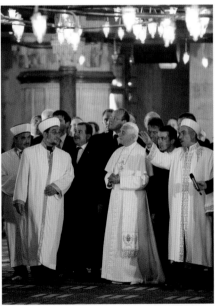

© Getty Images

while still a virgin, and they acknowledge the resurrection of the dead and God's Final Judgment (see *Relation of the Church to Non-Christian Religions*, 3).

The Church's Relationship with Other Non-Christian Religions

The Church is also in relationship with people who participate in religions that do not share belief in the one God, creator of all. Two such religions are Hinduism and Buddhism. Despite differences in belief, the Church acknowledges that the adherents of these religions search for the one God.

The Church recognizes that Hindus contemplate the divine mystery, which they express through mythic stories and philosophical insights. Buddhists have developed traditions of profound meditation and seek God in confidence and love. They recognize the temporary nature of this world and teach that humans can attain

Live It!
Common Commitment to Peace

The participants at the Day of Prayer for Peace in the World held in Assisi, Italy, on January 24, 2002, concluded their gathering by proclaiming their resolve to promote peace in the world. As part of this proclamation, the following commitment was read in several languages:

Violence never again!
War never again!
Terrorism never again!
In the name of God, may every religion bring upon the earth
Justice and Peace,
Forgiveness and Life,
Love!

These words challenge each of us to work for peace in the world. How can you make justice, peace, forgiveness, life, and love central in your everyday efforts to promote peace? Start by sharing this commitment with your family and friends, and invite them to join you in praying for peace in the world.

liberation from these limitations through their own efforts and with divine help (see *Relation of the Church to Non-Christian Religions*, 2).The Church deeply respects people of different religious traditions, as we can see in the following excerpt from Vatican Council II:

> She regards with sincere reverence those ways of conduct and of life, those precepts and teachings which, though differing in many aspects from the ones she holds and sets forth, nonetheless often reflect a ray of that Truth which enlightens all men. (*Relation of the Church to Non-Christian Religions*, 2)

The Church also sees herself connected with all people, even those affiliated with no religion, because all people are made in the image and likeness of God.

What is the Church's relationship with other religious traditions?

Article 27: Universality and Diversity

In chapter 4, "The Church Is One," we saw that unity does not mean uniformity. We can also say that universality does not mean uniformity. Rather, the Church encompasses great diversity.

The Church Reconciles and Embraces Diversity

Even though the Church of Rome is preeminent among particular churches, the Catholic Church is not Italian or even European. In Christ there is no exclusively African or Asian or American Church. Saint Paul indicated that the Church is a place where differences can be reconciled:

> So then you are no longer strangers and sojourners, but you are fellow citizens with the holy ones and members of the household of God, built upon the foundation of the apostles and prophets, with Christ Jesus himself as the capstone. Through him the whole structure is held together and grows into a temple sacred in the Lord; in him you also are being

canonize
The act by which the Church officially recognizes a deceased Catholic as a saint.

Latin Church
That part of the Catholic Church that follows the disciplines and teachings of the Diocese of Rome, especially the liturgical traditions. It is called the Latin Church because Latin has been the official language since the fourth century. The majority of the world's Catholics belong to the Latin Church.

built together into a dwelling place of God in the Spirit. (Ephesians 2:19–22)

Communion with God requires reconciliation rather than competition, rivalry, or division. We often find it comfortable to associate primarily with people who are like us—who think like us or act like us. For the Church to fully realize her catholicity, however, we must embrace, not erase, differences of culture, race, wealth, social class, or any other dividing characteristic.

The Saints: The Sign of the Church's Catholicity

We also see the Church's catholicity in the saints. Our saints have come from various walks of life and from many different places in the world. Thus the Church recognizes Saint Thomas Aquinas, the great Italian theologian and philosopher. She recognizes powerful kings and queens, such as Saints Louis of France and Elizabeth of Hungary, but also poor farmers, such as Saint Juan Diego of Mexico. As Pope, Saint John Paul II **canonized** Saint Andrew Dung-Lac and his companions, Vietnamese Catholics who suffered martyrdom during a time of persecution against the Church and her members. Pope Saint John Paul II himself was Polish, the first Eastern European Pope. Saints have included the twelve-year-old Saint Maria Goretti and the 105-year-old Saint Anthony of Egypt. Saints have included priests such as Saint John Vianney, popes such as Pope Saint Leo the Great and Pope Saint John XXIII, abbots and abbesses such as Saint Benedict of Nursia and Saint Brigid of Kildare, and married people such as Saint Elizabeth Ann Seton.

The Eastern Catholic Churches

The relationship between Roman Catholics and Eastern Catholics is an example of unity in diversity. Though the Eastern Catholic Churches (distinct from the Eastern Orthodox Church) have some rituals and practices that differ from those of the Roman Catholic Church, Eastern Catholics are in full communion with Rome. There are currently twenty-one Eastern Catholic Churches. These Churches refer to the Roman Catholic Church as the **Latin Church**.

Most of the Eastern Catholic Churches separated from the Roman Catholic Church as a result of the schism between the Orthodox and Catholic Churches in the eleventh century. As we have seen, the Eastern Orthodox Church is still not in full communion with the Catholic Church. Those Churches that have since returned to full communion with the Roman Catholic

Faith in Action
Wise Words from Saint Josephine Bakhita of Sudan

© Vicki Shuck / Saint Mary's Press

Valuing the catholicity of the Church can include reflecting on the lives of saints from different parts of the world. Saint Josephine Bakhita (1869–1947) was born in Sudan. She was kidnapped as a young child and spent her childhood in slavery. Bakhita, which ironically means "fortunate," is what her captors called her. The trauma of prolonged childhood slavery reportedly caused her to forget the name her parents had given her. At fourteen, she was bought by an Italian consul and came to Italy to live with his family, who treated her with love and respect at last.

In Italy, Bakhita met Catholic sisters, converted to Catholicism, and was baptized as Josephine. She eventually entered the order of the Canossian Sisters at the age of thirty-four. Her 1931 biography made her famous throughout Italy and beyond. She was canonized on October 1, 2000.

When you are going through a difficult time, consider meditating with the words of Saint Josephine Bakhita:

- "I have given everything to my Master: He will take care of me. . . . The best thing for us is not what we consider best, but what the Lord wants of us!"
- "O Lord, if I could fly to my people and tell them of your Goodness at the top of my voice: oh, how many souls would be won!"
- "If I were to meet the slave-traders who kidnapped me and even those who tortured me, I would kneel and kiss their hands, for if that did not happen, I would not be a Christian and Religious today."

(Quotations from the National Black Catholic Congress website)

icon
From a Greek word meaning "likeness," a sacred image of Christ, Mary, or the saints, especially in the artwork of the Eastern Churches.

iconostasis
A screen or partition with doors and tiers of icons that separates the bema, the raised part of the church with the altar, from the nave, the main part of the church, in Eastern Churches.

Church are called Eastern Catholic Churches. Although they do share much in common with the Orthodox Church because of their origin in the Eastern part of the Roman Empire, the Eastern Catholic Churches should not be confused with the Eastern Orthodox Church. Eastern Catholic Churches have different liturgical rites, customs, laws, devotions, and theological interests than the Latin Church, but they enjoy equal dignity with her.

Here are some examples of the ways Eastern Catholic Churches differ from the Latin Church:

- The use of **icons** is central in Eastern Catholic Churches.

- An **iconostasis** (a wall, with doors, decorated with icons) separates the altar from the rest of the church.

- Eastern Catholics make the Sign of the Cross by touching the forehead and the chest ("In the name of the Father and of the Son") and then the right shoulder before the left ("and of the Holy Spirit").

- The Eastern Catholic tradition celebrates the Sacraments, called mysteries, of Baptism, Confirmation, and the Eucharist at the same time. Thus when infants are baptized, they are also confirmed and receive the Eucharist by means of a few drops of the Blood of Christ.

- Married men can be ordained to the priesthood in the Eastern Catholic Churches.

This is an image of the front of an Eastern Catholic iconostasis. Notice the prevalence of the large icons. Can you identify who is pictured?

© Brian Singer-Towns / Saint Mary's Press

Additional Examples of Catholicity

Because the Church is universal, she is able to integrate diverse cultural elements and popular devotions into her unity. At the same time, the Church purifies or transforms cultural elements in the light of faith.

The Church's diversity is evident through the various pilgrimages, religious dances, and religious processions performed in various parts of the world. For example, pilgrims from all over the world travel to the shrine of Saint James in Santiago de Compostela, Spain. At Christmastime in Mexico, young people celebrate Las Posadas, a nine-day celebration that includes reenacting the story of Mary and Joseph's seeking shelter in Bethlehem before Mary gave birth to Jesus. Throughout the world believers

Pray It!

Peace Prayer

Jesus Christ calls all of us to unite as People of God. That means we must put aside the conflicts that divide us and promote peace through forgiveness and recognition of how much we all have in common. Use this beautiful and much-loved prayer, attributed to Saint Francis of Assisi, to ask God for the grace to promote peace and unity:

O Lord, make me an instrument of your peace.
Where there is hatred, let me sow love;
where there is injury, pardon;
where there is doubt, faith;
where there is despair, hope;
where there is darkness, light;
where there is sadness, joy.

O Divine Master, grant that I
may not so much seek to be consoled as to console;
to be understood as to understand;
to be loved as to love.

For it is in giving that we receive;
it is in pardoning that we are pardoned;
and it is in dying that we are born to eternal life. Amen.

© Godong / Alamy

dress in traditional clothing and join in colorful processions to celebrate the Feast of Corpus Christi.

Many of our devotions to saints and to Mary are closely tied to the history and culture of particular peoples. For example, Slavic people honor Saints Cyril and Methodius as the saints who evangelized the Slavs and helped to develop the Cyrillic alphabet, in which Slavic languages are still written today. The icon of Our Lady of Częstochowa (also known as the Black Madonna) has played an important role in Polish history. In Portugal, Mary is especially honored through her appearance at Fátima. Our Lady of Lourdes likewise has a particular devotion in France.

Chapter Review

1. Describe the two senses in which the Church is Catholic.

2. How is the Church Catholic in each of the three distinct meanings of the word *church?*

3. Why does the Church of Rome have special authority?

4. Why does the Church have a unique relationship with Judaism?

5. What are some beliefs shared by Islam and the Catholic faith?

6. What is the significant difference between the Eastern Catholic Churches and the Eastern Orthodox Church?

7. Identify three ways the practices of Eastern Catholic Churches differ from the practices of the Latin Church.

The Church Is Apostolic

Introduction

Thus far we have explored the first three Marks of the Church: One, Holy, and Catholic. In this chapter, we will explore the fourth Mark of the Church: Apostolic.

The Church is Apostolic because she is founded on the Apostles. Jesus sent his Apostles to continue his Father's mission, and he gave them the authority and power to do so. Because the Church is built on this apostolic foundation, she is indestructible. Christ governs the Church through the Pope and the bishops in communion with him—the successors to Peter and the Apostles. The Pope and the bishops united with him form the Magisterium—the living, teaching office of the Church. The Magisterium is entrusted with transmitting and interpreting Divine Revelation. The Church's handing on of the Gospel message and transmission and interpretation of Divine Revelation are known as Sacred Tradition.

Bishops are the successors of the Apostles through the fullness of the Sacrament of Holy Orders, which conveys sacred power to the bishops through the laying on of hands. Just as Jesus gave Peter specific authority, the Pope has full, supreme, and universal power over the Church.

The laity also has a vocation to spread the Good News of the Kingdom of God. Union with Christ and regular celebration of the Eucharist are key for Church members to carry out her mission. The laity's apostolate can take various forms through careers or family life.

Article 28: The Church Is Apostolic in Three Ways

We say that the Church is **apostolic** for three reasons:

apostolic
To be founded on the Twelve Apostles.

- She was and is built on the "foundation of the apostles" (Ephesians 2:20), who lived with and were taught by Jesus.

- With the help of the Holy Spirit, the Church preserves and hands on the teaching of the Apostles and their successors.

- The Church continues to be taught, made holy, and led by the Apostles through their successors: the College of Bishops, assisted by priests, in union with the Pope, the visible head of the Church.

How does it help you to know that the Church's teaching has been handed down in a direct line from the Apostles?

Article 29: The Apostles Continued Jesus' Mission

Has someone you love and respect ever asked you to do an important job? Did the job feel like an important responsibility? If so, then you have a small sense of how seriously Jesus' Apostles treated their mission when Jesus sent them out.

Who Were the Apostles?

You already know quite a bit about the Apostles. The Greek word *apostolos* literally means "one who is sent." Mark wrote, "He appointed twelve [whom he also named apostles] that they might be with him and he might send them forth to preach and to have authority to drive out demons" (3:14–15).

But the group known as Apostles was not limited to Jesus' twelve companions and witnesses of his Resurrection. We know that Christ called Saint Paul in a unique way (see Galatians 1:15) and sent him on a mission (see

Acts 26:16–18). Saint Paul wrote: "Am I not an apostle? Have I not seen Jesus our Lord?" (1 Corinthians 9:1). Although Saint Paul insisted that his authority as an Apostle was as great as that of any other Apostle (see 2 Corinthians 11:5), he also emphasized that all his strength and authority were based on God's grace only: "I will rather boast most gladly of my weaknesses, in order that the power of Christ may dwell with me. Therefore, I am content with weaknesses, insults, hardships, persecutions, and constraints, for the sake of Christ;

Faith in Action
Saint John Baptist de La Salle: Saint of the Schools

© Used with permission of the Institute of the Brothers of the Christian Schools

In seventeenth-century France, only the sons of rich families were educated. Education at that time meant being taught at home by a hired tutor, which few families could afford. Education was also considered unnecessary for poor children, many of whom would eventually learn a job through apprenticeship to an artisan—like a shoemaker, cabinetmaker, or baker. In reality, this meant that poor children under the age of fourteen or so were left to roam the streets while their parents worked long hours to support their families.

This bothered a young priest, John Baptist de La Salle (1651–1719). He saw that lack of education held many young people hostage to poverty and want. He also saw that they had no knowledge of Jesus Christ and of his love for them.

This young priest developed an educational system that met the needs of these children and the thousands that followed them. He gathered them into groups, according to their ages and abilities. He found teachers and taught them how and what to teach, including Christian doctrine. He chose to teach the children in their native language, French, rather than in the traditional Latin.

Saint John Baptist de La Salle followed Christ and ministered to those that society had left behind: its children. To continue to spread this work, he founded the Brothers of the Christian Schools (or De La Salle Christian Brothers). He is honored today as the patron saint of all teachers. Lasallian schools celebrate his life and work on May 15.

for when I am weak, then I am strong" (2 Corinthians
12:9–10).

Jesus Sent His Apostles
Just as the Father Sent Him

The Father sent his Son to offer us forgiveness of sin and
everlasting life: "God so loved the world that he gave his
only Son, so that everyone who believes in him might
not perish but might have eternal life" (John 3:16). Jesus
did not conduct his own mission apart from his Father.
Though the Holy Spirit was hidden from human eyes at
that time, he was intimately involved in the mission of
the Father and the Son.

In turn, Jesus sent his Apostles to continue his
Father's mission: "As the Father has sent me, so I send
you" (John 20:21). In doing so, he united them to the
divine mission. Just as Jesus relied on the power of his
Father, the Apostles relied on the power Jesus gave them.
He gave his Apostles great power and authority to serve
in his name and act in his person. The Apostles had the
authority to do the following:

Jesus commissioned the Apostles to continue his work on earth. How do you see the Church continuing Jesus' mission in the world today?

- proclaim the Kingdom of Heaven
  (see Matthew 10:7)

- heal the sick and cast out evil
  spirits (see Mark 6:13)

- raise the dead (see Acts 9:36–42)

- forgive sins in Jesus' name (John
  20:22–23)

The Apostles could do all these
things by the power of Christ. Peter
said to the man who was crippled,
"In the name of Jesus Christ the
Nazorean, [rise and] walk" (Acts
3:6). Here, the "name" of Jesus refers
to Jesus' authority and power.

After Jesus' Ascension, the
Apostles, with Peter as their leader

© Ugorenkov Aleksandr / istockphoto.com

and spokesman (see Acts 1:15–26, 2:14–21), led the first church in Jerusalem and held authority over other new churches. When a debate arose in some churches about whether all followers of Jesus should be required to be circumcised in accordance with Jewish Law, the Apostles made the final decision: Gentiles would not be required to follow Jewish Law with regard to circumcision (see 15:1–34).

> **Imagine you are one of the Apostles. How would you feel about Christ sending you out to continue his mission, just as the Father sent him?**

Article 30: Apostolic Tradition

The Church is very aware of her past, present, and future. That is, she is conscious of her responsibility today to honor the gifts received from successors of the Apostles in the past. She is also conscious that she must prepare leaders and all members of the Church for the future.

Appointing Successors

Jesus Christ, the fullness of Divine Revelation, commanded and entrusted the Apostles to tell all people and all nations what they had heard and seen regarding salvation. In this way, the teachings of Jesus have been

Live It!
Combining the Subjective and the Objective in Our Worship

Our Catholic faith is both objective and subjective. The objective part is God's Revelation, which is transmitted through Scripture and Tradition. The subjective part is how we respond to God's Revelation. We need both dimensions of faith.

Reciting the Nicene Creed at the Mass is a great opportunity for us to live out both aspects. Challenge yourself to understand the Nicene Creed more fully by studying the words. How can you reflect or apply the truths in your own life?

transmitted from generation to generation, proclaimed not only in word but also in action. As they moved from village to village, city to city, the Apostles, under the inspiration of the Holy Spirit, helped more and more people to believe in Jesus Christ. This handing on, or transmission, of the truths Jesus Christ taught is known as Sacred Tradition. Sacred Tradition will continue "under the inspiration of the Holy Spirit, to all generations, until Christ returns in glory" (*Catechism of the Catholic Church* [*CCC*], 96).

In chapter 4, "The Church Is One," we learned that Apostolic Succession is a source of unity in the Church. Let's look at Apostolic Succession more closely now. Once the time came to finish their work on this earth, the Apostles chose their successors, who were given the title *bishop*. To these successors the Apostles passed on the authority to teach and interpret Sacred Scripture and Tradition. This process is known as Apostolic Succession. In this way, the bishops and the entire Church, in her worship, teachings, and life, proclaim the redemption found in Jesus Christ. Through the worship, teachings, and life of the Church, she "perpetuates and transmits to every generation all that she herself is, all that she believes"[1] (*CCC*, 78).

Jesus entrusted the Apostles to continue his earthly mission. They in turn chose successors and passed on the authority to teach and interpret Scripture and Tradition.

© 2010 Monastery Icons

The Faith of the Church

Sometimes when we use the word *faith,* we speak of a personal act—"the free response of the human person to the initiative of God who reveals himself" (*CCC*, 166). For example, we might say, "She is a woman of great faith." Any faith-filled person, however, has received the faith from others. We cannot give faith to ourselves. And once we receive faith, we in turn must share it with others. Though faith or believing is a personal act, its source

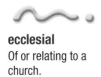

ecclesial
Of or relating to a church.

is the Church, who teaches each one of us. The faith of the Church precedes, supports, and nourishes the faith of individuals. Faith is both personal and **ecclesial**. If it were not for the Church's carefully preserving and passing down the faith, we would have no solid basis for our beliefs at all.

Passing Down the Apostolic Tradition

The Apostles handed on the Gospel message in two ways:

- **Orally** Before the Gospels were written down, the Apostles handed on the faith to the earliest Christians by preaching, providing examples of how to live, and establishing new Christian communities. The Apostles shared what Jesus taught them, what he did, and what they learned through the Holy Spirit.

- **In writing** The New Testament has divine authorship because the Apostles or their associates wrote the texts of the New Testament through the inspiration of the Holy Spirit. Because of this we know that the inspired books teach the truth. All of Sacred Scripture is living, not static.

   Sometimes we hear people question why the Church does not use the Bible alone as the source of

Primary Sources

Clement of Rome and Apostolic Succession

Saint Clement of Rome was Bishop of Rome (another title for the Pope) near the end of the first century AD. He was the fourth Pope after the death of Saint Peter, who may have ordained Clement himself. In a letter written around the year 96, Saint Clement describes the process of Apostolic Succession:

> The Apostles received the Gospel for us from the Lord Jesus Christ, Jesus the Christ was sent from God. The Christ therefore is from God and the Apostles from the Christ. . . . [The Apostles] appointed their first converts, testing them by the Spirit, to be bishops and deacons of the future believers. . . . If they should fall asleep, other approved men should succeed to their ministry. ("To the Corinthians," 42, 44)

authority. The written Sacred Scripture and the living Sacred Tradition do have one common source: God's Revelation in Jesus. But some elements of Sacred Tradition are not found in Sacred Scripture:

- Sacred Tradition gives us the exact list of books that we regard as Sacred Scripture. The early bishops, guided by the Holy Spirit, identified the writings that were inspired and therefore should be part of the official canon. The canon includes forty-six Old Testament books and twenty-seven New Testament books.

- The word *Trinity* is not used in the Bible. It is part of the Church's Tradition.

- Sacred Tradition includes the Church's answers to many contemporary questions, such as how to use genetic information, use technology, share resources, and so on.

To present the faith without error, the Magisterium authentically interprets the Word of God and applies it to new questions. The Church does this especially through the official proclamations of the bishops in union with the Pope. You will learn more about the Magisterium in chapter 9, "The Magisterium: The Teaching Office of the Church."

God's Revelation is present in both Sacred Scripture and Sacred Tradition. Together they provide the fullness of Revelation that is present in the Church.

Together "Sacred Scripture and Sacred Tradition make up a single sacred deposit of the Word of God (*Dei Verbum*, 10)" (*CCC*, 97). This deposit of the Word of God enables the Church to contemplate God, who is "the source of all her riches" (97). Sacred Scripture and Tradition never contradict each other, and we need both. Each helps us to understand the other more fully.

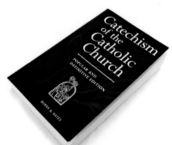

© Stephen Barnes / Religion / Alamy

What do you think is a pressing moral question facing our society today? What can you learn about the Church's teaching on this question?

episcopal
Of or relating to a bishop.

Article 31: The Successors to Peter and the Apostles

Let's look more closely at the bishops. These are the men who have succeeded the Apostles and are responsible for the Apostolic Tradition. Bishops have central roles in their own dioceses, but they also share a global responsibility for the Church with fellow bishops in communion with the Pope.

The Apostles and the Bishops

The Sacrament of Holy Orders is an essential element of Apostolic Succession. Jesus specifically gave authority to his Apostles when he gave them his Holy Spirit. Appearing to his disciples, Jesus breathed on them and said: "Receive the holy Spirit. Whose sins you forgive are forgiven them, and whose sins you retain are retained" (John 20:22–23).

Jesus' Apostles passed on the gift of the Holy Spirit to their successors through the laying on of hands. Thus Saint Paul reminded Timothy "to stir into flame the gift of God that you have through the imposition of my hands" (2 Timothy 1:6).

Pictured is a cardinal conferring the Sacrament of Holy Orders on a new bishop. Why is the laying on of hands a vital part of the Sacrament of Holy Orders?

Bishops, who are already ordained priests, receive the fullness of the Sacrament of Holy Orders. In the early Church, this fullness was known as the high priesthood. **Episcopal** consecration confers the office of sanctifying, teaching, and ruling on the bishop. The Sacrament of Holy Orders, through the work of the Holy Spirit, conveys sacred power from Christ to the man being consecrated as bishop.

Priests and deacons receive the Sacrament of Holy Orders, but their ordination does not make them successors to the Apostles, nor does it give them the authority of the bishops. The ordination of deacons, priests, and bishops is conferred

© ALESSIA PIERDOMENICO / Reuters / Landov

by the laying on of hands, followed by a prayer of consecration that asks God to pour forth the graces of the
Holy Spirit that the newly ordained man needs for his
ministry. The laying on of hands by the bishop who celebrates the ordination resembles the process of the early
Church. Ordination imprints a sacramental character on
the deacon, priest, or bishop. We will learn more about
ordination and the Church hierarchy in chapter 8, "The
Leadership Structure of the Church."

Peter and the Pope

Just as the mission of the Apostles continues in the mis-
sion of the bishops, so too Peter's role as the head of the
Apostles continues in the role of the Pope as head of the
College of Bishops.

Jesus entrusted specific authority to Peter: "I will give
you the keys to the kingdom of heaven. Whatever you
bind on earth shall be bound in heaven; and whatever
you loose on earth shall be loosed in heaven" (Matthew
16:19). Jesus' trust in Peter might seem surprising when
we recall that Peter clearly had human failings. At times
Jesus criticized Peter for having little faith (see 14:31) and
rebuked him sharply for thinking in human terms, not
in God's terms (see Mark 8:33). Peter's greatest failing
occurred when he denied three times that he knew Jesus
(see Luke 22:55–62).

Yet despite Peter's human failings, Jesus chose him
to be the solid rock of the Church. By giving him the
"power of the keys," as it is known, Jesus signified Peter's
authority to govern the Church. The power to bind and
loose refers to Peter's special authority to absolve sin,
make judgments about official doctrines, and make disciplinary decisions in the Church. This authority is also
given to the Apostles as a whole, with Peter as the head.

The Pope is the Bishop of Rome. He is the source and
foundation of unity in the Church and especially in the
College of Bishops. As Vicar of Christ and pastor of the
global Church, the Pope has full, supreme, and universal
power over the Church. Unlike the political checks-

and-balances system of the United States, the College of Bishops cannot veto the Pope or act apart from him. The bishops have no authority without him. The College of Bishops therefore acts in communion with the Pope.

Do you think someone with human failings and flaws can be a good leader? Why or why not?

Pray It!

© Dmitry Kalinovsky / Shutterstock

Intercessory Prayers on the Feast of Saints Peter and Paul (June 29)

Saint Peter the Apostle was the rock on whom Christ built the Church. Saint Paul the Apostle made many missionary visits to spread the Good News. Pray the following prayer from the Liturgy of the Hours for their feast day:

The Lord Jesus built his holy people on the foundation of the Apostles and the prophets. In faith let us pray:

Lord, come to the aid of your people.
You once called Simon, the fisherman, to catch men,
– now summon new workers who will bring the message of salvation to
   all peoples.
You calmed the waves, so your followers would not be drowned,
– guard your Church, protect it from all dangers.
You gathered your scattered flock around Peter after the resurrection,
– good Shepherd, bring all your people together as one flock.
You sent Paul as Apostle to preach the good news to the Gentiles,
– let the word of salvation be proclaimed to all mankind
You have the keys of your kingdom into the hands of your holy Church
– open the gates of that Kingdom to all who trusted in your mercy while
   on earth.

(The Liturgy of the Hours, page 1502)

Article 32: The Apostolate of the Laity

Every member of the Church has a vocation to the **apostolate**. That includes you! The word *apostolate* describes any Christian's activity that fulfills the apostolic nature of the whole Church when he or she works to extend the Reign of Christ to the entire world.

We Are Sent to Spread the Good News

The whole Church is apostolic, because she is in a communion of faith and life with the Apostles and because she is sent out into the world on a mission to spread the Good News of the Kingdom of God over all the earth.

Christ is the source of the apostolate for all members of the Church. Our relationship with Christ affects our ability to spread the Good News. Whether an ordained person or **layperson**, anyone who wants to engage in the apostolate must be in union with Christ. Participating in the celebration of the Eucharist is the soul of the apostolate.

The apostolate can take many forms for laypeople (also called laity), specifically because we live in the world, sharing the varied gifts given to us by the Holy Spirit. Every morning when we get up, we are sent out into the world, whether through going to school, working outside the home, or taking care of family. The essential nature of the apostolate is love. Every day we face small and big decisions that could result in a choice to love or not.

What Does a Lay Apostolate Look Like?

What is the difference between a career understood as an apostolate and one that is not? When a professional athlete understands his or her sports career as an apostolate, for example, the athlete will seek to become involved with the community and use time and money to improve the lives of others. We have all encountered some customer-service representatives who clearly do not view their work as an apostolate, but also others who

apostolate
The Christian person's activity that fulfills the apostolic nature of the whole Church when he or she works to extend the Kingdom of Christ to the entire world. If your school shares the wisdom of its founder, its namesake, or the charism of the religious order that founded it, it is important to learn about this person or order and his or her charism, because as a graduate you will likely want to incorporate this charism into your own apostolate.

laity (laypeople)
All members of the Church with the exception of those who are ordained as bishops, priests, or deacons. The laity share in Christ's role as priest, prophet, and king, witnessing to God's love and power in the world.

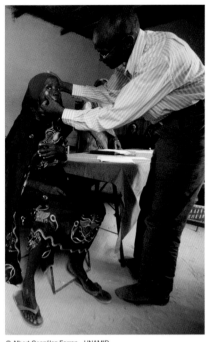

© Albert González Farran - UNAMID

try to improve the day of every person who places a call or comes in the door. How about a doctor who spends several weeks a year in a third-world country, helping people who do not have access to good medical care? How about a lawyer who takes on a good number of pro bono cases for clients who cannot pay?

Your life as a student can be an apostolate if you choose to make it so. How can you spread the Good News of Jesus Christ? How can you choose love in your life today?

This doctor is treating orphans in a refugee camp in Democratic Republic of the Congo. Currently your apostolate is to live out your Christian faith as a student. What might you envision your apostolate to be in the future?

Did You Know?

The Apostolate of Catholic Schools

© Used with permission of the Diocese of Allentown; Allentown, PA

The apostolate of Catholic education was almost exclusively the work of priests or consecrated religious in the first half of the twentieth century. Some schools were founded by a religious order or named after an inspiring Catholic, and these schools typically follow the charism of their founders or namesakes. Today Catholic education has become primarily a lay apostolate.

If you attend a Jesuit school, you may have learned to do things for the greater glory of God: the charism of Saint Ignatius Loyola, founder of the Jesuits. If you go to a high school run by the De La Salle Christian Brothers, you may have learned that you are always in the presence of God, a gift from Saint John Baptist de La Salle. Visitation schools are run by Sisters of the Visitation, an order founded in France in 1610 by Saint Jane Frances de Chantal and Saint Francis de Sales, who once said, "There is nothing so strong as gentleness and nothing so gentle as real strength."

Chapter Review

1. In what three ways is the Church Apostolic?

2. Describe how Jesus joined the Apostles to the mission the Father had sent him to carry out.

3. Define *Apostolic Succession*. Why is Apostolic Succession necessary?

4. How is faith both personal and ecclesial?

5. What is a bishop?

6. What specific authority did Jesus give Peter as the head of the Apostles?

7. What is a vocation that every member of the Church shares?

8. Why is Christ the source of the apostolate?

Unit 3

Leadership and Ministry within the Church

In unit 2, "The Church Is One, Holy, Catholic, and Apostolic," you learned that the Church is Apostolic and that Apostolic Succession helps to unite the Church. Christ commissioned the Twelve Apostles to go forth and spread the Gospel, and he designated Peter to lead the early Christians. Jesus Christ provided the Church with this visible, hierarchical leadership structure to guide her on the right path.

The clergy of the Church are her primary leaders. Through the grace of Holy Orders, the bishops—assisted by priests and deacons—govern, teach, serve, and sanctify the Church. They make Christ present to us through the Sacraments. The Pope, the Bishop of Rome, symbolizes the Church's unity as the leader of the entire Church, the successor to Peter.

The Pope and the bishops in union with him form the Magisterium: the living, teaching office of the Church. The Magisterium is solely responsible for authentically interpreting Sacred Scripture and ensuring that the Church remains faithful to the teaching of the Apostles.

Not everyone feels called to ordained ministry, but the Church calls each one of us to holiness. God calls some to the vocation of Marriage, and he calls others to profess vows as part of the specific vocation of consecrated life. We can live holy lives by following the evangelical counsels of obedience, chastity, and poverty, in ways suitable for whatever vocation God calls us to. Every baptized person shares in Christ's priestly, prophetic, and kingly offices.

The enduring understandings and essential questions represent core concepts and questions that are explored throughout this unit. By studying the content of each chapter, you will gain a more complete understanding of the following:

Enduring Understandings

1. God calls some men to ordained ministry and a life of service to the Church.
2. The role of the Magisterium is that of preaching and teaching the faith of the Apostles interpreted for the contemporary world.
3. Members of the laity grow in holiness and share in Christ's mission through a variety of vocations.

Essential Questions

1. Who comprises the hierarchy of the Church and why is it necessary?
2. How does the Magisterium help us to live our faith?
3. How do you share in Christ's mission?

Chapter 8

The Leadership Structure of the Church

Introduction

Like any organization, the Church needs clear and well-defined leadership. This leadership is provided by the clergy of the Church. The Church's leadership is a visible, hierarchical structure. The Pope, the Bishop of Rome, is the one leader of the whole Church, the successor to Peter. He symbolizes the Church's unity. The bishops of the Church, together with the Pope, are responsible for the spiritual welfare of the entire Church. But bishops are also the leaders in their own dioceses, where they are assisted by their coworkers, the priests and the deacons.

The ordained ministers of the Church, through the grace of Holy Orders, govern, teach, and sanctify the Church through the authority handed down from the Apostles, whose own authority came from Jesus Christ himself. Ordained ministers make Christ present to us through the Sacraments. Following Christ's example, they exercise leadership by service to the Body of Christ.

Article 33: The Church and Hierarchy

The Church is composed of two distinct but interconnected groups: the hierarchy and the laity. The hierarchy includes the Apostles and their successors, the Pope and bishops of the Church, along with their coworkers, the priests and deacons. Why do we call these ordained ministers the *hierarchy*? The leadership of the Church, as established by Christ, is hierarchical, meaning that her leaders and institutions are organized in a specific ascending order. Any group needs organized leadership, or chaos results.

This does not mean that bishops are more important than priests or that bishops and priests are more important than the laity. All members of the Church are equal in dignity. We are all simply called to different roles and ministries, but each of us contributes to building up the Body of Christ. In this chapter, and in chapter 9, "The Magisterium: The Teaching Office of the Church," we will examine the hierarchy and the Magisterium. In chapter 10, "Many Vocations to Holiness," we will turn our attention to the role of the laity.

© Bill Wittman / www.wpwittman.com

Hierarchical Leadership: Divine Authority and Service

The hierarchy consists of the ordained ministers of the Church: bishops (including the Pope), priests, and deacons. From the beginning of the Church, there have always been these three orders, or degrees, of ordained ministers. Only bishops can confer these three degrees of ordained ministry through the Sacrament of Holy Orders. These orders are absolutely necessary for the Church to exist. Without the hierarchy, the Church would falter, lacking the leadership instituted by Christ that makes him present in the Church through the Sacraments.

The Latin name for the bishop's chair is *cathedra*. This is why the church where the bishop is the pastor is called a cathedral.

At the top of the Church hierarchy is the Pope, who is a bishop with supreme power over the whole Church. Next are the bishops, whose authority depends on their union with the Pope. Priests, the bishops' coworkers, are the next level. Deacons, who work with priests in support of their bishop, carry out their ministries at the lowest level of the Church's hierarchy.

The Church is hierarchical because Christ himself set up this structure. Christ established the bishops as the successors to the Apostles, and the Pope as the successor to Peter, the head of the Apostles. The bishops represent Christ, as does the Pope in a unique way. Thus Christ's own divine authority flows through this hierarchical structure. As a result, the hierarchy has the spiritual authority necessary to govern, teach, and provide pastoral care for the Body of Christ.

Did You Know?

The Vatican Curia

© Saint Mary's Press / Brian Singer-Towns

The Pope leads the Church through the Vatican Curia, located in Vatican City, a sovereign city-state within the city of Rome. The Curia is a complex of offices that administer Church affairs. They include a Secretariat of State, nine Congregations, three Tribunals, eleven Pontifical Councils, and seven Pontifical Commissions. The following examples give you some sense of the Curia's activities:

- **Secretariat of State** Coordinates the Curia's offices and maintains diplomatic ties with foreign nations. (The Vatican, as a sovereign city-state, is recognized as a separate and independent country.)
- **Congregation for the Doctrine of the Faith** Oversees Catholic doctrine and publishes statements to clarify Catholic teaching.
- **Congregation for Bishops** Coordinates the appointment of bishops worldwide.
- **Apostolic Signatura** The highest Church court.
- **Pontifical Biblical Commission** Issues instructions on biblical interpretation.

As Americans we value equality and democracy, so we are naturally suspicious of hierarchies. However, we must remember that the hierarchy's order was established by Christ, and those within the hierarchy are not to express their authority in a domineering way. Christ himself defined how they must exercise their leadership, as we read in the Gospel of Mark:

> You know that those who are recognized as rulers over the Gentiles lord it over them, and their great ones make their authority over them felt. But it shall not be so among you. Rather, whoever wishes to be great among you will be your servant; whoever wishes to be first among you will be the slave of all. (10:42–44)

Beginning with Pope Saint Gregory the Great (Pope Gregory I, 590–604) and continuing with Pope Saint John Paul II, Pope Benedict XVI, and Pope Francis, popes have regularly referred to themselves as the Servant of the Servants of God, following the example of Christ.

Organizational Structure of the Church

The Church is generally organized into parishes and dioceses, surrounding the spiritual center of the Church in Rome. This structure reflects the ascending hierarchy of priests, bishops, and the Pope. Let's take a brief look at the different organizational levels in the Church's structure:

- **The Holy See** This term is a translation of the Latin *sancta sedes,* which literally means "holy seat." The word *see* refers to a diocese or seat of a bishop. The **Holy See** is the seat of the central administration of the whole Catholic Church, under the leadership of the Pope, the Bishop of Rome.

- **Diocese** A diocese is usually a certain geographic area governed by a bishop. There are more than 2,800 dioceses worldwide, with 195 dioceses in the United States. The universal Church is the communion of these dioceses worldwide.

Holy See
This term is a translation of the Latin *sancta sedes,* which literally means "holy seat." The word *see* refers to a diocese or seat of a bishop. The Holy See is the seat of the central administration of the whole Church, under the leadership of the Pope, the Bishop of Rome.

domestic church
A name for the first and most fundamental community of faith: the family.

- **Parish** A parish is a distinct community within a diocese. The bishop typically appoints one or more priests to care for each parish, although there are some exceptions.
- **Family** Because the family is where the faith is first taught and practiced, it can be thought of as the most basic level of the Church, sometimes called the **domestic church**.

As you can see, the number of Catholics increases at each level, culminating with the Holy See's responsibility for the spiritual care of all the world's Catholics. This responsibility would be overwhelming if it were not for the Holy Spirit, who guides and strengthens the leaders in their important roles.

What are some of the different ways your family first taught you about faith?

Article 34: The Pope: Visible Head of the Church

Is the Pope Catholic? People sometimes use this question as a reply to a question whose answer is obviously yes. This question works because the Pope and our Catholic faith fit so naturally and obviously together. When we see the Pope, we see the Catholic Church, because the Pope is the visible head of the Church.

Who Is the Pope?

Let's start with the fact that the Pope is first a bishop. That means he has all the rights and authority of a bishop, a successor of the Apostles. But the Pope is not just a bishop—he is the leader of all the bishops. Reviewing his chief titles can help us to clarify his unique identity and role as leader of the Church:

- **Successor to Peter** Christ established his Apostles as a permanent college with Peter at the head. The Pope is the successor to Peter, just as the bishops are the successors of the Apostles. Christ gave Peter the "power of the keys"—that is, the authority to govern the Church. This authority is passed down to each new Pope.

- **Bishop of Rome** During the lifetime of the first Apostles, the city of Rome was established as the spiritual center of the Church. The Apostles Peter and Paul, the two great leaders of the early Church, both ended up in Rome and were eventually martyred there. With rare exceptions, all the popes since Peter have lived in Rome. As the Bishop of Rome, the Pope is leader of the spiritual center of the Church.

- **Head of the College of Bishops** All the bishops of the world are united with one another, with the Pope as their head. As you have already learned, this body is called the College of Bishops, another name for the hierarchy. The Pope has the responsibility to provide leadership to the College of Bishops. In fact, the College

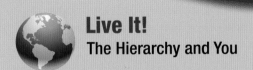

Live It!
The Hierarchy and You

Most of us have little direct contact with the hierarchy of our Church. But you can take some steps to establish a closer connection with them that will enrich your own life:

- Pray for the Pope and the bishops. We pray for them at each Mass, but you could include them in your daily prayers as well. These leaders bear great responsibilities, and our prayers can help them.
- Pray with the Holy Father's prayer intentions for each month. You can easily find these online.
- Read the teachings of the bishops. A great place to start is with *Stewardship and Teenagers: The Challenge of Being a Disciple* (United States Conference of Catholic Bishops, November 14, 2007). This statement, written for young people, offers some good practical suggestions about how to share your talents with others and how to grow more deeply in your personal relationship with Christ.

of Bishops has no authority unless it is united with the Pope. As head of the College of Bishops, the Pope has the authority to appoint bishops throughout the world.

© AFP / Getty Images

The Pope is the Bishop of Rome and holds a special responsibility and authority to lead the Church.

- **Vicar of Christ** The Pope is the Vicar of Christ, meaning that he acts for Christ, as Christ's human representative on earth. Bishops are also called vicars of Christ, but when this phrase is used in the singular, it refers to the Pope. Just as Christ himself is the single head of his Body, the Church, so too the Pope is the visible and rightful head of the Church. The Pope is especially the visible sign of Christ's presence on earth. He is a personal sign and guarantee of the Church's unity in her belief, her Sacraments, and her authority, which originated with Peter and the Apostles. Catholics all over the world, as well as many world leaders, look to the Pope for guidance and inspiration.

- **Pastor of the Universal Church** The Pope has the responsibility for the big picture: ministry to Catholics throughout the world. Christ gives the Pope full, supreme, and universal power over the entire Church so that he may carry out this tremendous responsibility.

As you can see from these titles, the Pope has a key role in the hierarchy of the Church. We look to him in a unique way for guidance and inspiration on our common journey as disciples of Christ.

Blessed John Henry Newman and Papal Supremacy

If the Pope is the supreme head of the Church, why don't we see this teaching more clearly in the New Testament, or in the work of early Church writers? Writing in the nineteenth century, <u>Blessed John Henry Newman</u> (1801–

1890) argued that this early silence was only natural, as the conditions necessary to reveal this teaching had not yet developed.

Newman pointed out that the early Churches were too scattered and too concerned with local issues, such as poverty and the threat of persecution, to be led by one clearly identified pastor of the whole Church. During the fourth and fifth centuries, however, conditions changed. Persecutions came to an end, and Christianity even became the official religion of the empire. Bishops could gather in Ecumenical Councils to clarify theological beliefs. Given these developments, it was natural for the authority of a single, clearly identifiable head of the Church to grow stronger and function more openly.

By appointing Peter as the head of the Church, Jesus established the principle of papal supremacy from the beginning. So the Church of Rome and its bishop were accorded special recognition from the early days of the Church. However, the universal authority of the Bishop of Rome, the Pope, emerged clearly only later, when the time was right.

What do you know about the current Pope?

Article 35: The Role of the Bishops in the Church Hierarchy

Have you had a chance to meet the bishop of your diocese—perhaps at your Confirmation or at a parish or school liturgy? A bishop's life is a busy one, and his calendar is usually full. Bishops are frequently on the road to be with their people. This is because the hierarchy—the bishop in communion with the Pope—has the task of teaching, sanctifying, and governing the Church.

Some Basics about Bishops

Let's review some basic facts about bishops. When Christ first called his Twelve Apostles, he formed them as a permanent group, or college, with Peter as their head. The

province

A grouping of two or more dioceses with an archbishop as its head.

bishops, as successors to the Apostles, receive this same apostolic authority through the fullness of the Sacrament of Holy Orders. Together they form a college, with the Pope at their head, and are entrusted with faithfully passing down the Apostolic Tradition. They do this by authentically teaching the faith, celebrating divine worship—especially the Eucharist—and acting as the pastoral leaders in their own dioceses. The bishops are assisted in these responsibilities by the priests and deacons of their dioceses.

Each bishop is the visible head of a particular church, or diocese. Within his diocese, a bishop is the visible source and foundation of unity. In other words, the bishop is a living symbol that his particular church is unified with the universal Church. This unity comes through Apostolic Succession, through sharing the same truths, and through celebrating the same Sacraments. The *episcopacy* or *episcopate* is another term for the bishop's governance of his church.

All bishops are ordained as priests before they become bishops. When a position for a new bishop opens, the Pope appoints a priest or bishop to fill this position. These men are recommended by local bishops, a papal representative, and the Vatican's Congregation for Bishops. If the newly appointed leader is a priest rather than a bishop, then he is consecrated as a bishop, usually by an archbishop.

You may have wondered about some related terms. An archbishop governs a particularly important diocese (including large cities such as New York or Los Angeles) and presides over meetings and gatherings of the other bishops in his **province**. A cardinal is a senior Church official, usually a bishop, appointed by the Pope to serve as a member of the college of cardinals, the body responsible for electing the Pope. The major offices responsible for governing the Church are headed by cardinals.

Sanctifying Office of the Bishops

As the representative of Christ and the Church, the bishop sanctifies the Church, or makes her holy, by overseeing the administration of the Sacraments in his diocese. He is especially responsible for the celebration of the Eucharist—notice how his name is mentioned in the Eucharistic Prayers of every Mass. Every priest's authority to celebrate the Sacraments flows from the sacramental authority of the bishop.

© KHAM / Reuters / Landov

The bishop also plays a special role in celebrating other Sacraments. You most likely have been, or will be, confirmed by a bishop. Bishops are the ordinary celebrants of Confirmation in the Latin Church. A bishop is also the only person who can ordain priests and deacons, because the Sacrament of Holy Orders continues the ministry of the Apostles through Apostolic Succession.

Local bishops have the authority to ordain new priests and deacons. Why is it important for a bishop to ordain the priests and deacons who will serve in his diocese?

The Governing Office of the Bishops

As a vicar of Christ, a bishop has the authority to govern his particular church. He sets guidelines and establishes procedures for things such as the requirements for receiving the Sacraments or how the priests and deacons of the diocese are prepared for their ministries. The bishop does this work with the help of many other people, including the priests, deacons, and lay ecclesial ministers of the diocese. However, he has the final authority and responsibility for all decisions affecting the spiritual and practical welfare of the diocese. He serves the People of God, promotes our true interests, and helps us to reach the goal of salvation. In this he follows the example of Jesus, who came to serve, not to be served (see Mark 10:45).

A bishop has the ultimate governing authority in his own diocese. But that does not mean he is free to make

collegial
Characterized by the equal sharing of responsibility and authority among the members of a group who form a college. The bishops of the Church together with the Pope at their head form a college, which has full authority over the Church.

whatever decisions he wants. He must use his authority in communion with the whole Church under the guidance of the Pope.

In their governing, bishops show a special concern for the poor, for those who are persecuted for their faith, and for missionaries throughout the world. The Catholic Campaign for Human Development, for example, is an initiative of the United States bishops that empowers the less fortunate to help themselves.

The Collegial Nature of the Bishops

A bishop is primarily responsible for his own diocese, but he also is concerned for churches throughout the world, especially those most in need. In this context, a bishop's relationship with other bishops is **collegial**. This means that they share equally in the authority to make decisions affecting the Church in a particular country or region or even the worldwide Church. These decisions are always made in union with the Pope.

The collegial nature of the episcopate is especially clear when bishops gather together with the Pope in an Ecumenical Council to settle, after careful and open discussion, questions of major importance for the entire Church. Bishops also meet in synods or provincial councils at a more local level. In 2009, for example, Pope Benedict XVI convened a synod of African bishops. The bishops in the United States meet twice a year. We see another powerful symbol of their collegiality when bishops gather to consecrate a new bishop.

An Early Christian Understanding of the Role of Bishops

The letters of Saint Ignatius of Antioch, written around the year 100, are a particularly important witness to the hierarchical structure of the early Church, as well as the crucial role of the bishop in passing down the faith. Saint Ignatius was a Church Father who lived at a time when there was much debate and confusion about Christian belief. He insisted that Church members follow closely the teachings and authority of the bishops and thus of Christ himself. The following quotations come from letters he wrote as he was being escorted to Rome for execution because of his refusal to renounce his faith in Christ:

> "Do nothing without the bishop and the presbyters."

> "We should look upon the bishop even as we would upon the Lord Himself."

> "Do all things in harmony with God, with the bishop presiding in the place of God."

> (In Bart D. Ehrman, editor and translator, *The Apostolic Fathers*, pages 247, 225, and 247)

© Holy Transfiguration Monastery; Brookline, MA; used with permission

How do the quotations from Saint Ignatius of Antioch help you to understand the role of the bishop in the Church?

Article 36: The Priesthood

The Church leader you probably know best is the priest (or priests) of your parish. Perhaps your school also has a priest chaplain. As the bishop's wise coworker, your priest shares in your bishop's authority in service to your parish. He and the other priests of the diocese work in union with your bishop. Together they are responsible for the spiritual and practical welfare of the whole diocese.

In the early Church, the term *presbyter* was more commonly used for the ordained ministers we now call priests. In Greek this term literally means "elder" and originally referred to the older, more experienced community leaders. That is why you will sometimes hear the priests in your diocese referred to as the **presbytery** or **presbyterate**.

presbytery, presbyterate
The name given to priests as a group, especially in a diocese; based on the Greek word *presbyter*, which means "elder."

The Priest's Authority and Responsibility

You have learned that the bishops share the authority of the Apostles and thus of Christ. In turn they share their authority with the priests as coworkers. Together with their bishop, priests are responsible for a particular diocese. The bishop gives individual priests the authority over a specific parish community or sometimes over an office within the diocese (such as the diocesan office of divine worship).

All of us who are baptized participate in Christ's priestly office. This is called the common priesthood of the faithful. But the priesthood of the ordained priest, sometimes called the ministerial priesthood, differs in its essence from the priesthood of the faithful. The Sacrament of Holy Orders confers a sacred power on the priest—power that he is to use to serve the faithful. He represents Christ to the community, serving in the name and in the person of Christ. He exercises his service to the People of God through his teaching, divine worship, and pastoral leadership.

The priest's primary role is that of sacramental minister. He presides over our parish celebration of the Eucharist on Sundays and weekdays and offers the faithful the grace of the Sacraments of Baptism, Penance and Reconciliation, Anointing of the Sick, Matrimony, and Confirmation. (Only priests and bishops may celebrate the

Primary Sources

The Heavenly Vocation of the Priest

Saint Gregory of Nazianzus was an accomplished theologian and Doctor of the Church who is especially known for defending the doctrine of the Trinity against early heresies. In this passage, he explains the heavenly vocation of the priest:

[A priest is] the defender of the truth, who stands with angels, gives glory with archangels, causes sacrifices to rise to the altar on high, shares God's priesthood, refashions creation, restores it in God's image, recreates it for the world on high, and, even greater, is divinized and divinizes.

Eucharist, Penance and Reconciliation, Anointing of the Sick, and Confirmation.) But priests also have many other responsibilities. They oversee the religious education in their parish and Catholic school if there is one. They visit the sick and offer spiritual care to those who need it. They oversee the work of the parish staff and make sure the parish buildings are taken care of. By now you can probably guess that their work is never done.

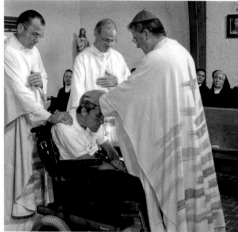

© Bill Wittman / www.wpwittman.com

Yet just as the bishop must concern himself with the universal Church as well as his particular diocese, the priest's mission is not restricted to his parish. Through the Sacrament of Holy Orders, he also participates in the universal mission of the Apostles, whom Christ sent out "to make disciples of all nations" (Matthew 28:19).

The laying on of hands by a priest or bishop is a part of the Sacrament of Anointing of the Sick. What other Sacraments have the action of the laying on of hands?

Likewise, just as the bishops in union with the Pope share a collegial relationship, so too the priests of a particular diocese, in union with their bishop, have a collegial relationship with one another. We see a sign of their collegiality when priests, after the bishop, place their hands on a priest candidate during the Rite of Ordination.

Finally, the authority of a priest also has a personal character. Through the Sacrament of Holy Orders, a priest receives the sacred power to act as Christ's representative. This power is most apparent to us when the priest offers the Eucharist in the person of Christ. In every celebration of the Eucharist, the priest makes Christ's offering of his life on the cross present and immediate in our own time.

How Does a Man Become a Priest?

How does a man become a priest? First, no man can choose to become a priest—rather, each priest is called by God. He must be a baptized man. Any man who

discernment
From a Latin word meaning "to separate or to distinguish between," the practice of listening for God's call in our lives and distinguishing between good and bad choices.

feels God might be calling him to the priesthood must submit his desire to the authority of the Church, who then determines whether he is in fact being called. Only Church authority has the responsibility and the right to call someone to receive the Sacrament of Holy Orders.

Someone who feels called to the priesthood typically goes through an unofficial process of **discernment**, which includes praying, gathering information, and seeking advice from wise and trusted people. If he then still believes he has a vocation to the priesthood, he begins the formal process outlined in general terms here:

- **Candidacy** This is a formal period of discernment with other men who are considering the priesthood. Also known as pre-theology, this period generally lasts two years.

- **Seminary study** Sponsored by his diocese, a candidate then enters seminary for priestly formation and theological studies. This stage generally lasts four years, and then the candidate works one year in a parish of the diocese.

- **Transitional Diaconate** About a year before he is scheduled to be ordained to the priesthood, a seminarian is ordained to the Transitional Diaconate (different from the Permanent Diaconate, which you will read about in the last section of this chapter). The

transitional deacon makes **vows** of **celibacy** and obedience to the bishop at this point.

- **Priesthood** When the bishop determines that he is ready, the transitional deacon is ordained to the priesthood by the bishop.

> **What does your parish do to support men who are called to be priests? What can you do personally to support them?**

Article 37: The Diaconate

You may be familiar with the ministry of deacons (also called diaconal ministry). Shortly after Vatican Council II ended, Pope Paul VI restored the diaconate as a permanent order in the Church. The number of permanent deacons is growing as more men are called into this ministry of service.

Most permanent deacons are not full-time Church ministers. They earn their living by working in the world, just as most of the laity does. And unlike priests or transitional deacons, permanent deacons can be married and raise families. This may seem confusing, but it is similar to the way deacons ministered in the early Church. Today's deacons are examples of service to the Church and the world, just as the deacons of the early Church were.

What Is a Deacon?

A deacon is ordained for ministry and service. *Diakoinia* is the Greek word for "service" that appears in New Testament writings. This word indicates the primary role of the deacon: to be of service to the Church and to the world. Deacons' ordination by the bishop confers on them the grace to serve in the ministry of the Word, in the Church's worship, in pastoral governance, and in acts of charity. In these works of service, the deacon is directly responsible to the bishop of the diocese.

vow
A free and conscious commitment made to other persons (as in Marriage), to the Church, or to God.

celibacy
The state or condition of those who have chosen or taken vows to remain unmarried in order to devote themselves entirely to the service of the Church and the Kingdom of God.

catechesis, catechists

Catechesis is the process by which Christians of all ages are taught the essentials of Christian doctrine and are formed as disciples of Christ. Catechists instruct others in Christian doctrine and for entry into the Church.

© Bill Wittman / www.wpwittman.com

Deacons, though ordained, often are married, have children, and have careers outside of the Church. How is this a gift in their service of the Word as preachers and teachers?

Deacons share in Christ's mission and grace in a special way. The Sacrament of Holy Orders leaves an imprint (or character) that shapes their lives to the life of Christ, who was himself a deacon in the sense that he humbled himself to become a servant of all (see Philippians 2:7–8, Mark 10:45).

Service of the Deacons

Deacons serve the Church in three primary areas: the liturgy, the Word, and charity.

- **In service of the Liturgy** A deacon is an ordinary minister of the Sacrament of Baptism, along with a priest or bishop. He also blesses marriages in the Sacrament of Matrimony. He assists with celebration of the Eucharist and distributes it.

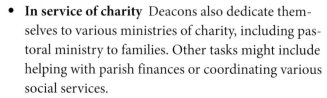

- **In service of the Word** Deacons give homilies and may lead celebrations of the Liturgy of the Word. They also carry out **catechesis** and other teaching responsibilities. For example, a deacon may lead a Bible study at your parish, serve as a school chaplain, or offer religious instruction to children, youth, or adults. Through these activities deacons participate in ongoing evangelization and contribute to the missionary activity of the Church.

- **In service of charity** Deacons also dedicate themselves to various ministries of charity, including pastoral ministry to families. Other tasks might include helping with parish finances or coordinating various social services.

History of the Diaconate

How did the diaconate begin? The title *deacon* is used in the New Testament (see 1 Timothy 3:8–13), although the precise functions of the deacons at that time are unclear to us today. We can trace the diaconate back to the Apostles' selection of seven men to assist them with charitable ministries in the early Church, as described in <u>Acts of the Apostles 6:1–7</u>. <u>Saint Stephen</u>, the first Christian martyr, was one of these seven men, and today he is the patron saint of deacons. <u>Saint Ignatius of Antioch</u>, writing around the year 100, referred to deacons as a distinct group alongside bishops and presbyters.

Over the centuries the importance of the diaconate as a separate ministry declined in the Latin Church. By modern times the diaconate was only a transitional stage in preparing for the priesthood. The Second Vatican Council, however, restored the Permanent Diaconate in

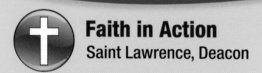

Faith in Action
Saint Lawrence, Deacon

© Nicolo Orsi Battaglini / Art Resource, NY

<u>S</u>aint Lawrence was a deacon martyred in Rome as part of the Roman Empire's persecution of Christians. As a student of theology in Zaragoza, in present-day Spain, Lawrence encountered a famous and well-respected teacher who went on to be elected Pope Sixtus II in 257. Upon his election, Sixtus II ordained Lawrence as a deacon and appointed him archdeacon of Rome. This was a serious responsibility. As the archdeacon of Rome, Lawrence was entrusted with caring for the treasury of the church and distributing alms to the poor.

One traditional story of Lawrence shows us how seriously he took his responsibilities. During the Emperor Valerian's persecution of Christians, Roman authorities demanded that Lawrence give up the Church's treasures to the empire. Lawrence replied that he would need three days to collect the Church's riches. During that time, he distributed much of the Church's property to the poor. Then he gathered together the poor and the sick of Rome and presented them to the authorities, calling them the treasures of the Church.

Lawrence died a martyr. The Roman authorities put him to death by slowly roasting him over a fire. A well-known legend about his death says that Lawrence barely felt the flames, because he already burned with so much love for God. According to this legend, Lawrence may even have joked to his executioner, "Turn me over—I'm done on this side." Then he died praying for the conversion of Rome and the spread of the Good News.

the Latin Church. The Eastern Catholic Churches have always maintained the Permanent Diaconate.

A 2013 survey commissioned by the United States Conference of Catholic Bishops estimated that there are some 18,500 deacons in the United States, with nearly fifteen thousand of them actively engaged in service. Ninety-three percent are married, and 94 percent are over the age of fifty.

Deacons Are Called to a Life of Holiness

In his 1967 apostolic letter on the Permanent Diaconate, Pope Paul VI called on deacons to devote themselves to

Pray It!

Prayer for Deacons

During the Ordination of deacons, the bishop prays over them as part of the Ordination liturgy. The following is a selection from that prayer. You can pray it at any time to support the ministry of deacons around the world.

Send forth upon them, Lord, we pray,
the Holy Spirit,
that they may be strengthened
by the gift of your sevenfold grace
for the faithful carrying out
of the work of the ministry.

May there abound in them every Gospel virtue:
unfeigned love,
concern for the sick and poor,
unassuming authority,
the purity of innocence,
and the observance of spiritual discipline.

. . . .

may they remain strong and steadfast in Christ,
so that by imitating on earth your Son,
who came not be served but to serve,
they may be found worthy to reign in heaven with him.

(Rites of Ordination of a Bishop, of Priests, and of Deacons
[Second Typical Edition], 277)

a special holiness of life. This special holiness included committing themselves to the following activities:

- carefully studying and meditating on Scripture
- frequently attending the Mass, on a daily basis if possible
- receiving the Eucharist frequently, and participating in Eucharistic Adoration
- frequently receiving the Sacrament of Penance and Reconciliation
- performing a daily examination of conscience
- developing a special devotion to <u>Mary, Mother of God</u>
- participating in the Liturgy of the Hours

> (Adapted from *The Sacred Order of Deacons [Sacrum Diaconatus Ordinem]*, 26)

Chapter Review

1. What does it mean to say that the Church is hierarchical? Why is it necessary for the Church to be hierarchical?

2. In what way are the Holy See, the diocese, the parish, and the family related in the Church's hierarchy?

3. In what way is the Pope the visible sign of the Church's unity?

4. In what way is the Pope the successor to Peter?

5. In what specific ways does a bishop sanctify the Church?

6. What are some examples of the collegial relationship of the bishops?

7. Describe the relationship between a bishop and a priest.

8. Describe the responsibilities of a priest.

9. Explain what a deacon is, and describe his three primary areas of service.

Chapter 9

The Magisterium: The Teaching Office of the Church

Introduction

In the previous chapter, we learned that the bishops have the duty to celebrate divine worship, especially the Eucharist, and to guide their particular churches as pastors. In this chapter, we will examine the duty of the bishops as the Magisterium to authentically teach the faith.

The Church's Magisterium has an obligation to interpret the Word of God, whether it takes the form of Sacred Scripture or Sacred Tradition. The Magisterium also ensures that the Church remains faithful to the teaching of the Apostles. The work of the Magisterium helps us as Church members to grow in our understanding of the faith. The Church's teaching allows us to be confident that we will not be led astray. The *Catechism of the Catholic Church (CCC)* is an important and helpful resource for learning what the Church teaches.

The Church has the gifts of indefectibility and infallibility. Her indefectibility means she will remain faithful to Christ's teaching until the end of the world. If you remember, *infallibility* means that her pastors, the Pope and the bishops in union with the Pope, are without error when they definitively proclaim a teaching related to faith or to the moral life.

The Church has many teachings. But we can identify which of these truths are the most central, because there is an order or hierarchy to them. The Church's emphasis on truth challenges relativism, a philosophy that claims that truth depends only on a person's opinion or viewpoint.

Article 38: What Is the Magisterium?

Let's review our basic knowledge of the Magisterium. The word *Magisterium* echoes the Latin word *magister*, which means "master" or "teacher." The Magisterium is the name given to the official teaching authority of the Church. That is, the Magisterium's task is to interpret and preserve the truths of the faith transmitted through Sacred Scripture and Sacred Tradition. The bishops in communion with the Pope form this body. Together they are responsible for preserving and passing on the faith handed on by the Apostles.

© MAX ROSSI / Reuters /Landov

What Does the Magisterium Teach?

The Magisterium has the right but also the duty to preserve and share the Church's teaching. The Magisterium interprets and preserves the heritage of faith contained in Sacred Scripture and Sacred Tradition—but it does not change the heritage of faith. It serves us by ensuring that we will not be led astray. We can be confident we have received the truth that allows us to have a relationship with God and that leads to our salvation.

The *Catechism* is one tool the Church uses to present the faith. The *Catechism* describes itself as "an organic synthesis of the essential and fundamental contents of Catholic doctrine, as regards both faith and morals, in the light of the Second Vatican Council and the whole of the Church's Tradition" (11). When we look at the *Catechism,* we can see that its presentation of the faith, like that of many earlier catechisms, is built on four pillars:

- **Pillar I: The profession of faith (the Creed)** The first part of the *Catechism* expands on the Nicene Creed by exploring its concepts in great depth. Much of the material covered in this book comes from this first pillar.

- **Pillar II: The sacraments of faith** This second part explains how God's salvation was brought about through Jesus Christ and the Holy Spirit. It shows us that salvation is made present in the sacred actions of the Church's liturgy, especially in the Seven Sacraments.

- **Pillar III: The life of faith (the Commandments)** The third part explains that we can achieve eternal happiness by freely choosing right conduct with the help of God's grace and Law. Right conduct fulfills the two Great Commandments to love God and neighbor, as explained through the Ten Commandments.

- **Pillar IV: The prayer of the believer (the Lord's Prayer)** The last part of the *Catechism* examines the meaning and significance of prayer in our lives as Church members. It especially examines in depth the Lord's Prayer, the Church's quintessential prayer, which Jesus gave to us.

When you want to know what the Church teaches, the *Catechism* is a good place to start.

Because God created us with a longing for him, we have the obligation to search for the truth about God and his Church. We are then also obliged to embrace and assent to the truth preserved by the Magisterium.

What is one question you have about a mystery of faith or a Church teaching? Where might you turn for an answer?

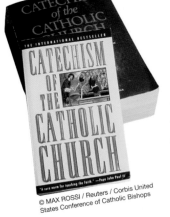

© MAX ROSSI / Reuters / Corbis United States Conference of Catholic Bishops

Article 39: Sacred Tradition, Sacred Scripture, and the Magisterium

The Church perpetuates and transmits to all generations all that she is and all that she believes through her doctrine, life, and worship. The Holy Spirit helps all members of the Church as we grow in our understanding of the Church's heritage of faith contained in Scripture and Tradition. We develop this understanding through the following means:

- **Theological inquiry** Vatican Council II explained, "Theological inquiry should pursue a profound understanding of revealed truth; at the same time it should not neglect close contact with its own time that it may be able to help these men skilled in various disciplines to attain to a better understanding of the faith" (*Pastoral Constitution on the Church in the Modern World* [*Gaudium et Spes, 1965*], 62).

- **Contemplation and study** Vatican Council II also described how contemplation and study help to deepen our understanding of the faith: "There is a growth in the understanding of the realities and the words which have been handed down. This happens through the contemplation and study made by believers, who treasure these things in their hearts (see Luke 2:19,51) through a penetrating understanding of the spiritual realities which they experience, and through the preaching of those who have received through Episcopal succession the sure gift of truth" (*Dogmatic Constitution on Divine Revelation* [*Dei Verbum, 1965*], 8).

- **The teaching of bishops** When all the bishops in union with the Pope, called the Magisterium, speak on faith and morals, their teachings are guided by the Holy Spirit and are infallible, or without error. This

Primary Sources

Pastoral Constitution on the Church in the Modern World

These are the opening words from the Vatican II's *Pastoral Constitution on the Church in the Modern World* (*Gaudium et Spes, 1965*):

The joys and the hopes, the griefs and the anxieties of the men of this age, especially those who are poor or in any way afflicted, these are the joys and hopes, the griefs and anxieties of the followers of Christ. Indeed, nothing genuinely human fails to raise an echo in their hearts. (1)

infallibility assures us that the teaching of the bishops represents the truth of salvation.

Sacred Tradition, Sacred Scripture, and the Magisterium are so closely connected that none can stand apart from the others. Through the action of the Holy Spirit, all three work together to help bring about salvation.

Why do you think Jesus used keys as a symbol of spiritual authority?

How has studying Catholicism helped you to deepen your faith?

© Private Collection / Bridgeman Images

Article 40: Indefectibility and Infallibility

The Church is both indefectible and infallible—meaning that she is incorruptible and without error. The Church as a whole possesses these charisms even though individual members of the Church have faults and make mistakes.

Did You Know?

The Galileo Controversy

© De Agostini Picture Library / G. Dagli Orti / Bridgeman Images

In 1633, Church officials condemned the Italian scientist Galileo Galilei for teaching that the earth revolves around the sun, because this idea appeared to contradict biblical statements that the earth stands still while the sun moves (see, for example, Joshua 10:13).

In his reflections on the affair in 2000 during his papacy, Pope Saint John Paul II concluded that Church officials mistakenly confused scientific and revealed knowledge by using Sacred Scripture to make a judgment about a scientific fact—something that the Church is not competent to do.

Indefectibility

The **indefectibility of the Church** means that the one Church established by Jesus will remain uncorrupted and faithful to Christ's teachings until the end of human history. Jesus gave this promise of indefectibility to the Church when he said to Peter, "You are Peter, and upon this rock I will build my church, and the gates of the netherworld shall not prevail against it" (<u>Matthew 16:18</u>). Jesus promised that not even the powers of death would be able to overcome the Church. The gift of indefectibility belongs to the Church alone, not to any individual member of the Church.

indefectibility of the Church
The Church's remaining uncorrupted and faithful to Christ's teachings, until the end of human history.

Vatican Council I, in the nineteenth century, declared that under the leadership of Peter and his successors as popes, the Church will remain "indestructible until the end of time" ("The Bishop of Rome Is Peter's Successor"). More recently, Vatican Council II taught that by "the power of the Holy Spirit the Church is the faithful spouse of the Lord and will never fail to be a sign of salvation in the world" (*Church in the Modern World*, 43). The Church remains faithful to Christ's teaching until the end of time so that all people can achieve salvation and communion with the Trinity. Even at the final tribulation, when Christ comes again, the Church will remain firm.

By now you might be wondering how the Church has the gift of indefectibility even though individual members of the Church still have defects. For an answer we can look to the early desert monks and nuns, who had a favorite saying from the Book of Proverbs: "Though the just fall seven times, they rise again" (<u>24:16</u>). These men and women went to the desert to dedicate themselves to a life of holiness, but they knew they would often fall short. By God's grace, however, they rose again each time and went on trying.

All of us, all human beings, are sinners. Even the Pope sins. He regularly receives the Sacrament of Penance and Reconciliation from a father confessor.

Knowing that we are all sinners, we nevertheless trust in Christ's promise that his Church, the Bride of Christ, will always remain faithful to him.

Infallibility

The Church's indefectibility and her infallibility are related. If the Church is without defect, she must also be without error, infallible, in her teachings. You have learned that infallibility is the Holy Spirit's gift to the whole Church by which the leaders of the Church—the Pope and the bishops in union with him—are protected from fundamental error when teaching on a matter of

Faith in Action
Archbishop Fulton Sheen: A Television Saint?

© Everett Collection

It is 8 p.m. on a Tuesday in 1955. Your family has settled in front of the television in your living room. Your family must choose between watching the famous comedian Milton Berle or an auxiliary bishop of New York, Fulton J. Sheen. Which one would your family choose?

You might be surprised by how many families would have chosen Bishop Sheen's program, *Life Is Worth Living*. Speaking with only a blackboard and chalk as a visual aid, Bishop Sheen (later made an archbishop) applied principles of Catholic theology and philosophy to the everyday lives of his viewers. Catholic and non-Catholic families alike tuned in for his wise insight and spiritual guidance during the tumultuous 1950s and 1960s.

Archbishop Fulton J. Sheen (1895–1979) was born in a small town in Illinois. He had a great capacity for education, a great talent for public speaking, and a great love for Christ and the Gospel. After studying theology in Belgium and Rome, he taught at the Catholic University of America in Washington, DC. When he was ordained a priest, he resolved to spend one hour in prayer each day before the Blessed Sacrament. He kept that resolution his entire life.

Archbishop Sheen delighted people with his sense of humor. When he accepted an Emmy Award for his television show, he said, "I feel it is time I pay tribute to my four writers—Matthew, Mark, Luke, and John." He has been proposed as a candidate for sainthood. In a first step toward canonization, he was declared venerable in 2012 by Pope Benedict XVI.

faith and morals. This infallibility includes all elements of doctrine. The gift of infallibility ensures that the truths of the faith are preserved for all generations, are correctly taught, and are properly observed by the faithful. The gift of infallibility can take more than one form.

For many people, the most familiar form of the Church's infallibility is the gift of papal infallibility. Specifically, as the supreme pastor and teacher of all the faithful, the Pope may proclaim infallible teaching on his own authority. When a pope makes such a definitive teaching, we say it is issued *ex cathedra*, which is a Latin term meaning "from the chair." The term refers to the Pope's authority as the successor to Peter, an authority symbolized by the image of the Pope sitting in Peter's chair. The Pope's gift of infallibility applies only in very specific circumstances: when the Pope officially acts as the Church's supreme pastor and with the authority of the Apostles to define a specific matter of faith or morality for the belief of the whole Church. When the Pope makes such a pronouncement, he is speaking as the supreme teacher of the universal Church, not as a private individual.

Not everyone knows about a second form of the Church's gift of infallibility. The worldwide College of Bishops has this gift of infallibility when, in union with the Pope, it agrees that a certain doctrine regarding faith and morals must be definitively held by the faithful. This infallible authority is most clearly expressed when the bishops meet in an Ecumenical Council, a gathering of all Catholic bishops that is convened by the Pope and acts under his authority and guidance. The last Ecumenical Council was Vatican Council II, which was convened by Pope Saint John XXIII in 1962 and concluded in 1965 under Pope Venerable Paul VI.

An example of the first form of infallible authority occurred in 1950 when, as Pope, Venerable Pius XII (1876–1958) proclaimed *ex cathedra* that the Assumption of Mary is a dogma of faith, a teaching that every Catholic must acknowledge as true. An example of the second

© Everett Collection / MONDADORI PORTFOLIO / Walter Mori / Sergio del Grande

form of infallibility, exercised by the bishops in union with the Pope, is a teaching from the Council of Chalcedon (AD 451). At that time Christians had been debating the exact relationship between Christ's human and divine natures. Guided by the teaching of Pope Saint Leo I, the Council of Chalcedon stated infallibly that Christ's two natures exist "without confusion, change, division, or separation" *(Christ, the Eternal King [Sempiternus Rex Christus], Encyclical of Pope Pius XII on the Council of Chalcedon, 23).*

How does the gift of infallibility help to deepen your faith in Church teachings?

Article 41: The Magisterium and Truth

The Church's teachings can seem overwhelming to someone learning them for the first time. We might want to ask ourselves which of these teachings and truths we *really* need to know. It is helpful to realize that the Church has a hierarchy or order of truths. This hierarchy of truths makes it possible for us to identify which truths are most fundamental and then to see how other truths are connected to them.

The Hierarchy of Truths

When we refer to the hierarchy of truths, we don't mean that some truths are less relevant to our faith; rather, some truths are more central and fundamental, and these illuminate other truths. The Trinity is the central mystery of the Christian faith and is "the source of all the other mysteries of faith, the light that enlightens them" (*CCC*, 234).

As believers we must see that all the Church teachings are interconnected and that it would be impossible to isolate and disregard one teaching without also disregarding other truths of the faith associated with it.

Dogmas are those doctrines that are central to Church teaching. They have been defined by the Magisterium and are given the fullest weight and authority. Dogmas express the truths we need to know for our salvation, but they do not involve intellectual belief alone. Their truth contributes to our spiritual and ethical growth. The opposite is also true: as we grow in our spiritual and ethical lives, we will come to understand dogmas better.

Changing Guidelines for Changing Circumstances

The Magisterium interprets and preserves the heritage of faith contained in Scripture and Tradition, but it does not change it. However, various disciplinary, liturgical, and devotional traditions can be changed under the guidance of the Magisterium. For instance, the Church's guidelines on fasting and abstinence have changed over the years.

Your grandparents may remember when Catholics abstained from meat every Friday, all year, not just during Lent. For centuries the Church had taught the faithful to abstain from eating meat on Fridays in order to commemorate Jesus' suffering and death. In 1966, however, in his *Apostolic Constitution on Penance (Paenitemini)*, Pope Venerable Paul VI adjusted the law on fasting and abstinence. He spoke of the danger of purely external practices and emphasized that acts of penitence, such as abstinence and fasting, should be intimately related to our inner conversion, prayer, and works of mercy. He called the Church to consider new penitential practices that are suited to the times and to the goal of inner conversion. He also asked all of us to voluntarily adopt penitential practices that turn us away from sin and prepare us to encounter God. This is one example of how the hierarchy can adjust guidelines for spiritual practice to respond to changing circumstances in the world.

Truth and Relativism

Any suggestion of a universal truth can seem suspicious to some people today. So we can be tempted to look at a Church teaching as simply one viewpoint among many. Sometimes we mean to just be tolerant and inclusive by hesitating to say what is true and what is not. Without realizing it, however, we can come to believe that truth is actually relative—that it depends on a person's opinion or viewpoint. This way of thinking is called relativism.

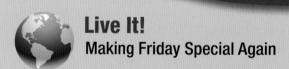

Live It!
Making Friday Special Again

Our bishops teach us to make every Friday a special day of penance and spiritual discipline in order to commemorate the suffering and death that Jesus underwent for our sakes. They encourage us to choose something that is personally meaningful. Consider some of these options:

- Continue the ancient tradition of abstaining from meat on every Friday, not just Fridays in Lent. This can be a great weekly reminder (for yourself and others) of your Catholic identity, as well as a reminder not to become too attached to the things of this world.
- Commit to saying extra prayers.
- Commit to a "spiritual fast" from music, television, or computer time to focus better on growing in your spiritual life.
- Commit to volunteer work that helps the less fortunate.
- Commit to extra acts of kindness or thoughtfulness at home or school.

When we look more closely, though, we can see why relativism cannot be an accurate philosophy. Relativism is built on the premise that there is no absolute truth. But of course this premise needs to be absolutely true for relativism to even work. Do you see how relativism inherently contradicts itself?

In the words of the *Catechism*: "God is Truth itself, whose words cannot deceive. This is why one can abandon oneself in full trust to the truth and faithfulness of his word in all things" (215). From your study of the Genesis accounts of Creation and the Fall, you may remember that the first sin came out of a lack of trust in God—specifically, the suggestion by the serpent that the all-loving God was keeping something good from the first humans. But we know that God wants all good things for us, and these good things include Truth.

Pray It!

The Vocation of the Clergy and Laity of the Church

Use this prayer to ask God to help everyone—from the Church hierarchy to all laypeople—to fulfill their vocations, their calls from God:

Let us pray

. . . .

for all bishops, priests, and deacons;
for all who have a special ministry in the Church, and for all God's people.

Almighty and eternal God,
your Spirit guides the Church and makes it holy.
Listen to our prayers
and help each of us
in his or her own vocation
to do your work more faithfully.
We ask this through Christ our Lord.
Amen.

(*Roman Missal*, page 152)

Be aware of the opposing philosophy of relativism as you talk about your faith. Spend some time thinking about how you can differentiate between respecting and accepting people with contradictory beliefs and accepting the contradictory beliefs themselves.

Chapter Review

1. Define *Magisterium* and explain its significance for the Church.

2. What are believers required to do in response to the teachings of the Magisterium?

3. What does it mean to say that the Church is indefectible?

4. What does it mean to say that the Church is infallible?

5. What is the central mystery of the Christian faith?

6. Explain the hierarchy of truths.

Many Vocations to Holiness

Introduction

Christ calls all of us to a life of holiness. To live holy lives, we are called to follow the evangelical counsels of obedience, chastity, and poverty—each of us in our own way. Laypeople share in Christ's priestly, prophetic, and kingly offices. Laity who are called to the vocation of marriage have the responsibility of raising children in the faith. This is why the family is often called the domestic church.

When a person makes a public profession of the evangelical vows, he or she enters the consecrated life. Life in a religious order or community is a common form of the consecrated life. These communities are characterized by the rhythm of daily prayer. Religious communities today can trace their origins to the spirituality of the desert hermits in Egypt, a form of consecrated life that still exists. New forms of consecrated life are also emerging, including secular institutes and a revival of consecrated virgins.

chastity
The virtue by which people are able to successfully and healthfully integrate their sexuality into their total person; recognized as one of the fruits of the Holy Spirit. Also one of the vows of religious life.

evangelical counsels
The call to go beyond the minimum rules of life required by God (such as the Ten Commandments and the Precepts of the Church) and strive for spiritual perfection through a life marked by a commitment to chastity, poverty, and obedience.

Article 42: The Evangelical Counsels

You might be aware that Roman Catholic diocesan priests make promises of celibacy and obedience to their bishop as part of the Sacrament of Holy Orders. And religious priests, brothers, and sisters make lifelong vows of poverty, **chastity**, and obedience. But did you know that every Christian is called to make a commitment to these virtues?

On our path to holiness, all Christians are called to follow the three **evangelical counsels**: poverty, chastity, and obedience. However, men and women who publicly profess these vows and commit to a stable state of life have a vocation to the consecrated life. Let's take a closer look at what it means to live the evangelical counsels.

Poverty

Do you remember the Gospel account of the rich young man who wanted to follow Jesus? Jesus told him, "Go, sell what you have, and give to [the] poor and you will have treasure in heaven; then come, follow me" (Mark 10:21). Does that mean all of us are called to give up all our possessions? No—but the evangelical counsel of poverty does call each of us to focus on spiritual riches, not material wealth. We must not become attached to money and material things, because they can so easily become the focus of our lives. As Jesus warned his disciples, "Amen, I say to you, it will be hard for one who is rich to enter the kingdom of heaven" (Matthew 19:23). We can quickly fall into the trap of focusing on having the newest clothes or getting the latest gaming system. Christ calls every Christian to be "poor in spirit" and to use money and possessions in a moderate and healthy way.

When a person in the consecrated communal life takes a vow of poverty, however, she or he literally does give up the right to individual possessions, promising to share possessions in common with the community. For example, if religious sisters or brothers receive pay for a job, some or all of the paycheck usually goes to their community, not to the individual. Diocesan priests do not take a vow of poverty, but they are called to follow the evangelical counsel of poverty by living a simple lifestyle.

Chastity

Chastity is the healthy integration of our sexuality into our whole person. This virtue is also one of the fruits of the Holy Spirit. Every baptized person is called to lead a chaste life according to our state of life, with Jesus as our model. To be chaste does not mean denying or suppressing our sexuality, but rather integrating it in the right way. We are all called to control our sexual desires, rather than having them control us.

© The Crosiers / Gene Plaisted, OSC

Jesus told the rich young man, "Go, sell what you have . . ." (Mark 10:21). Why do you think Jesus told the rich young man that he had to sell everything to have treasures in Heaven?

For young people like you, chastity means complete abstinence before marriage. You are called to develop a purity of heart, keeping away from sexual fantasies and pornography. In our sexually permissive society, living a chaste life is a huge challenge. But you can develop this virtue with daily effort and with the help of God's grace, including the sacramental graces of Baptism and the Eucharist. The results are worth it. Chastity helps you to develop more respect for the beautiful gift of your own sexuality, and this respect will allow you to share that gift in a full and joyful way when the time for marriage arrives.

You may be surprised to learn that married couples are also called to chastity. Most obviously this means that a husband and wife must be sexually faithful to each other—that is, they must not commit acts of adultery or even engage in nonsexual romantic relationships with someone who isn't their spouse. But it also means that a husband and wife must practice sexual control with each other. If the couple is using natural family planning, for example, to space out the birth of children for serious reasons, they must abstain from sexual relations for certain days every month. This practice allows a couple to develop self-discipline and a healthy respect for each other's bodies. It also encourages them to discover non-sexual ways to be intimate.

Those who are called to the ordained priesthood and to the consecrated life live chaste lives through their vow of celibacy. This means that they commit to not getting married, to not having sexual relations with anyone for the rest of their lives. Before men who are preparing for priesthood take the vow of celibacy, the bishop gives them the following instructions, which give us insight into the call to celibacy:

> You will exercise your ministry committed to the celibate state: know that celibacy is both a sign and a motive of pastoral charity and an inspiration to it, as well as a source of spiritual fruitfulness in the world. Compelled by the sincere love of Christ the Lord and embracing this state with total dedication, you will cling to Christ more easily with an undivided heart. You will free yourselves more completely for the service of God and man, and minister more effectively in the work of spiritual rebirth. (*Rites of Ordination of a Bishop, of Priests, and of Deacons* [Second Typical Edition], 267)

© Image Source / Corbis

We can all take part in fun activities that respect our call to live chaste lives. What activities do you and your friends like to do that help keep you pure of heart?

Celibacy is a major life commitment. Those who make this commitment have spent years discerning whether this is their call. But living a celibate life allows people to dedicate themselves to God and to their ministry in a very special way. And through this commitment, they provide all of us with a living example of the importance of living a chaste life.

Obedience

All Christians are called to obey Christ—this is the very definition of being a disciple. But this also means that we have a duty to obey the Church's Magisterium. The Pope and bishops are the vicars of Christ, his representatives to the Church and the world. Christ gave them divine authority to teach us God's revealed truth, and it strange, because in our democratic society we place high value is our duty to obey their teaching. This idea might seem on our independence. We don't like it when others tell us what to do. But Jesus himself gave us the example of this type of obedience when he surrendered to his Father's will: "He humbled himself, / becoming obedient to death, / even death on a cross" (<u>Philippians 2:8</u>).

Ordained ministers and those in the consecrated life make special, lifelong vows of obedience. Priests and deacons promise to obey the bishop of the diocese. They commit to being the bishop's representatives, teaching and administering as directed by their bishop. Consecrated people in a religious community similarly promise special obedience to their religious superiors.

> **How do you already follow the evangelical counsel of obedience? What can you start to do today?**

Article 43: The Priestly, Prophetic, and Kingly Mission of the Laity

As a young person, you are part of the laity. And as a layperson, you should realize that as a member of the Church, the Body of Christ, you have a very important role in God's plan of salvation.

When we talk about the laity, we refer to all the members of the Church except for those who have been ordained. In chapters 8 and 9, "The Leadership Structure of the Church" and "The Magisterium: The Teaching Office of the Church," you learned how ordained ministers participate in the hierarchy. The hierarchy's primary role is to provide leadership for the Church. But the laity's primary role is to witness to God's love throughout the whole world.

You are to be Christ's hands and feet and voice and ears in sharing the Good News of the Gospel with your friends, classmates, family members, and people in your community. You are in a unique position to help influence the world's social, political, and economic realities to reflect God's will. You have both the right and the duty to help others know the saving message of Christ. Sometimes people can hear the Christian message only through laypeople. Your ministry and the ministry of the hierarchy work together to continue Christ's mission in the Church and the world.

So even though you are not ordained to Holy Orders, in your own way you participate in the priestly, prophetic, and kingly ministries of Christ as a layperson. Let's look more closely at what these ministries, or "offices," mean.

The Priestly Office of the Laity

The laity share in Christ's priesthood. Through the graces of Baptism and Confirmation, we are united with Christ in serving the world, fulfilling our call to holiness. This is called the common priesthood of the faithful. Just as the

Live It!
Praying with Your Family

Getting along with family members isn't always easy. One way to support healthy and loving family relationships is by learning to pray together. Consider some of these suggestions:

- Pray at meal times. Beginning a family meal by thanking God is a great way to turn our thoughts away from the busyness of the day and to focus for a few moments on how our Creator blesses and sustains us. Praying before meals at a restaurant can be a powerful witness of our faith to others.

© Don Hammond / Design Pics / Corbis

- Pray before leaving on a trip.
- Pray for family members in your own private prayer.
- Pray the Rosary or Angelus together with family members.
- Pray together at bedtime. This can be a wonderful opportunity to instruct younger siblings in some of the basics of the faith. Bedtime prayers help to instill habits of being grateful for the day's blessings and of turning over worries and problems to God before going to sleep.

priest offers the sacrifice of the Mass to God, laypeople too can offer daily work, family life, and leisure activities—if carried out in the Spirit—as a spiritual sacrifice to the Father. Developing a life of prayer and offering intercessions for the needs of others are two more ways we can participate in Christ's priestly office.

The ministerial priesthood is clearly different from the common priesthood of the faithful. The Ordination of priests confers on them a sacred power for the service of the faithful. Only ordained ministers can exercise this sacred power through their teaching, sacred liturgy, and pastoral leadership. The laity may also assist in certain specific ministries of the Church, including lectoring, serving, and singing in the choir.

© Bill Wittman / www.wpwittman.com

The Prophetic Office of the Laity

Christ fulfills his prophetic office through not only the priests and bishops but also the laity. Christ works through the laity as witnesses and provides us with the sense of faith *(sensus fidei)*—that is, readiness to accept the true teaching of the Church in faith and morals. To be a prophet means to share God's Word with those who need to hear it. The laity are called to be witnesses to Christ in every circumstance of our lives and with every person we meet. In this way, we can bring the Good News of salvation to all corners of the world. Here are some ways the laity can participate in the prophetic office of Christ:

There are many ways young people can contribute to the liturgical life of the Church. What opportunities do you have to serve in your school or Church liturgies?

- Laypeople are involved in evangelization, proclaiming Christ through words and through the witness of their lives.

- Capable and trained laity may also collaborate with the hierarchy as catechists and religion teachers.

- Laypeople are playing an increasingly important role in providing a Catholic voice on television, radio, Internet sites and blogs, social media, and other new media.

- The laity also have the right and duty to make their opinions known, in a respectful manner, to their pastors on matters relating to the good of the Church.

The Kingly Office of the Laity

The laity are also called to share in Christ's kingly office. What does it mean to be a leader, from God's point of view? It starts with the self-discipline to consistently choose what is good and right. It continues with our commitment to follow God's call with all our strength and soul for our entire lives. And it means always serving those most in need. As a layperson you are called to lead others by the example of your moral choices, by your

Did You Know?

The Laity's Role in Establishing a Culture of Life

© Alexander Raths / Shutterstock.com

In his 1995 encyclical *The Gospel of Life (Evangelium Vitae)*, Pope Saint John Paul II challenges us to take part in the ongoing battle between a culture of death and a culture of life in our society today. He discusses several ways laypeople—including young people—can promote the culture of life:

- caring for the weak in our society, including AIDS patients, the elderly, and the disabled
- teaching and promoting chastity, including methods of natural family planning
- supporting single mothers
- encouraging health care personnel, including doctors, pharmacists, and nurses, to resist the temptation to manipulate lives or be agents of death
- influencing political and legislative processes to pass laws that respect the dignity of every life
- rethinking labor or other social policies to give families adequate time to care for babies, ill family members, or the elderly

commitment to God's will in your life, and by following Christ's example of leading through service.

You may also know laypeople who assist the hierarchy in governing the Church. Some laypeople provide this help in the parish through membership on various committees. Others support the bishops when they meet in councils and synods.

How have you exercised Christian leadership in your school, parish, and community?

Article 44: The Vocation of the Laity

In what specific ways do you live out your call to holiness? Each of us has unique opportunities to share Christ's love with the world and to continue his saving mission. As a layperson you have relationships with people who may have never gone to church or met a priest. Perhaps you can begin to see why the laity's work and vocation are very important. Let's look at some of the ways the laity participate in Christ's mission.

The Work of the Laity

A primary way laypeople participate in Christ's mission is through their own work. All laypeople are called to seek the Kingdom of God by doing God's will within their chosen work, whether they are parents, nurses, lawyers, or computer programmers. This also includes being a student! By doing their work well and being honest, friendly, caring, and joyful in schools and workplaces, the laity give witness to the Kingdom of God.

Another primary way laypeople participate in Christ's mission is through the vocation of marriage. The vocation of marriage is natural to human beings. A married couple has a natural vocation to have children and to raise their children in a way that respects each child's vocation to follow Jesus.

From the beginning of Christianity, some laypeople have chosen to renounce the great good of marriage in order to follow Christ as a single, celibate person. Both the call to marriage and the call to virginity for the sake of the Kingdom come from the Lord himself. The call to renounce marriage may take the form of a dedication to the consecrated life (discussed later in this chapter). Yet many laypeople live as committed single people without consecrating themselves to that choice. Committed single life involves a permanent, celibate gift of self to God and one's neighbor. Committed single people are often especially close to Jesus' heart and serve God and neighbor with great dedication.

© Rob Marmion / Shutterstock.com

We are all called to bring Christ into the work we do. What careers are you considering in your life? How can you show the love of Christ through those careers?

As Christians we all have a duty to work with civil authorities to create a society where truth, freedom, solidarity, and justice reign. The work of laypeople who are called to political office or other influential positions in society is especially important in accomplishing this. Because their decisions influence the lives of so many other people, they have a special responsibility to work for the common good, to act in harmony with Church teaching, and to be witnesses and agents of peace and justice.

The Family: The Domestic Church

Did you wake up in church this morning? A Christian family is called a "domestic church." Raising a Christian family is a unique and special way the laity participate in Christ's mission. The Christian home is the place where children first hear the Word of God and the call to faith. In families we learn how to share in the Trinity's communion of love through prayer, moral living, and service to others. The Christian family is the domestic church because it is the first and best teacher of human virtues and Christian charity.

The family as a type of Church has always been significant in Christian history. In the earliest days of Christianity, when the head of a household converted to Christianity, his or her household also converted (see Acts 16:15,31–33; 18:8). The early Church literally met in people's houses (see Romans 16:5, 1 Corinthians 16:19).

Parents have a special role in the family. Obviously they have a duty to provide for the physical and spiritual needs of their children as much as they can. But in our culture, it is very easy to focus on the physical needs—maybe even too easy to focus on material things—and neglect the spiritual needs. Parents must remember that they are the first proclaimers of the faith to their children. They teach their children the virtues and set a good

Pray It!

Prayer Honoring Saint Gianna Molla

© Society of Saint Gianna Beretta Molla

Gianna Beretta Molla (1922–1962) was an Italian pediatrician, wife, and mother. Facing a difficult delivery of her fourth baby, she made clear that if the doctors could save only one person, they should save her child. The baby was successfully delivered, but Gianna died from complications. She was canonized in 2004.

You, Lord Jesus, were for Gianna a splendid example. She learned to recognize you in the beauty of nature. As she was questioning her choice of vocation she went in search of you and the best way to serve you.

Through her married love she became a sign of your love for the Church and for humanity. Like you, the Good Samaritan, she cared for everyone who was sick, small or weak. Following your example, out of love she gave herself entirely, generating new life.

Holy Spirit, Source of every perfection, give us wisdom, intelligence, and courage so that, following the example of Saint Gianna and through her intercession, we may know how to place ourselves at the service of each person we meet in our personal, family and professional lives, and thus grow in love and holiness. Amen.

institute
An organization devoted to a common cause. Religious orders are a type of religious institute.

hermit
A person who lives a solitary life in order to commit himself or herself more fully to prayer and in some cases to be completely free for service to others.

example by their own lifestyle. They further evangelize their children by bringing them into the life of the Church from their earliest years. Parents should teach their children to pray and to discover their vocation as a child of God. They must always teach their children that our first duty as Christians is to follow Jesus, our Lord and Savior.

Children in turn can help parents to grow in holiness. Living in a family, we can learn from one another the joys of work, love, forgiveness, and self-sacrifice.

How do you help your parents to grow in holiness? How do they help you to grow in holiness?

Article 45: The Consecrated Life: Religious Orders

Have you gotten to know a priest, brother, or sister who is a member of a religious order (sometimes called a religious community)? The names of religious orders are sometimes based on the name of the person who inspired or founded the order. Franciscans (<u>Saint Francis</u>), Dominicans (<u>Saint Dominic</u>), and Benedictines (<u>Saint Benedict</u>) are a few examples. The members of these orders have made a formal, public vow to live out the evangelical counsels of poverty, chastity, and obedience in a stable state of life recognized by the Church—thereby entering into one form of the consecrated life.

The Beginning of Religious Orders

Members of religious orders live communal lives, publicly profess the evangelical counsels, share a liturgical character, and belong to **institutes** recognized by the Church. By their desire to more closely follow Christ, they witness to the union of Christ with the Church.

In the first centuries of the Church, there was a great monastic movement involving **hermits** who went to the desert to dedicate themselves to following Christ more closely. These were people whom God had called to withdraw from the world for a life of prayer and solitude. Some hermits gradually formed communities. <u>Saint Pachomius</u> is usually credited with founding the first monastic community around the year 320 (the word *monastic* is derived from the Greek word for "alone"). People belonging to these communities were called **monks** and nuns. Religious life first developed in Syria and Egypt from these monastic movements.

Eventually these communities became known as religious orders. A religious order can have both consecrated lay members (religious brothers and sisters) and consecrated ordained members (priests) who live communal lives and follow a common religious rule. Consecrated laymen in religious orders are called **brothers**, and consecrated laywomen are called **sisters** (or sometimes nuns). All religious orders in the Roman Catholic Church must be approved by the Pope.

Variety of Religious Orders

New religious orders can emerge in response to changing conditions. In the Middle Ages, the Dominicans responded to a need for teachers and preachers. The Franciscans were established because <u>Saint Francis of Assisi</u> sought to restore a life of simplicity to the Church. The Jesuit order developed in response to the need to reform certain practices in the Catholic Church after the upheaval of the Protestant Reformation.

The founders of religious orders impart a certain charism to their community. The Christian Brothers follow <u>Saint John Baptist de La Salle's</u> emphasis on the education of the young, particularly those in greatest need. The Dominicans focus on preaching and teaching, following the example of their founder, <u>Saint Dominic</u>.

Religious orders took a leading role in evangelizing non-Christian lands. Examples include the Jesuit missions in the Far East, as well as the Dominican and Franciscan efforts in the Americas. Many religious communities today continue to do missionary work through-

monk
A male member of a religious community who lives a life of prayer and work according to a specific rule of life, such as the Rule of Saint Benedict.

(religious) brother
A layman in a religious order who has made permanent vows of poverty, chastity, and obedience.

(religious) sister
A laywoman in a religious order who has made permanent vows of poverty, chastity, and obedience.

out the world, including working for justice in places where there is a great deal of injustice.

Some religious orders and congregations are devoted primarily to prayer and contemplation. Rather than being actively engaged in the world, these communities follow the ancient monastic path of separating from the world so their members can avoid the world's distractions and more fully commit themselves to pursuing holiness through prayer and study.

Faith in Action
Presentation Sisters

MISS NANO NAGLE.

© Private Collection / Bridgeman Images

Nano Nagle (1718–1784) was born to a wealthy Irish family. At that time, Ireland was ruled by the Anglican monarchy of England, and it became illegal both to operate Catholic schools in Ireland and to travel overseas for Catholic education. Nagle's parents were able to smuggle her and her sister to France to receive a Catholic education.

Although Nagle was drawn to the religious life in France, she eventually chose to return to Ireland to serve her people. The English penal laws still prohibited Catholic schools in Ireland, so Nano secretly set up schools for poor Irish children. She also ministered to the elderly and sick at night, earning her the nickname Lady of the Lamp. She eventually established a religious order that became known as the Presentation Sisters of the Blessed Virgin Mary.

Today the Presentation Sisters have ministries on every continent. Following Nano's charism, they are involved in education, health care, and the promotion of social justice. In South Dakota, for example, the Presentation Sisters have established three hospitals and sponsor one college. They continue to advocate on social justice issues, including calling for the abolition of the death penalty.

Prayer as the Rhythm of the Religious Life

The daily life of all religious orders is characterized by regular prayer, especially the prayers of the Liturgy of the Hours (also known as the Divine Office). The Hours are designed to make the whole course of the day and night holy through praising God, and they fulfill <u>Saint Paul's</u> exhortation to "pray without ceasing" (<u>1 Thessalonians 5:17</u>). Priests are also required to pray the Liturgy of the Hours daily. Other consecrated people, permanent deacons, and the laity can also join in praying the Liturgy of the Hours, because it is the public prayer of the Church. The Divine Office focuses heavily on Psalms and also includes hymns, Scripture readings, prayers, and responses.

© Bill Wittman / www.wpwittman.com

Prayer is an integral part of the life of vowed religious. Through their continual prayer, they both pray for the needs of God's children and model a devotion to prayer for all the members of the Church.

The Liturgy of the Hours in the Roman Rite includes seven Hours. Morning prayer (also referred to as Lauds) and evening prayer (also referred to as Vespers) are the primary hours.

Third Orders and Lay Associates

Third Orders are associations of laypeople connected to a particular religious order in the Church. These laypeople do not take public vows of chastity, obedience, and poverty. In fact, many have families of their own. But they do practice the religious order's spirituality, and they typically assist with the ministries the order carries out. Three examples are the Franciscan Third Order, the Dominican Third Order, and the Carmelite Third Order.

Other lay associations are connected with religious orders but are not called Third Orders. For example, laity associated with the Christian Brothers are called LaSallian associates. Maryknoll, the missionary institute, has lay associates who serve as lay missioners.

Which religious order's ministry and spirituality is most attractive to you?

Article 46: Other Types of Consecrated Life

Religious orders may be the most familiar form of the consecrated life, but they are not the only form. Other forms of the consecrated life include life as a hermit, consecrated virgin or widow, or a member of a secular institute or society of apostolic life. The variety of possibilities is a testimony to the work of the Holy Spirit in the Church. He calls people to different ways of living out the evangelical counsels.

Thomas Merton was a well-known spiritual writer and Trappist monk who chose to spend the last years of his life as a hermit.

© Photograph of Thomas Merton by John Howard Griffin courtesy of the Merton Center and used with permission of the Griffin Estate.

Hermits: The Eremitic Life

Do you sometimes feel a need to be alone, to find some peace and quiet away from the constant busyness of life? If so, perhaps you can relate somewhat to the life of the hermit.

Hermits don't necessarily profess the evangelical counsels publicly, but they separate themselves from the world to focus on prayer and penance. The degree of separation varies. Even though some hermits live very secluded lives, virtually all hermits

Primary Sources

A Story from the Desert Fathers

Because hermits are by nature solitary, we don't have many stories or details about the lives of those who seek the eremitic life. Benedicta Ward, a modern-day theologian, offers us this tale from traditions surrounding the early Christian hermits:

> The devil appeared to a monk disguised as an angel of light and said to him, "I am Gabriel, and I have been sent to you." But the monk said, "Are you sure you weren't sent to someone else? I am not worthy to have an angel sent to me." At that the devil vanished. (*The Desert Fathers*, page 165)

today have some degree of human contact. Essentially hermits are a witness to the interior aspect of the mystery of the Church. The hermit's focus on complete union with God reflects the Church's perfect union with Christ.

The **eremitic** tradition began around AD 250 with men who lived in the Egyptian desert. (The term *eremitic* is derived from the Greek word for "desert.") Saint Anthony of the Desert, also known as <u>Saint Anthony of Egypt</u>, is the best known of the Desert Fathers who lived and prayed alone in the desert. Some women, such as Sara and Syncletica, who lived in the fourth century, were also called to this vocation.

eremitic
Relating to the life of a hermit, characterized by self-denial and solitude.

secular
Relating to worldly concerns rather than religion.

The spirituality of hermits is a spirituality of the desert—a life of solitude and purification. Models for this spirituality include Israel's forty years of wandering in the desert, the prophet Elijah's time in the desert, and John the Baptist's and Jesus' forty days in the desert. However, a hermit is not focused on himself or herself only. Though the hermit is alone, his or her prayer life is universal. He or she prays for the good of the whole world.

Consecrated Virgins and Widows

Consecrated virgins and widows are women—who either never married or were later widowed—who dedicate themselves to a life of celibacy for the sake of the Kingdom of God. Such a woman is betrothed mystically to Christ and is an image of the Church and a sign of the Church's love for Christ. She is consecrated by the bishop of her diocese but remains fully in the world, working in her **secular** job. She supports the Church through her prayers and volunteer work, but she is not required to take on specific duties.

© Photo by Mary Devlin; used with permission of the Catholic Diocese of Sioux Falls, SD

Secular Institutes

Secular institutes are communities of people who live consecrated lives but whose daily work takes place within the world. They are a powerful witness to Gospel values in society, and they share in the work of evangelization. Members of secular institutes share annual retreats, meetings, and daily common prayer.

Caritas Christi, for example, is an organization of single Catholic women who desire to follow Christ more closely while still working in their secular jobs. Their inspiration is <u>Saint Catherine of Siena</u>, who desired to serve the Church while remaining in the world. As Pope, Venerable Pius XII officially recognized such groups in 1947.

Societies of Apostolic Life

Societies of apostolic life, also called apostolic societies, are not strictly speaking a form of the consecrated life, but they are similar to religious orders. Apostolic societies are composed of laity or clergy who usually live in community for a particular purpose but do not make public religious vows. Maryknoll, also called the Catholic Foreign Mission Society of America, is an apostolic society dedicated to foreign missions. The Oratory of Saint Philip Neri, a congregation of priests and lay brothers founded in the late 1500s in Rome, fosters a greater devotion to prayer, preaching, and the Sacraments. The mission of the Paulist Fathers is to evangelize North America in ways appropriate to our distinct cultures.

Chapter Review

1. What are the three evangelical counsels? How are different groups in the Church called to follow the counsels?

2. What is the special mission of all laypeople?

3. Describe how the laity shares the priestly, prophetic, and kingly mission of Christ.

4. In what ways is the family the domestic church?

5. Describe how the work of the laity participates in the mission of Christ.

6. Name two characteristics that all religious orders share.

7. What are some needs that have been fulfilled by religious orders throughout history?

8. How does the Liturgy of the Hours help to fulfill Saint Paul's admonition to pray without ceasing?

9. Define the terms *hermits, consecrated virgins, secular institutes, Third Order,* and *societies of apostolic life.*

The Church's Mystery and Mission

Thus far we have looked at the Church as Christ's continued presence in the world. We have examined the four Marks of the Church and considered her leadership structure and vocations to holiness. But fundamentally the Church is a mystery. We can never fully understand this mystery, but we can explore it by examining images of the Church as well as her mission of salvation.

Sacred Scripture gives us three important images that help us to more deeply contemplate the mystery of the Church: the People of God, the Body of Christ, and the Temple of the Holy Spirit. These images remind us of the close relationship between the Church and each Divine Person of the Trinity. They also help us to understand Sacred Scripture and the liturgy, especially the Mass.

With these important images in mind, we turn to questions about the Church's mission of salvation. Why be a Catholic? Does someone have to be Catholic to be saved? Christ established the Church as the means of salvation. Other faith traditions do have elements of holiness and truth, but the Catholic Church alone has the fullness of these means of salvation. She must always seek to apply Sacred Scripture and Sacred Tradition to the changing conditions of the world. Evangelization—the primary focus of the Church's mission—is the proclamation of Christ in word and deed. To carry out her evangelizing mission, the Church must actively engage with modern life and culture.

The enduring understandings and essential questions represent core concepts and questions that are explored throughout this unit. By studying the content of each chapter, you will gain a more complete understanding of the following:

Enduring Understandings
1. We can better understand the mystery of the Church through several images presented in Sacred Scripture.
2. The fullness of Jesus Christ's Church is found only in the Catholic Church, which is necessary for salvation.
3. In order to transform the world into the Kingdom of God, the Church must engage the world through evangelization and inculturation.

Essential Questions
1. How does or should a typical parish mirror the images of the Church to the contemporary world?
2. How can those who do not belong to the Catholic Church be saved?
3. What is the role of inculturation in the process of evangelization?

Chapter

11 Images of the Church

Introduction

We can explore the mystery of the Church through three important images from Sacred Scripture: the People of God, the Body of Christ, and the Temple of the Holy Spirit. These images help us not only to grasp more fully the Mystery that is the Church (because metaphors are frequently used in the Church) but also to understand Sacred Scripture and the liturgy, especially the Mass.

First we look at how the Church is the People of God. When we talk about the People of God, we potentially include every person on the planet. Under the first covenant, membership was a birthright. Under the New Covenant, Christ invites all people to have faith in him and to be baptized so that we can belong to the People of God—so that we can form one family.

The Body of Christ is a second important way to understand the Church. This name reveals the extremely close relationship between Christ and believers as well as the intimate relationship among the believers themselves.

Finally, we look at the Church as the Temple of the Holy Spirit, an image that emphasizes how the Church is a dwelling place for the Holy Spirit. For the Jewish people, God dwelt in the Temple. Saint Paul said that the Holy Spirit now lives in the Church and in each one of us (see 1 Corinthians 3:16–17).

Article 47: The Church Is the People of God

Where do you feel that you belong? Groups to which you belong can tell others something about you. Saying you belong to the drama club suggests that besides loving theater or acting, you likely also feel at home with the other members of that club who share your interest. To say you belong to the Asian American student association suggests that you appreciate the company of others who want to know more about your shared cultural heritage. Likewise, to say you belong to the People of God conveys the message that it is important to you to spend time with others who share your relationship with Christ—that you see yourself as part of the Catholic Church.

God Wants All People to Be His

Imagine that at Baptism everyone receives an official welcome booklet. It begins: "Welcome to the People of God! Here is what you need to know about us!" What would it say? Perhaps it would include some of the following points:

- God creates every human being with a desire for him, and he continuously calls each person to himself. By nature we are religious beings. God made us to live in communion with him and to find happiness through this communion. There is a place for every person in the People of God.

- We are called the People of God not because we claim God (no one owns or claims God) but because God claims us.

- We become members of this People by Baptism.

- Our Head is Jesus Christ, the Messiah.

- As members we enjoy the dignity and freedom of the children of the Father.

- The Holy Spirit dwells in our hearts.

- Our law is given by Jesus: "I give you a new commandment: love one another. As I have loved you, so you also should love one another" (John 13:34).

  - Our mission is to infiltrate the world, bringing it salt (a precious commodity that enhances and preserves) and light (the light of Christ).

  - Our destiny is nothing less than the Kingdom of God.

Amazingly, the People of God is a community to which every one of us is welcome and truly belongs—no particular skills or talents needed. God invites all people to belong to the People of God, to form one family. Welcome to the People of God.

The People of God in the Old and New Covenants

God chose the people of Israel to be his People, and he made a covenant with them. Jews become part of the Chosen People by birth. When Christ offered the New Covenant at the Last Supper, he created the new People of God, the Church, based on this New Covenant. Followers of Christ become members of this People not through physical birth but through the spiritual birth of Baptism and their faith in Christ, who invites all human beings to be part of this People. God offers membership in the Church to all, so that we can become one family, one People of God.

The People of God Are United

If you have ever been part of a recreational sports league or another activity in which anyone can participate, you know you will find participants at all levels of ability and interest. It can be difficult for the coach or leader to meet everyone's needs.

Because the Church draws people from all parts of the world, she includes people with different customs, languages, and levels of understanding and interest. How then has she become a global community of more than one billion people? It is no surprise that this unity comes from the Trinity. That is, the universal Church is united through the unity of the Father, the Son, and the Holy Spirit.

What can you learn about your own close relationships through the example of the unity of the Trinity and the universal Church?

© Bill Wittman / www.wpwittman.com

What diversity exists within your parish community?

Faith in Action
Mother Laura, Colombia's First Saint

© Luis Benavides / AP / Corbis

Saint Laura of Saint Catherine of Siena was born María Laura Montoya Upegui in Jericó, Colombia. To support herself and her widowed mother, she became a school teacher. She had always devoted time to prayer and to the Eucharist, but it was not until she was forty years old that she felt free to follow a missionary call to serve the indigenous peoples of Colombia. She longed to become "an Indian with the Indians to win them all for Christ" ("Laura Montoya Upegui [1874–1949]"). With four other women, she formed a congregation, the Missionaries of Mary Immaculate and Saint Catherine of Siena, devoted to the service of the Indians. The community became popularly known as the Lauristas.

Serving the Indians meant learning their customs and living with them in respect and love, often in primitive conditions. It also meant teaching them to read and write and helping to defend them against racial discrimination and violation of their rights.

In 2013, Mother Laura was canonized by Pope Francis, a fellow South American. He said that Saint Laura "teaches us to be generous to God . . . and to make the joy of the Gospel shine out in our words and in the witness of our life" ("Holy Mass and Canonizations," 2). Today Mother Laura's community continues to work deep in the Amazon, in the Democratic Republic of the Congo, and on the streets of Haiti.

Article 48: The Church Is the Body of Christ

If the phrase "Body of Christ" brings more than one image to mind, then you may be on your way to understanding this complex central image of the Church. By now you have often been told that the Church is the Body of Christ. When you learned about the Body of Christ in preparation for First Communion, your study probably focused on the important truth that we receive the Body and Blood of Christ in the Eucharist. The intimate union we have with Christ in the Eucharist is a good foundation for learning about the close relationship we can have with him through his Body, the Church.

Pray It!

Prayers of Petition

Do your classes begin with a prayer? If so, perhaps the person who leads prayer invites you and your classmates to mention someone or something you would like the whole class to pray for. By these prayers of petition, you participate in the Church as the Body of Christ. You call others to communion with the Father, the Son, and the Holy Spirit, and you also affirm that we are in prayerful communion with people near and far, known and unknown, through Christ's Body.

Use the Morning Offering—a much-loved prayer of petition—and add your own intentions:

O Jesus,
through the Immaculate Heart of Mary,
I offer You my prayers, works,
joys and sufferings
of this day for all the intentions
of Your Sacred Heart,
in union with the Holy Sacrifice of the Mass
throughout the world,
in reparation for my sins,
for the intentions of all my relatives and friends,
and in particular for the intentions of the Holy Father.
Amen.

Christ told us, "Whoever eats my flesh and drinks my blood remains in me and I in him" (John 6:56).

We know that during the Consecration in the Mass, the bread and wine become the Body and Blood of Christ. This change is called **Transubstantiation**. Christ himself is present in a true, real, and substantial manner. Receiving the Eucharist intensifies the union we always have with Christ, as he dwells in us and we dwell in him.

Communion in Christ with Others

Because we, as members of the Body of Christ, are in intimate communion with Christ as individuals, we are also all closely related to one another. People of diverse backgrounds, languages, countries, and experiences belong to the Body of Christ. We are united in Christ. Comparing the Church with the human body illustrates how intimate our relationship is with Christ and with other Church members.

We not only come from many different places, but we also possess different gifts and, therefore, assume different roles in the Church. We contribute to the Church in different ways, much like the leg and foot contribute to the good of the human body differently than an ear or an eye does.

Because we belong to Christ and are in communion with him, we grow in love and other virtues. This growth makes us more sensitive to fellow members of the Body as well as to all people. As a community (meaning "people in communion"), we share joys and sorrows, and we try to show special concern for members most in need, especially people who are poor and persecuted. As Saint Paul explained so well, "If [one] part suffers, all the parts suffer with it; if one part is honored, all the parts share its joy" (1 Corinthians 12:26). Things that sometimes divide us, such as gender, race,

Transubstantiation

In the Sacrament of the Eucharist, this is the name given to the action of changing the bread and wine into the Body and Blood of Jesus Christ.

Through the Eucharist, we share in the Body of Christ in a special way. How does physically receiving the Body and Blood of Christ unite us with him and one another?

© Bill Wittman / www.wpwittman.com

or socioeconomic status, do not matter in the Body of Christ. Saint Paul reassured us, "You are all one in Christ Jesus" (Galatians 3:28).

Christ Is the Head of the Body

Christ is also the Head of the Body, which is the Church. Christ lives in and with her. The Church receives her life from Christ. She lives in him and for him. Christ unites the members of the Church with his life so that we all may come to resemble him more and more. He unites us with his suffering, death, and Resurrection. Amazingly, when we bring our suffering to Christ, he transforms it. He has the power to bring new life out of suffering and sacrifice.

In addition to gaining eternal life for us, Christ also conquered evil in a significant way. Evil never wins in the end. Good always does. This truth does not mean we do not suffer in life. It means we suffer with Christ in hope of new life, trusting that Christ can bring good from painful experiences. No matter how bad a situation seems, Christ can transform it and bring new life.

Exploring the nature of the Church as the Body of Christ, with Christ as her Head, helps us to understand ourselves as members of this Body. The head helps the body to grow; Christ helps us to grow toward him. Just as a person's head and other body parts make up one body,

Primary Sources

We Are Part of a Greater Whole

In 1999, the leaders of Israel and Palestine signed a historic accord intended to promote peace in the Middle East. Shortly after, Pope Saint John Paul II addressed young people of Israel and Palestine, the greatest hope for future peace among those conflicting peoples. Although conflict continues to disrupt the Holy Land today, the Pope's wise words offer a timeless reminder that we must work together in the one body of humankind:

> None of us is alone in this world; each of us is a vital piece of the great mosaic of humanity as a whole. ("Message of the Holy Father to the Young People of Israel and Palestine")

Christ and the Church are one Body and together make up the "whole Christ."

Of course, membership in the Body of Christ does not mean that the Church's members always act in a way that reflects this union. Saint Paul scolded early Christian Churches when he saw unloving behavior that did not promote unity. He found factions and divisions in the Christian community. For example, when some Christians were not sharing their food with the poor, Saint Paul made this point: "Now you are Christ's body, and individually parts of it" (1 Corinthians 12:27). It was no accident that Saint Paul concluded his instruction on being the Body of Christ with his great instruction on love (see 1 Corinthians, chapter 13). Love is the way to fully become what we receive—the Body of Christ.

The Church Is the Bride of Christ

Although Christ and the Church are one, we also talk about the Church and Christ in terms of a personal relationship, both to distinguish between the Church and Christ and to reveal their unity. Specifically, we describe Christ as the bridegroom who loves the Church, his bride. What is incredible about this union is that Christ gave himself up for his bride, the Church, in order to make her holy and to join her with himself in an everlasting covenant.

Saint Paul compared the intimate relationship between a husband and wife with the intimate relationship between Christ and the Church: "Husbands, love your wives, even as Christ loved the church and handed himself over for her to sanctify her" (Ephesians 5:25–26). This image may be hard to understand at first. Saint Paul himself went on to say, "This is a great mystery, but I speak in reference to Christ and the church" (5:32).

The unity of Christ the bridegroom with the Church, his bride, also reveals to us something about the intimate relationship God intends for a husband and wife. The relationship between Christ and the Church can be described as two becoming one flesh (see *Catechism of the*

© Russell McBride / iStockphoto.com

When a man and woman are married in the Sacrament of Holy Matrimony, they make an everlasting covenant to love and care for each other. In the same way, Christ has made a covenant with the Church to love and care for her for all eternity.

Catholic Church, [CCC], 796). This is the case for a husband and wife too. In his **Theology of the Body**, Pope Saint John Paul II teaches us not to shy away from a deeper understanding of the sexual imagery involved in this comparison. For a married couple, sexual intercourse is a profound sign of unifying love: a sign of the total self-giving of each spouse, and of the profound mystery of the two becoming one flesh. Thus Christian Marriage becomes an effective sign or Sacrament of the covenant of Christ and the Church, and the faithfulness of each spouse to the other gives witness to God's faithful love (see *CCC*, 1617, 1648).

How does the example of a faithful Christian marriage help you to understand Christ's relationship with the People of God?

Article 49: The Church Is the Temple of the Holy Spirit

In trying to explain to early Christians the mystery of the Church, Saint Paul offered this image: "Do you not know that you are the temple of God, and that the Spirit of God dwells in you? . . . The temple of God, which you are, is holy" (1 Corinthians 3:16–17). In the Old Testament and other accounts of Jewish history, the Temple was the building in which God was present to the people of Israel in a special or unique way. Thus Saint Paul was saying that the Holy Spirit is present in a unique way now in the Church.

Art Resource, NY

Ancient Israelites believed that God dwelt in the innermost part of the Temple, foreshadowing the Church as the dwelling place of the Holy Spirit.

The Holy Spirit Is the Soul of the Church

The Holy Spirit is the center of the Church's life. Another way to say that is to say the Spirit is the soul of the **Mystical** Body of Christ. The Holy Spirit is the source of the Church's life, unity, gifts, and charisms. The Holy Spirit is present in the Body of Christ, the Church. Jesus Christ has poured the Holy Spirit out on all the members of the Church, making the Holy Spirit part of everything the Church is and does.

The Holy Spirit is the source of the Church's life and is active in the liturgy. He reveals Christ's presence in the community gathered, in the proclamation of Sacred Scripture, in the priest who presides, and in the physical signs of the liturgical celebration. But the Holy Spirit is at work even before that, preparing us to receive Christ in the liturgy. And the Holy Spirit does more than just reveal Christ in the liturgy. Through the Holy Spirit, the saving work of Christ is actually made real and present in the liturgy. The Holy Spirit also brings us into communion with Christ. This gift of communion builds up and animates the Church and increases her holiness.

Theology of the Body
The name given to Pope Saint John Paul II's teachings on the human body and sexuality delivered during his papacy via 129 short lectures between September 1979 and November 1984.

mystical
Having a spiritual meaning or reality that is neither apparent to the senses nor obvious to the intelligence; the visible sign of the hidden reality of salvation.

Live It!
Our Bodies Are Not Our Own

You may remember that Saint Francis of Assisi considered all of creation to be his brothers and sisters. He called the sun Brother Sun and the moon Sister Moon. He called his body Brother Donkey because, in his view, it carried him around from place to place. On his deathbed Saint Francis apologized to Brother Donkey for not taking very good care of his body. He realized, too late, that his body was a great gift from God. His body deserved respect and proper consideration.

Think of your body as a Temple of the Holy Spirit, and consider some implications. Do you give it the right food, enough rest, and proper exercise? Do you get regular physical and dental check-ups? Do you take unnecessary risks that might result in bodily harm to you or others? Spend a few moments asking yourself these questions. Choose one way to live a healthier lifestyle. Then start soon!

The Holy Spirit empowers the members of the Church to acquire and develop human virtues. These are "stable dispositions of the intellect and the will that govern our acts, order our passions, and guide our conduct in accordance with reason and faith" (*CCC*, 1834). The four pivotal human virtues, called the cardinal virtues, are prudence, justice, fortitude, and temperance. All other human virtues can be grouped around these four. The Holy Spirit also gives us talents and skills that enable us to contribute to the Church's mission.

When Jesus told his Apostles about the Holy Spirit, he used the word *advocate*. A human advocate speaks or writes in your favor, supports you, and recommends you.

Did You Know?

Dwelling Places of the Holy Spirit

© Christopher Futcher / iStockphoto.com

Long ago, as a young king of Israel, David realized something: "Here I am living in a house of cedar, but the ark of God dwells in a tent!" (2 Samuel 7:2). But he was not the king who would build a suitable house for God. His son, the wise and wealthy Solomon, would build the great Temple of Jerusalem.

Jesus foretold that the Temple would not stand, and it was indeed destroyed by the Romans in AD 70. But Jesus reassured us that we ourselves would become the dwelling places of the Holy Spirit:

"Whoever believes in me, as scripture says:

'Rivers of living water will flow from within him.'"

He said this in reference to the Spirit that those who came to believe in him were to receive.

(John 7:38–39)

Being a dwelling place for the Holy Spirit means respecting ourselves and others in body, mind, and heart. It means not harboring anger or envy or bitterness, but instead offering hope and love, helpfulness and prayer. It means being a place where the Holy Spirit can say, deep in our hearts, "Here, I am at home."

Imagine how much more the Holy Spirit does for us! The next time you are in a difficult situation, call on the Holy Spirit.

Chapter Review

1. How can someone become a member of the People of God?

2. How is the Church—which numbers over one billion people globally—unified?

3. How does belonging to the Body of Christ make us grow in love?

4. Explain why the Church is the Bride of Christ.

5. What connection is there between the Temple of the Jewish people and the Church as the Temple of the Holy Spirit?

6. How is the Holy Spirit the source of the Church's life?

© Kirk Strickland / iStockphoto.com

When we care for our bodies through exercise, rest, and proper diet, we are caring for the Temple of the Holy Spirit that God has given us.

12

The Church and Salvation

Introduction

In our society today, we sometimes find people who say that all religions are generally the same. With this in mind, let's turn now to this question: Why be a Catholic? In this chapter, we will recall that Christ established the Church as the means of salvation. Although other faith traditions do have elements of sanctification and truth, the Catholic Church alone has the fullness of these means.

These truths lead us to a second question: Does someone have to be Catholic to be saved? We will learn that God offers salvation to all people, including those who, through no fault of their own, have never heard of Christ or his Church. We will also learn that salvation can be attained in non-Catholic Christian churches and ecclesial communities, but only through these communities' relationships to the fullness of the Catholic Church.

We will then consider a final question: Why belong to any organized religion? We find that because humans are social by nature, so too human salvation is social—God offers us salvation through the community of the Church.

Article 50: The Fullness of Truth and Salvation

It is comforting to assume that most people will go to Heaven, regardless of their religion. According to this way of thinking, it doesn't really matter if we are Catholic, as long as we try to be good. This idea can seem very open-minded and tolerant, but before accepting it, we should ask a deeper question: Is this assumption true, or is it just based on wishful thinking?

The First Letter to Timothy tells us that God loves all people and "wills everyone to be saved." The passage goes on to say that God wills everyone "to come to knowledge of the truth"(2:4). In other words, it is through knowledge of the truth that we are saved. The truth is in fact a person, Jesus Christ, who is the one true path to salvation. Salvation begins with God's loving initiative. The Father sent his only Son to atone for our sins. Jesus freely gave himself so that salvation would be possible for all people. God has entrusted that truth to the Church, and thus the Church has the obligation to proclaim that truth to the world. This obligation inspires and gives life to the Church's missionary activity.

The Fullness of the Church of Christ

In unit 2, "The Church Is One, Holy, Catholic, and Apostolic," we explored the four Marks of the Church. As we look at what these Marks tell us about the Church, we must keep in mind that the fullness of Jesus Christ's Church is found in the Catholic Church only. The Catholic Church, led by the Pope and the bishops in communion with him, is the only Church with the fullness of the four Marks. However, when we affirm that the Church is One, Holy, Catholic, and Apostolic, we do so with humble hearts. We pray knowing the members of the Church struggle with sin. We pray also with the knowledge that holiness and truth can be found outside the visible organization of the Catholic Church.

The fullness of Christ's Church includes the following:

© CORBIS

- the fullness of Revelation, which is transmitted through Scripture and Tradition
- the fullness of the Sacraments
- the fullness of the ordained ministry

The Catholic Church alone has retained the fullness of these means of salvation.

One saint who reached this conclusion was Blessed John Henry Newman. A brilliant English intellectual closely associated with Oxford University, Newman was originally a priest in the Church of England. Along with other influential Anglican leaders, Newman launched the Oxford Movement, an effort to recover the roots of the Anglican Church in the earliest Church and the Apostolic Succession. Newman's intense study of early Church history, however, eventually led him to conclude that only the Catholic Church had preserved the fullness of the Apostolic Tradition. Despite discouraging social pressure, Newman followed his convictions. He was received into the Catholic Church in 1845 and was eventually made a cardinal by Pope Leo XIII. In 2010, he was beatified by Pope Benedict XVI.

When an infant is baptized, what are the parents hoping for and promising to do for their child?

The Church Is Necessary for Salvation

Christ is the one path to salvation (see John 14:6), and he is present to us in the Church. Jesus established the Church as a visible organization through which he communicates his grace, truth, and salvation. Jesus himself explained that it is necessary to join the Church through Baptism in order to be saved: "Whoever believes and is baptized will be saved; whoever does not believe will be condemned" (Mark 16:16). He also said, "No one can enter the kingdom of God without being born of water and Spirit" (John

© CURAphotography/Shutterstock.com

3:5). Thus salvation comes from Christ, who is our Head, through the Church, which is his Body.

The Church Is a Sacrament

The Church in this world is the sacrament of salvation, the sign and instrument of the saving union between God and humans. You might be asking, "How can the Church be a sacrament—aren't there only Seven Sacraments?" Yes, there are seven official Sacraments of the Church, but the idea of sacrament is bigger than that. A sacrament is a visible sign of God's invisible grace.

Two Latin terms can help us to understand the mystery of the Church as sacrament: **sacramentum** and **mysterium**. Both terms originally translated the Greek word *mysterion*. Over time the term *sacramentum* came to refer to the visible sign of the hidden reality of salvation, and *mysterium* came to refer to the hidden reality itself. The first or primary sacrament is Jesus Christ. This is because he, more than anyone or anything, makes

sacramentum
The visible sign of the hidden reality of salvation.

mysterium
The hidden reality of God's plan of salvation.

Pray It!

See the Body of Christ

When you look around at everyone gathered with you at Sunday Mass, of course you see the people you know–possibly friends from school, relatives, or a former teacher or catechist. You likely also see many people you don't know. An elderly couple might be sitting in the front pew, possibly a family with a crying baby, maybe a teenager whom you've never met, and possibly a young adult by himself or herself. All the people gathered with you are a part of the Body of Christ, each bringing his or her own gifts, troubles, joys, and pains. The next time you go to Mass, take a moment to notice the wonderful and diverse Body of Christ, and ask Christ to help you recognize him in those around you:

> To Jesus, who called us friends:
> Let me be a true friend to you today,
> seeing you in everyone around me,
> those I know, and those I don't.
> Let my words and my actions
> tell the world how much I love you.
> Amen.

(*The Catholic Youth Prayer Book*, page 15)

visible God's presence in the world. He himself is the mystery of salvation, and his saving work is made visible to us through the Seven Sacraments. It is through the Sacraments that the Holy Spirit spreads the grace of Christ throughout the Church.

The *Catechism of the Catholic Church (CCC)* explains, "The Church, then, both contains and communicates the invisible grace she signifies" (774). She is a sacrament because she makes visible the invisible communion we share with God—Father, Son, and Holy Spirit. When we call the Church the sacrament of salvation, we emphasize that it is through the Church that we come to know God and are saved. Because the Church shows us God's love for all people everywhere, we can add *universal* to the description: The Church is the "universal sacrament of salvation" (*Dogmatic Constitution on the Church* [*Lumen Gentium*], 48).

The Church is a sacrament of communion with God and unity among people. The Church is a sign of this communion and also is the means by which this communion comes into being. The primary focus of the Church is union with God for all its members. Union with God also brings unity among people. The Church is the instrument Christ uses for the salvation of the whole world. Because the Church is a sign of God's grace and redemption, and because the Church actually brings God's grace and redemption, we say that the Church herself is a sacrament.

What is one way in which the Church shows you God's love for everyone, everywhere?

Article 51: Salvation for Those outside the Church

Church leaders such as Saint Cyprian have taught that "outside of the Church there is no salvation." Does this mean only Catholics can be saved? Although that might seem like a logical conclusion, the actual answer is no. Let's consider why this is not so.

Salvation Is Offered to All People

God desires that all people be saved. His Son, Jesus Christ, died for the sake of all of us. As a result, salvation in Christ is a real possibility for all people, including those who are not Christian. Think of all the millions of people, both now and in the past, who never had the chance to join the Church or who never heard the Gospel message. If the Church is necessary for salvation, how could such people be saved?

The missionary work of the Church extends to everyone, whether or not they are Catholic. What are examples of the missionary work of the Church?

The Church has answered this question. People outside the Church may still be saved if, through no fault of their own, they do not know the Gospel of Christ or his Church, but they nevertheless sincerely seek God and, moved by his grace, try

© DELOCHE / BSIP / Superstock

Primary Sources

Saint Cyprian on the Necessity of the Church for Salvation

Saint Cyprian (ca. 200–258) converted to Christianity as an adult. He later became bishop of Carthage, in Africa, before being martyred during the persecution of Christians in the Roman Empire. In this excerpt, he explains why the Church is necessary for salvation:

> Thus too the Church bathed in the light of the Lord projects its rays over the whole world. . . . She extends her branches over the whole earth in fruitful abundance; she extends her richly flowing streams far and wide; yet her head is one, and her source is one. . . . By her womb we are born; by her milk we are nourished; by her spirit we are animated. . . . He cannot have God as a father who does not have the Church as a mother. ("The Unity of the Catholic Church")

to do his will as they know it in their conscience. They are offered salvation in a way that is fully known to God alone. We can say, therefore, that salvation is available to those outside the Church through God's grace.

Grace and Truth Outside the Visible Boundaries of the Church

Because of God's great mercy, saving grace is available outside the visible boundaries of the Church. This grace outside the Church, however, still comes from Christ, as a result of his sacrifice, and it is communicated by the Holy Spirit. It is connected with the Church of Christ in a way that is not fully clear to us.

As we have said, many elements of sanctification and truth can be found outside the visible boundaries of the Church. The Holy Spirit works through non-Catholic churches and ecclesial communities to offer salvation to their members. For example, if someone is baptized in another Christian denomination in the name of the Father, Son, and Holy Spirit, the Catholic Church recognizes that person's Baptism as valid. If that person converts to Catholicism, he or she is not "rebaptized" in the Church. But the ability of these communities to offer salvation ultimately depends on the fact that the fullness of Christ's grace and truth has been preserved in the Catholic Church.

The Church's Continuing Mission

If salvation is possible outside the visible boundaries of the Church, should the Church give up her missionary activity and assume that God will offer all people salvation through their own religious traditions? Not at all. The Church still has the sacred duty, and the right, to preach the Gospel to all people. This task comes from Jesus himself: "Go, therefore, and make disciples of all nations" (Matthew 28:19). The Church has been given this missionary mandate to share with all people the fullness of truth that has been entrusted to her. This missionary mandate is part of who the Church is.

In regard to non-Catholic Christians, the Church's missionary efforts should help to lead us to the goal of Christian unity. Her mission also involves a respectful dialogue with non-Christian religions. This dialogue allows Church members to better appreciate the elements of holiness and truth in those religions, and those elements can in turn to be raised up and completed in the full light of the Christian Gospel.

What is one thing you can start doing to participate in the Church's missionary mandate?

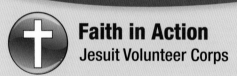

Faith in Action
Jesuit Volunteer Corps

The Church has lived out her missionary mandate throughout her history, and she continues to do so today. One group that has embraced the missionary work of the Church is the Jesuit Volunteer Corps (JVC). JVC is made up of men and women twenty-one years of age or older who commit for one year (or two years, if working internationally) to serve those in need, work for peace and justice, and live in community with other JVC members. Some work with Jesuit organizations and schools, and others work in social and pastoral ministry in Jesuit parishes. But all of their work is grounded in the teachings of the Catholic Church. The Jesuit Volunteer Corps is committed to four core values: social justice, simple living, community, and spirituality. JVC volunteers live out the missionary mandate of the Catholic Church by sharing God's love in both action and example.

Currently a few hundred volunteers are serving throughout the United States and also in six developing countries across the globe. Volunteers serve and live in solidarity with people who are elderly, homeless, abused, and mentally ill, as well as others who are marginalized by society. Many volunteers have education and experience in teaching, law, health care, and language fluency. If you are interested in applying to work with the JVC when you are old enough, you can start to research the organization now to learn how your own interests and career plans might be of service.

Article 52: Who Needs Organized Religion?

Have you ever heard people say they feel closer to God when they are alone with nature than when they sit in a church? Others might say they don't like all the rules of organized religions and feel they have the right to worship God in their own personal way. The best response to such beliefs is a simple question: Is this how God wishes to be worshipped? It is true that God wants us to know him in all aspects of our lives. But Sacred Scripture and Tradition teach us that God wishes to be worshipped by people joined together in communities, not just by isolated individuals.

The Social Nature of Humans and of Salvation

Each one of us is created to live in community and to build relationships. We all share a longing for true friendship and love. The reality is that we cannot attain true happiness in isolation. We need one another to offer

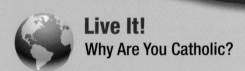

Live It!
Why Are You Catholic?

Has anyone ever asked you why you are Catholic? How did you respond? Answering this question can be a daunting task if you are not familiar with your faith and the teachings of the Church. Fortunately, you can prepare for this question in several ways:

• Consult the *Catechism of the Catholic Church.*
• Reflect on what you have learned in this class.
• Talk with your pastor, school chaplain, and campus ministry staff.
• Pose the question to adults who are committed to the Church.

Each one of us is called to be able to share our faith in a true and meaningful way. The best way to share your Catholic faith with others is to know your faith. If you prepare, you will be able to explain to others why you are Catholic, in a way that can help them to come to love and appreciate the Church.

support and encouragement and to provide an example for following Christ. Our social nature is a gift from God, and it is one essential reason why God saves us by calling us together as one group, one family—the Church. In fact, the goal of salvation itself is ultimately about relationship. The goal is communion with God and unity among all people.

© Bill Wittman / www.wpwittman.com

It is important to know that as individual human beings we cannot save ourselves. We depend completely on Christ's free gift of grace. Christ distributes this gift through the community of the Church. We encounter Jesus in community when we hear the Gospel proclaimed. In fact, Christ assured us that we encounter him when we gather in community: "Where two or three are gathered together in my name, there am I in the midst of them" (Matthew 18:20).

Gatherings like World Youth Day can strengthen and renew our faith. National and diocesan gatherings of Catholic youth can be equally moving. Take advantage of the opportunity to participate in one of these gatherings.

Communal and Individual Worship

When we participate in the Mass, the Eucharist, we are part of a community at many different levels. We are part of the liturgical assembly, those who gather throughout the **Liturgical Year** to celebrate the **Paschal Mystery**. We are part of the local church or diocese. And we are part of the People of God throughout the world. The liturgical celebration itself is essentially communal rather than individual. It is the work of the whole Christ, the Head, in union with the Body, the Church. In the sacrifice of the Eucharist, the whole Church offers herself in union with Christ's sacrifice. The liturgy unites us not only with Christ and the Church on earth but also with the worshippers in Heaven—angels and those humans who have attained Heaven.

Of course it is also true that we can, and indeed should, worship God through our own individual devotions, whether inside or outside a church building. As we have said, God desires to know us in all parts of our lives.

Liturgical Year
The Church's annual cycle of feasts and seasons that celebrate the events and mysteries of Christ's birth, life, death, Resurrection, and Ascension, and forms the context for the Church's worship.

Paschal Mystery
The work of salvation accomplished by Jesus Christ mainly through his Passion, death, Resurrection, and Ascension.

Our personal, private worship should both draw us to communal prayer and complement the communal worship of the Church (see Matthew 6:5–6). In other words, even when we pray on our own, we should be preparing for communal prayer and keeping in mind the needs of the larger community.

We are social by nature. Think of how we came into existence and how we depend on one another to survive and thrive in this world. But our need for community extends beyond our relationships with other human beings. We were created by God, and we are constantly being called into communion with him. Communion with God and unity with all people are the goal of God's plan for us, and the Church is the means through which his goal will be accomplished. We all need organized religion, but more specifically we need the Church. It is through the Church that we can achieve our God-given destiny.

Did You Know?

Communal Worship in the Book of Revelation

© Photoservice Electa / Universal Images Group / Superstock

The Book of Revelation offers many different examples of heavenly communal worship. It begins by portraying the communion of the Persons of Trinity: God the Father sitting on his throne; the Son, portrayed as the Lamb, standing near him; and the Holy Spirit as a stream of water flowing from God's throne.

The Book of Revelation goes on to depict all of creation's involvement in the worship of God. The four living creatures represent all of nature (see 4:6–8), and the twenty-four elders represent both the old (Twelve Tribes) and the new (Twelve Apostles) covenants (see 4:10–11). Angels worship alongside the elders and the creatures (see 7:11–12). The 144,000 worshippers (based on the symbolism of the Twelve Tribes) represent the new People of God (see 7:1–9). Finally, "a great multitude, which no one could count, from every nation, race, people, and tongue" stand before God's throne and worship (see 7:9).

Chapter Review

1. In what sense is the Church necessary for salvation?

2. What does it mean to say that the fullness of the Church of Christ is found in the Catholic Church?

3. Can a person who has never heard of Christ or his Church still be saved? Explain.

4. Can the Holy Spirit be active outside the visible boundaries of the Catholic Church? Discuss examples.

5. How are the social needs of human beings related to the way God offers us salvation?

6. In what ways is the Church's worship communal?

Chapter

13 The Church and the World

Introduction

In this chapter, we will begin to deepen our understanding of Apostolic Tradition and of how the Church applies Sacred Scripture and Tradition to the changing conditions of the world. We will also explore in greater depth what it means for the Church to read "the signs of the times" (Matthew 16:3) and interact with the modern world. Finally, we will turn our attention to evangelization, the primary focus of the Church's purpose and mission. Evangelization is the proclamation of Christ through both word and deed, and it requires active engagement with modern life and culture. This means both using resources that help us to share the Gospel message and working to transform modern culture when it stands counter to that message.

Article 53: Engaging the World

As we discussed in unit 2, "The Church Is One, Holy, Catholic, and Apostolic," the Church was entrusted with the task of handing down the Apostolic Tradition, the truths of the Catholic faith transmitted through Scripture and in Church teachings. Together Sacred Tradition and Sacred Scripture form a single deposit of the Word of God, in which the Church encounters God. Through her teaching, life, and worship, the Church gives to each generation all that she is and all that she believes. One of the ways she does this is through Apostolic Succession, by

Pray It!

Saint Joseph

Did you know that Saint Joseph is a patron saint of the Church? Joseph, the husband of Mary and the adoptive father of Jesus Christ, was named patron saint of the Church in 1847 by Blessed Pope Pius IX. During his life, Joseph helped to raise and protect Jesus. As the patron saint of the Church, Joseph continues to help the Body of Christ, the Church. The next time you pray, ask Saint Joseph to continue his protection of the Church:

Blessed Joseph, husband of Mary, be with us this day.
You protected and cherished the Virgin;
loving the Child Jesus as your Son,
you rescued him from danger of death.
Defend the Church, the household of God,
purchased by the blood of Christ.
Guardian of the holy family,
be with us in our trials.
May your prayers obtain for us
the strength to flee from error
and wrestle with the powers of corruption
so that in life we may grow in holiness
and in death rejoice in the crown of victory.
Amen.

(*Handbook of Indulgences*, Bishops' Committee on the Liturgy, USCCB, page 43)

which the Apostles handed on Sacred Tradition to their successors, the bishops in union with the Pope.

Reading the Signs of the Times

The Church has the responsibility of looking at the particular circumstances of each generation and then interpreting them in the light of Sacred Scripture and Tradition. In the Gospel of Matthew, we read that Jesus scolded the Jewish religious leaders because they could not "judge the signs of the times" (16:3). Vatican Council II echoed Jesus' words in its *Pastoral Constitution on the Church in the Modern World* (*Gaudium et Spes*, 1965): "In every age, the church carries the responsibility of reading the signs of the times and of interpreting them in the light of the Gospel, if it is to carry out its task"(4). It is not enough for the Church to proclaim the Gospel message. She must be able to apply that message to the issues each generation faces. The Church must also speak to each generation in a manner that is understandable and that answers the questions people have about this life and the life to come.

Interpreting the signs of the times in light of the Gospel also brings the Church into dialogue with different cultures as well as generations. Vatican Council II offered the following insight into how the Church interacts with different cultures in changing times and how the Church also remains constant in her mission:

> There are many links between the message of salvation and culture. In his self-revelation to his people, fully manifesting himself in his incarnate Son, God spoke in the context of the culture proper to each age. Similarly the Church has existed through the centuries in varying circumstances and has utilized the resources of different cultures to spread and explain the message of Christ in its preaching, to examine and understand it more deeply, and to express it more perfectly in the liturgy and in the life of the multiform community of the faithful. . . . The Church is faithful to its traditions and is at the same time conscious of its universal mission; it can, then, enter into communion with different forms of culture,

thereby enriching both itself and the cultures themselves. (*The Church in the Modern World*, 58)

In our present world, the Church must apply a Gospel perspective to issues such as international conflicts, health care reform, economic justice, and technology. The essential Gospel message does not change, but it requires wisdom and discernment to understand how it applies to these and other difficult issues in modern culture.

What is one "sign of the times" today that you think merits the Church's attention?

© amanaimages/Corbis

What opportunities do new technologies offer us to share the love of Christ?

Article 54: Engaging Modern Culture

The Catholic Church has a responsibility to be active in the modern world, promoting and proclaiming the truth that has been entrusted to her. To carry out this important work, the Church must take advantage of the latest technologies and cultural developments. But she must not only utilize the appropriate development of modern society but also transform the culture when it comes in conflict with the Gospel message. As part of her prophetic mission, the Church often finds herself in the position of standing counter to developments in our modern society.

Bringing Christian Values into Politics

The prophetic mission of the Church also extends to the arena of what we might call "political issues." You probably are familiar with the concept of the separation of church and state, which means that the government does not support a particular religion or establish a national religion. The Church, however, still has both a right and a responsibility to bring Christian values into the public debate on various social, political, and economic issues. The Church is careful not to advocate for specific political candidates or parties; instead she addresses specific issues that affirm or stand counter to the Gospel message. This activity does not conflict with the separation of church and state. On the contrary, it strengthens the public debate and dialogue.

Faith in Action
Catholic Relief Services

© Rick D'Elia for Catholic Relief Services

Catholic Relief Services (CRS), based in Maryland, is an international relief agency sponsored by the United States Conference of Catholic Bishops. After World War II, when European refugees began to return to their devastated homelands, CRS formed to offer aid, through the generosity of millions of American Catholics.

Its mission in developing countries is to break the cycle of poverty through proactive solutions such as agricultural initiatives, community banks, health education, and clean water projects. CRS volunteers—including high school and college students—also respond to natural disasters throughout the world by helping victims rebuild and begin again. Why? CRS President Carolyn Y. Woo explains:

> [In the midst of disaster] you find God in the helping hands that emerge from every corner. You find God in the sense of community lost and now so suddenly found. You find God in the words of comfort and encouragement. . . . You find Catholic Relief Services at the scene of disasters around the world because you, the Catholic community in the United States, tell us that God is there. That is where we all must be—helping, comforting, encouraging. ("When Disaster Strikes, God Is There in You")

CRS's guiding principles echo the principles of Catholic social teaching. In particular, the mission of CRS echoes the principle of solidarity: "We are all part of one human family—whatever our national, racial, religious, economic or ideological differences—and in an increasingly interconnected world, loving our neighbor has global dimensions."

One Pressing Issue: The Culture of Death

The Church applies a Gospel perspective to respond to many issues in modern society. But the most pressing issue the Church addresses in the public arena is the value and dignity of every human life. When any public group promotes social or political policies that threaten God-given human rights, the Church has a responsibility to speak out publicly. Thus the Church works to address poverty, environmental issues, and other social ills that threaten the dignity of the human person.

The Church especially works to transform what Pope Saint John Paul II called the "culture of death" (*The Gospel of Life [Evangelium Vitae]*, 19). The prevalence of abortion and the growing acceptance of euthanasia are elements of this culture of death. The Church recognizes that from the moment of conception to natural death, all human life is sacred and should be treated with care and dignity. For this reason, the Church stands firm in promoting a culture of life. At the heart of this is an effort to

Did You Know?

Faithful Citizenship

Every four years since 1976, the United States Conference of Catholic Bishops has issued a statement on the responsibilities of Catholics to society. Each new edition of this statement summarizes the consistent and challenging message found in Church teachings. The United States bishops remind all members of the Church of our responsibility to promote the common good, most especially the dignity and sacredness of the human person. One way we do this is by being active in the political arena. The bishops provide guidance on how parishes and individuals can do this in a way that respects the political process and is consistent with the teachings of the Church.

© vichinterlang / iStock.com

educate people to have a profound respect for the sacredness of every human life. The Church also called for new programs to care for the sick and elderly, and for political action against unjust laws that do not respect the right to life of innocent persons.

What is one thing you can do to confront the culture of death and transform our society into a culture of life?

Article 55: Evangelization and Inculturation

The Church has a responsibility to engage modern culture and promote the teachings of Christ. What issues in the world today stand counter to the truth and love of Christ?

Pope John Paul II called Catholic youth to share their faith with their peers who did not know Christ. How is your life a witness to your faith in Christ?

The Church has a missionary mandate to help all people to share in the communion of the Holy Trinity. Evangelization is the primary way we accomplish this mission, proclaiming Christ both by our words and by the witness of our lives.

In Pope Saint John Paul II's encyclical *Redemptoris Missio* (1990), which he wrote during his papacy, he identifies three circumstances in which the Church must evangelize in the world today. In the first circumstance, the Church must reach out to cultures, communities, and groups where Christ and the Gospel message are not known or where people lack the ability to adequately proclaim the faith. The Church has a responsibility to actively share the Gospel message in these situations. The second circumstance includes active and vibrant Christian communities. The Church evangelizes these communities by continuing to carry out "her activity and pastoral care" (33). The third circumstance relates to individuals or groups who have been baptized in the faith but no longer actively live it or even consider themselves

© PAUL HANNA / Reuters / Landov

members of the Church "and live a life far removed from Christ and his Gospel. In this case what is needed is a 'new evangelization' or a 're-evangelization'" (33).

Examples of Evangelization

It was the evangelizing activity of Jesus and the Apostles that carried the Church into the world, and their evangelizing activity continues in the Church today. Therefore everyone in the Church has a responsibility to share the Good News of Jesus Christ. The laity are called upon to evangelize both at home and at work. Such ordinary settings can help to make their witness particularly effective. Spouses evangelize within the family by witnessing the faith and love of Christ to each other and to their children.

Young people like you are some of the best evangelists for other young people, especially if you evangelize by the witness of your life. The witness of a teen committed to living a chaste life is a powerful witness to Gospel

Live It!
Taking Part in Evangelization

How can you participate in the Church's mission to evangelize? Consider the following:

- **Recommit to personal holiness.** Nothing turns people away from faith faster than someone who preaches the faith but doesn't practice it. While you share your faith, make sure that every day you take opportunities to grow in holiness. Saint Mother Teresa, for example, spent a great deal of time in prayer every day, in addition to her public work of caring for others.
- **Respect other traditions.** All people, including non-Christians, are God's children. Proclaim Christ, but also listen to the truth that exists in other religious traditions, and then explore how that truth relates to Christ.
- **Recommit to evangelization.** It is difficult and a little scary to proclaim the truth of our own faith these days. But, deep down, people are hungry for the truth. Most often others will respond positively to your own witness if they see that it genuinely brings you peace and joy.

values in our age. The witness of a young man or woman who has earned a reputation for always telling the truth when others easily rely on convenient white lies is equally striking.

Religious orders have long played an important role in the evangelical mission of the Church. Notable efforts have included the Franciscans and Dominicans in the Spanish colonies of Mexico and California, as well as the missions of the Jesuits in the Far East. Today the evangelical efforts of religious men and women can take many forms. For example, some evangelize through the witness of their special love of God, as expressed by their dedicated lifestyle. Other religious, such as Saint Mother Teresa's Missionaries of Charity, do not attempt to actively convert to Christianity the poor whom they serve. But through their selfless acts of service, they evangelize by witnessing to their love of Jesus. Saint Teresa of Calcutta (1910–1997) said: "I'm evangelizing by my works of love. . . . That's the preaching that we are doing, and I think that is more real."

Men in ordained ministry—deacons, priests, and bishops—share in the evangelical mission of the Church in a special way. Bishops "are directly responsible, together with [the pope], for the evangelization of the world, both as members of the College of Bishops and as pastors of the particular churches" (*Redemptoris Missio*, 63). Priests are entrusted with both the pastoral care of a specific community and the evangelization of those who do not yet know Christ. They evangelize through their example of a life devoted to Christ, through their ministry of preaching, and especially through their role in the celebration of the Sacraments.

Inculturation

Through her evangelization the Church seeks to inculturate the Gospel message. So what is inculturation? Inculturation involves a respectful encounter between the Christian faith and a particular culture. The process is a two-way street: (1) it integrates particular cultural values into the life of the Church, and (2) it proclaims the Gospel message in different cultural contexts, allowing it to "take flesh" in each people's culture.

One challenge of inculturation is the assimilation of the Gospel message into different cultural contexts without betraying the fundamental truths of that message. Here are a few examples of the inculturation of the Gospel message:

- Pope Saint John Paul II suggested that traditional African ancestor worship was a preparation for the African people to understand and accept the Christian belief in the Communion of the Saints.

- Lakota Catholics such as Black Elk saw traditional Lakota ceremonies as a preparation for Christianity. Black Elk thought the Lakota were better prepared to understand Christ's sacrifice through their experience of the Sundance, a ceremony in which participants voluntarily endure suffering for the benefit of their people.

© John A. Sundby Photography

- The Church allows different liturgies, popular devotions, prayer forms, and devotions to various saints and to Mary to express the unique cultural conditions of areas throughout the world.

Principles of Evangelization

As you have read, *Redemptoris Missio* presents three conditions or circumstances in which the Church is called to evangelize in the world today. So how do we evangelize in these situations? Each of us can embrace numerous elements or principles that help us to evangelize those who have never heard the Gospel message, those who are active in their faith, or those who have moved away from the Church:

- **Boldness and respect** Christians should respect religious freedom and local cultures. We must seek to inculturate the Gospel message, but we should not be afraid of proclaiming the truth of Christianity, even if some see us as narrow-minded or intolerant (see *Redemptoris Missio*, 2–3).

- **Technological developments** We have the ability to communicate in ways that were not possible even fifteen years ago. We must be willing to use the latest technologies in proclaiming the Gospel.

- **Commitment to personal holiness** The earliest Christian missionaries were successful not because of new techniques of preaching, but because of the holiness of the preachers (see *Redemptoris Missio*, 90).

- **Reaching out to people of all ages** The Gospel message applies to everyone, no matter what age, so we must make an effort to evangelize all people. As a young person, you have the unique ability to share the Gospel message with your peers and to challenge them to live according to Gospel values.

Primary Sources

Pope Saint John Paul II's Message to Young People at World Youth Day in 1989

Pope Saint John Paul II, a friend to young people everywhere, initiated World Youth Day in 1985. Since then, World Youth Day has been celebrated nearly every year in individual dioceses, and every two or three years young people gather from all over the world to celebrate World Youth Day with the Pope. At the 1989 World Youth Day, held in Santiago de Compestela, Spain, Pope Saint John Paul II explained why young people have a special call to share the Good News:

> You young people are the first apostles and evangelizers of the world of youth. . . . So many of those of your own age do not know Christ, or do not know Him well enough. So you cannot remain silent and indifferent! You must have the courage to speak about Christ, to bear witness to your faith through a life-style inspired by the Gospel. . . . Christ needs you! ("Message of the Holy Father John Paul II to the Youth of the World on the Occasion of the IV World Youth Day," 2)

Evangelization is central to the mission of the Church and is the responsibility of all her members. It is important for us to continually recommit ourselves to this mission and to be willing to expand the tools we utilize to reflect the changing times in which we live.

© SUCHETA DAS / Reuters / Landov

Chapter Review

1. What does it mean to say the Church reads the signs of the times?

2. Explain the difference between the culture of death and the culture of life.

3. What role do Catholics play in public policy debates?

4. What are some specific ways a layperson might evangelize at home or in the workplace?

5. What is inculturation?

6. What are the characteristics of evangelization as presented in *Redemptoris Missio*? How might you live out some of them in your own life?

The Missionaries of Charity put love into action through their care of those who are most in need. What are ways you show love through action?

The Church and Young People

In this unit, we will look at some implications of what you've learned about the Church for your own life. Jesus called his Apostles to follow him, built a relationship with them, and sent them out into the world to further his mission. You too have been called to the Church, to Christ. You are as free to choose your response as the Apostles were. If you respond to Christ's call and follow him, your relationship with him will grow. He also wants you to share the Good News with others in ways that utilize your gifts and talents.

How is Jesus Christ calling you? You might be looking for something momentous, like the flash of light that knocked Saint Paul to the ground on the road to Damascus (see Acts, chapter 9). But Paul's story is so memorable because it was unusual. Jesus Christ calls most of us through the ordinary events of our daily lives. To hear his call and then grow in our relationship to Christ, we need to read Sacred Scripture prayerfully, receive grace through the Sacraments, and make friends with those who can support our growth in faith.

Christ is calling you to go into the world as his disciple, with the help of the Holy Spirit. Being his disciple means being part of his mission, in large and small ways. Sometimes discipleship will bring you into conflict with the values of our society, and you may find it difficult to overcome the pressure to conform to cultural expectations. This is why prayer and participation in the Sacraments are so important. Both will help you to make good everyday choices to reach your goal: life in communion with the Trinity.

The enduring understandings and essential questions represent core concepts and questions that are explored throughout this unit. By studying the content of each chapter, you will gain a more complete understanding of the following:

Enduring Understandings
1. We are each called to be part of the Catholic Church.
2. We come to learn more about God through others and through the life of the Church.
3. Christ calls each of us to become a disciple with the help of the Holy Spirit.

Essential Questions
1. How are the Church and God's love for us related?
2. How do prayer, Sacred Scripture, and the Sacraments support our life in Christ?
3. Considering your gifts and talents, what is your role in the Church as a disciple right now?

Chapter

14

You Have Been Called

Introduction

What is it like to receive a call from God? Consider the various ways the Apostles were called. Saint Peter was fishing and having a bad time of it when Jesus invited him to put out his nets again. Saint Matthew was a tax collector hanging out with his friends when Jesus approached him. We know that Jesus called his Apostles to be in relationship with him and later sent them out to share the Good News with others. If we pay attention, we will notice Jesus calling to us in the ordinary events of our lives.

To first hear our call and then to keep our relationship with Christ alive, we need some gifts and skills. We need to learn how to read Sacred Scripture in a prayerful way. We need to receive grace from the Sacraments. We need to know and practice various ways to pray. Sacred Scripture and Sacred Tradition help us to understand God's Revelation, which is essential for our lives as Christians. If you are like most Catholic teens in the United States, God called you to new life in Christ through the Sacrament of Baptism, and you have since received graces from other Sacraments.

God constantly calls all of us into communion with himself and others. The Church's call means that we will come to know God more intimately and come to have significant relationships with others who are his disciples. You are called to be part of this convoked assembly, the Church. Finding friends who can support your growth in faith is important. Your Catholic school and your parish provide many opportunities to meet these friends.

Article 56: Called by God to Belong to the Church

Perhaps at some point in your life, you received a wonderful gift. It could have been something material, something you had wanted for a long time but could never have asked for. Or perhaps it was a relationship with a great friend or a new sister or brother. When you look back at that moment, you might think: "Why me? I would never have expected that I would be given such a gift or that something so wonderful would have happened to me!"

Recall that the Church is the convocation or assembly of people whom God calls together to be in a special relationship with him. God calls everyone to the unbelievable gift of the Church. God's desire to be in relationship with us is extraordinary. The additional gifts we receive as members of the Church are due to God's love. He created the world, and all of humanity, out of love. He created us and gives us free will. We must freely respond to his call because he will not force us to come to him and receive his gifts. In addition to receiving gifts from the Church, we need to give the gift of ourselves to God and the Church.

Your Call from God

You might think that being called by God would be a dramatic, startling experience involving angels or a cloud or a trumpet blast, followed by God's instructions about what to do next. Saint Paul did have a spectacular call that even caused him to be blind for a time, but for most of us, God's call is more subtle.

Most Catholic teens began the Christian life as infants, through the Sacrament of Baptism. Perhaps this is the case for you. If you were baptized as an infant, you couldn't knowingly respond to God's call, but your parents and godparents were able to do so. Your parents brought you to Baptism just as their parents may have brought them. As Jesus said, parents "know how to give good gifts" to their children (Matthew 7:11). Think of

Sacred Chrism
Perfumed olive oil consecrated by the bishop that is used for anointing in the Sacraments of Baptism, Confirmation, and Holy Orders.

Age of Reason
The age at which a person can be morally responsible. This is generally regarded to be the age of seven.

all the good things parents do for their children, such as providing them with an education as well as the basics of food, clothing, and shelter. At the Baptism of infants, parents promise to do an additional good thing. They promise to help their children come to know God and participate fully in the Church.

Your Life in the Sacraments

Through the Sacrament of Baptism, you were incorporated into the Church. As you were immersed in the waters of Baptism, or as the waters were poured over your head, you died and rose with Christ and were freed from Original Sin in the name of the Father and of the Son and of the Holy Spirit. You were anointed with **Sacred Chrism**, incorporated into the Body of Christ as priest, prophet, and king. Your white garment symbolized that you had "put on" Christ, and your candle, lit from the Easter candle, symbolized that Christ has enlightened you as the light of the world.

At about age seven or eight, the **Age of Reason**, many of you received the Sacraments of Penance and Reconciliation and the Eucharist for the first time. In the Sacrament of Penance and Reconciliation, you received God's mercy for sins you had committed against him and his Church. You learned how to examine your conscience,

Primary Sources

A Palm Sunday Message of Joy from the Pope

In his Palm Sunday Homily, his first major service since his election just ten days earlier, Pope Francis addressed young people and renewed the special commitment his predecessors had made to them:

> Dear young people, I saw you in the procession as you were coming in; I think of you celebrating around Jesus, waving your olive branches. I think of you crying out his name and expressing your joy at being with him! You have an important part in the celebration of faith! You bring us the joy of faith and you tell us that we must live the faith with a young heart. . . .
> ("Homily of Pope Francis: Celebration of Palm Sunday of the Passion of Our Lord," 3)

confess sins to the priest, and complete your penance.

When you received your First Communion, the Eucharist, you received the Sacrament that is at the center of our faith. You were able to be in a special communion with Jesus and, through him, with the Father and the Holy

© Bill Wittman / www.wpwittman.com

Spirit as well. Receiving this Sacrament every week nourishes your spiritual life, protects you from sin, and unites you more fully with the Body of Christ.

You may have already received the Sacrament of Confirmation, or maybe you have yet to receive it. Through this Sacrament you receive the Gifts of the Holy Spirit. Baptism, Confirmation, and the Eucharist together are called the Sacraments of Christian Initiation.

Receiving the Eucharist for the first time is a special experience. How did your family celebrate this event?

Learning More about God and His Church

Your parents are giving you the gift of a Catholic education. You are learning more about God and his Church through religion classes, books like this one, retreats, liturgical experiences, and the positive examples of adults and other students who are serious about their faith. These adults, particularly, are there to answer your questions about the faith, to direct you to additional information about the Church, and to help you apply a teaching to real-life situations.

When someone doesn't know what the Church is all about, he or she can find it difficult to recognize God's call, to actually live out that call, and to share the Good News with others. But we know that God calls everyone throughout their lives. When God call us, he calls us to the Church. Part of why the Church is exciting is because it is an assembly of people whom God has called and who have responded by saying yes. With all those others who have responded to God's call, we are one family through faith and Baptism. We are united in love by the Holy Spirit. We are the Body of Christ in the world.

> **What adults have played an important role in promoting your faith life and your participation in the Church?**

Article 57: Christ Enriches Us through Participation in the Life of the Church

God wants to give you his love, and your parents have provided you with opportunities to gain the skills and knowledge you need to grow in faith. You have many opportunities to deepen your relationship with Christ and to receive his grace. Sacred Scripture, the Sacraments, and personal prayer are three important ways Christ offers us to get to know him and to receive his grace.

Sacred Scripture

Today we are inundated by words. We can use the Internet to look up any topic that interests us. We are in constant communication with one another. Cell phones seem to be a necessity of life now. We can text, post, and tweet to our heart's content—at times ignoring the person next to us!

So when we call Jesus the Word of God, are we saying that he is just one word among many in our lives? No. We are saying that he is the unique Word through which God has chosen to speak to us. The *Catechism of the Catholic Church (CCC)* explains: "Christ, the Son of God made man, is the Father's one, perfect, and unsurpassable Word. In him he has said everything; there will be no other word than this one" (65).

In reading and praying with Sacred Scripture, we not only learn more about Jesus and his life, death, Resurrection, and Ascension, but we also encounter Jesus himself. Reading and praying with Sacred Scripture is a skill as well as a grace. It takes time and involves patience and commitment. But if we listen, we will hear Jesus offering us hope and encouragement in our lives. If some particular words speak to you during your study of Sacred Scripture, hang

© Aldo Murillo / iStockphoto.com

"The Church 'forcefully and specifically exhorts all the Christian faithful . . . to learn "the surpassing knowledge of Jesus Christ," by frequent reading of the divine Scriptures'" (*CCC*, 133).

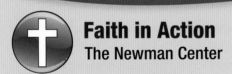

Faith in Action
The Newman Center

© Monkey Business Images / Shutterstock.com

When do you think you will finish your study of the Catholic faith? after Confirmation? after high school? The correct answer is . . . never!

Why is the study of your faith, including deeper ways to live out your faith, a lifelong task? The Catholic faith is about the mystery of God in your life. You can only begin to grasp this mystery by growing into it. You may know facts about the faith, such as the Ten Commandments or the Beatitudes, but your understanding of these facts will grow as you grow. A faithful adult understands the Ten Commandments far better than a child does. A teen understands the two Greatest Commandments—to love God and to love others as yourself—much better than a nine-year-old does.

Blessed John Henry Newman, who converted to Catholicism, believed that education at the university level should include the study of theology, once called "the queen of the sciences." The influence of Cardinal Newman and his book *The Idea of a University* (1854) spread widely among Catholic educators in the late nineteenth century and beyond. His ideas inspired the foundation of the first Newman Clubs at Oxford University in England in 1888 and at the University of Pennsylvania in 1893.

Today Newman Centers are found at many secular colleges and universities. Often the center includes a chapel for the celebration of Sunday Mass, as well as rooms for lectures and group study on topics of concern to Catholics. Non-Catholic students are also welcome in the Newman Center.

on to them. Repeat them in your mind. Take them along with you. Sacred Scripture is a gift from God, but in order to appreciate the gift, we need to open the book.

Scripture is an essential element of our lives as Christians, for as Saint Jerome said, "Ignorance of the Scriptures is ignorance of Christ"[1] (*CCC*, 133).

The Sacraments

We are called to receive the Sacraments because they are gifts from Christ that bring us face-to-face with God. We don't see God in a visual sense, but we know he is with us and loves us. We encounter grace most fully in the Sacraments, and through grace we participate in God's divine life, the life of the Trinity. When we celebrate the Sacraments with the necessary attitude of openness to God's love, we are able to recognize God's presence more clearly. The Sacraments are efficacious signs of grace. The graces proper to each Sacrament are truly present.

The Gospels show us how Christ instituted the Sacraments, established the meaning of each Sacrament, and commissioned his disciples to celebrate them. As you learned briefly in unit 2, "The Church Is One, Holy, Catholic, and Apostolic," the Sacraments fall into three categories:

1. The **Sacraments of Christian Initiation** are Baptism, Confirmation, and the Eucharist, because these three Sacraments form the foundation of Christian life. Baptism is the first Sacrament we celebrate, because it makes us members of Christ and part of the Church. Confirmation strengthens us and is necessary to complete baptismal grace. The Eucharist nourishes us with Christ's Body and Blood in order to transform us into the image of Christ and enable us to live as his disciples. The Eucharist is the high point of Christian life, and all the Sacraments are oriented toward it.

2. The **Sacraments of Healing** are the Sacraments of Anointing of the Sick and Penance and Reconcilia-

tion. Through them the Church continues Jesus' mission to heal and forgive sins.

3. The **Sacraments at the Service of Communion** are Holy Orders and Matrimony. These Sacraments contribute to the Church's mission primarily through service to others.

Our response to God's call means having an active liturgical life. In turn, God calls us through this life. We should also witness other people as they receive the Sacraments. Attending the Sacrament of Matrimony, being present during Baptisms, or attending a friend's Confirmation strengthens our own faith and relationship to the Body of Christ.

© The Crosiers / Gene Plaisted, OSC

Prayer

Through the Church, God calls us to be people of prayer—yet another gift to us. Notice the picture of Jesus knocking on a wooden door. Strangely, this door does not have a handle on the outside. Jesus cannot open the door from his side. The person on the inside has to open the door to Jesus. Prayer is something like that picture. Prayer is a door to Christ that we can open at any time, but it

Pray It!

Saint Ignatius's Prayer for Generosity

We usually need to ask God to help us grow in holiness. This prayer is a good model:

Lord, teach me to be generous.
Teach me to serve you as you deserve;
to give and not to count the cost,
to fight and not to heed the wounds,
to toil and not to seek for rest,
to labor and not to ask for reward,
save that of knowing that I do your will.
Amen.

aspiration
A short prayer meant to be memorized and repeated throughout the day. The word comes from the Latin *aspirare*, "to breathe upon." In this way, we can heed Saint Paul's injunction to pray without ceasing and continually turn our thoughts toward God.

must be opened from the inside, where we are. Only you can open the door of your life to Christ, through prayer.

Learning how to pray takes practice and guidance, and people pray in many different ways. Luckily there is no "one size fits all" way to pray. To develop a habit of praying every day, you might begin by choosing a time in the morning when you can say a short prayer asking Jesus to bless your day. In the evening, ask his help for the things that did not go so well. Ask him to be with you tomorrow. And he will be there waiting—right behind that door that only you can open.

Remember, prayers do not have to be long, elaborate, or formal. Saint John Cassian was a monk who wrote that his own favorite kind of prayer was called arrow prayer. An arrow prayer is short, direct, and focused. It flies straight and true to God. Arrow prayers are somewhat like what we call **aspirations** (which literally means "breathings") today. Perhaps you have heard some of these examples: "My Jesus, mercy" or "Jesus, Mary, and Joseph." The name of Jesus, prayerfully repeated, is a prayer. Saint John Cassian's favorite prayer was: "O God,

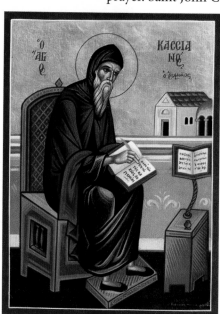

© Hagiographer: Nun Kassiane, Holy Monastery of the Annunciation, Patmos, Greece; Publishers: Aperges & Co, www.aperges.com

come to my assistance. O Lord, make haste to help me." He taught that this prayer is always necessary and helpful. If we are sad, we need God's help to overcome our sadness. If we are happy, we need God's help to express and share our happiness. Centuries later the Church still says this prayer at the beginning of the Liturgy of the Hours. You might like to pray this arrow prayer or make up your own to encourage you to pray often.

Prayer is vital. Without it we fail to follow the lead of the Holy Spirit and we fall into sin. Prayer cannot be separated from our lives. As Saint Paul explained, God calls the Church to pray constantly, "giving thanks always and for everything in the name of our Lord Jesus Christ to God the Father" (Ephesians 5:20). We can accomplish this when we unite prayer with the everyday things we do. It is always possible to pray because the Risen Christ is always with us.

> **What might be an arrow prayer you can easily remember and pray during the day?**

Article 58: Called to Community

From the Book of Genesis, we know that God created both a woman and a man because, as he declared, "It is not good for the man to be alone" (2:18). Through the account of the Fall, we learn that God wants his people to live in harmony with him, with creation, and with one another.

God wants us to be in communion with him and others, and he wants us to have friends that bring us closer to him. The desire to be in relationship with others is wired into us. Even as infants, we are most drawn to the image of a human face. We have all experienced loneliness, another indicator of our need for others and for God.

The people in our lives are also gifts from God, and they are ways for God to communicate with us. You may have heard someone say, "He is such a Godsend." Perhaps you have personally found that you feel much better after you talk an issue through with a friend than if you stew about it on your own. Friends can help us to learn about God's love and mercy just by who they are and how they care about us.

True Friends Help Us to Grow in Faith

The Book of Proverbs says this about friendship: "There are friends who bring ruin, / but there are true friends more loyal than a brother" (18:24). True friends help us to grow in faith and as members of the Body of Christ.

Even if we have experienced betrayal by friends before, each of us will find companions who embrace us as we are and help us to be all we can be. True friends do the following:

- build us up and encourage us in our gifts and talents rather than envy them
- support us and do not put us down, especially in front of others
- tell us the truth and do not make false promises
- keep confidences—in fact, breaking confidences is one of the quickest ways to lose a friend
- share our values
- support us as we grow in faith

Live It!
Get Involved in Your Faith

© Bill Wittman / www.wpwittman.com

Do you participate in your parish's youth ministry or your school's campus ministry? In both ministries, you are likely to encounter other teens who share your desire to grow in faith. Many may be seeking a break from some of the social pressure they feel in other settings. They may also want to make good friends with whom they can explore the life God calls us to. Parish-based youth ministries and school-based campus ministries provide opportunities for you and other young people to understand the Gospel message and discern how to apply its truths in daily life today. These ministries can also help you to get more involved in practices of faith such as praying, serving others, and participating in the Sacraments. Look at your parish bulletin or talk to your campus ministry team about ways you can get involved and meet other Catholic young people.

Some people have a lot of friends. Others are happier with two or three good friends. Of course, to find good friends, you need to be a good friend.

Where Can You Find True and Faithful Friends?

Where can you find a true friend who can help you to grow as a Catholic? You have plenty of opportunities to meet Catholic friends today. Your school is a primary example. You may have already made friends in class, at lunch, or in extracurricular activities. Many parishes offer activities for teens as well as other ministry opportunities that bring adults and teens together. Parish or school retreats provide opportunities for socializing and for deeper discussion with other teens. You may find a friend who shares your values and interests through volunteering with parish or school service groups whose members may tutor, coach, serve at food kitchens, or visit people who need company.

In the Church, we find service opportunities related to each of its three meanings, which you studied in chapter 1, "The Origin of the Church": the assembly gathered for liturgy, particularly for the Eucharist; the diocese; and the worldwide Church. In the first context, your own parish, service may take the form of helping in a food bank, working at a social event for older people or children, or participating in a service event outside the parish with other parishioners.

In what service projects have you participated? How does service bring us closer to God and to other members of the Body of Christ?

Service opportunities also occur on a diocesan level. Sometimes teens from several parishes gather for a larger service opportunity. A diocese may then send teens from different parishes on projects. Finally, some service groups that work at the

© Bill Wittman / www.wpwittman.com

local parish or diocesan level have national or even global outreaches. Teens travel to other parts of the country to help people to recover from natural disasters or may even go to other countries and build homes. How exciting it would be to participate in activities at your parish and then someday be one of the thousands of young people participating with the Pope in World Youth Day. It is very possible.

We Are Members of the Body of Christ

God has called us into a big family of faith, the People of God. As members of the Body of Christ, we are never alone. Even hermits are intimately connected with the rest of the Body of Christ. The Church is diverse, with members from every nation and people. We can rejoice in what we have in common—our Catholic faith and relationship with God—and also the diversity of gifts we exchange with our brothers and sisters in the faith.

Did You Know?

Catholics Are Not All the Same, Thank God!

© Palmer Kane LLC / Shutterstock.com

As human beings we want to belong. Yet in everyday life we can find ourselves defining ourselves and others by our differences rather than by what unites us.

Recall the image of the Church as the Body of Christ. Each person who belongs to the Body offers something unique, and each person's gifts are important. Instead of defining yourself and others by your differences, and seeing these differences as negatives, try to see these very differences as gifts—evidence of God's creativity touching your life. If every snowflake is different, why shouldn't every human being, including you, be different as well?

If you are confident in your giftedness, you will all the more welcome and accept the uniqueness you find in others. You will not lose anything, but you will gain more understanding of the infinite diversity of God's creative power. Each one of us is gifted in different ways, yet we are all God's children.

When God calls to us, he provides us with many opportunities to learn about him and different ways to respond to him. We can come to know him through reading Sacred Scripture, receiving the Sacraments, praying, and spending time with the people in our lives. As we take advantage of the gifts he has given us, we learn more about the Church and what it means to be a disciple. In the last chapter of this book, "Sent with the Holy Spirit," we will examine what being a disciple involves in daily life and how the Holy Spirit supports us as we are sent to share the Good News of Jesus Christ.

Chapter Review

1. Explain why God's call to us is a gift.

2. Why did Jesus call his Apostles?

3. What are the effects of the Sacrament of Baptism?

4. Why does Saint Jerome say that if we are ignorant of the Scriptures, then we are ignorant of Christ?

5. What is the relationship between the picture on page 223 and the life of prayer?

6. How do we know that God created us to be in community with others?

7. Why is a member of the Body of Christ never alone?

Chapter 15

Sent with the Holy Spirit

Introduction

In the previous chapter, "You Have Been Called," we looked at how you are called to the Church, to Christ. Once you have gotten to know him, Christ sends you out into the world as a disciple with the help of the Holy Spirit. Discipleship is an ongoing call that brings you closer to Jesus. But discipleship does not mean simply following Jesus in an abstract way; it also means following him as a servant. Being a disciple of Jesus means being part of his mission. It means being salt and light for the world and sharing your God-given talents for the sake of others. Many of your ordinary skills can make a big difference in the world.

Discipleship takes place in daily life. Sometimes it will require you to act in a way that is counter to the values of the culture that surrounds you. Prayer and the sacramental life are key aspects of discipleship. Good everyday choices resemble "the little way" of Saint Thérèse of Lisieux.

Each Divine Person of the Trinity—Father, Son, and Holy Spirit—contributes to the well-being of the Church, but our study has focused on the contributions of the Holy Spirit to the Church. Christ does not send you out alone. He sends you with the Holy Spirit. Making good choices involves living with our goal in mind: life in communion with the Trinity.

Article 59: You Are Sent as a Disciple

The author of the First Letter of John wrote to the earliest Christian disciples: "Children, let us love not in word or speech but in deed and truth" (3:18). Consider some ways you as a young person can take these words to heart and live out your discipleship, not in words or speech, but in actions from the heart.

Salt and Light

> You are the salt of the earth. But if salt loses its taste, with what can it be seasoned? It is no longer good for anything but to be thrown out and trampled underfoot. You are the light of the world. A city set on a mountain cannot be hidden. Nor do they light a lamp and then put it under a bushel basket; it is set on a lampstand, where it gives light to all in the house. Just so, your light must shine before others, that they may see your good deeds and glorify your heavenly Father. (Matthew 5:13–16)

In this passage from the Gospel of Matthew, Jesus tells us that we are sent to be salt and light for the world. What does it mean to be salt or to be light? Why would he compare his disciples to salt rather than another spice? Why would Jesus say, "You are the light of the world" (Matthew 5:14)? Let's explore these metaphors.

Of all the spices, salt may be the most necessary and the tastiest. On its own it has a very strong bite. But when mixed with other foods, its zest enhances the other flavors in the foods. Christ calls us to bring out the true flavor and goodness of the world not only in ourselves but in others.

When Jesus said, "You are the light of the world," he explained that people do not hide light under a bushel basket. Rather, they put it on the lampstand "where it gives light to all in the house" (Matthew 5:15). In this way, Jesus was telling us that we each have talents and gifts to share with others, and we should not hide them or keep them to ourselves.

How Can You Be Salt and Light for the World?

What skills do you have? Can you read and write and solve math equations? Are you learning how to drive? Maybe you speak more than one language or have played the violin for a time. Perhaps you play basketball, tell great jokes, or are a good listener.

Service takes many forms. You can help out at a homeless shelter, visit a nursing home, or hold a fundraiser, like a car wash, to raise money for a charity.

Speaking to a stadium of thirty thousand youths, Pope Benedict XVI explained why all young people are an important part of the Church:

© Bill Wittman / www.wpwittman.com

> My appeal to you today, young people . . .
>
> is this: do not waste your youth. Do not seek to escape from it. Live it intensely. . . . You, young people, are not just the future of the Church and of humanity, as if we could somehow run away from the present. . . . The Church needs you, as young people, to manifest to the world the face of Jesus Christ, visible in the Christian community. Without this young face, the Church would appear disfigured. ("Meeting with Youth; Address of His Holiness Benedict XVI," 7)

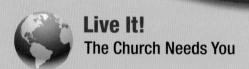

Live It!
The Church Needs You

Speaking to a gathering of young people, Pope Benedict XVI urged, "Do not waste your youth" ("Meeting with Youth: Address of His Holiness Benedict XVI," 7). You probably can't wait to grow up and try new things, but the Pope encourages you to embrace your youth today in a way that reveals Christ to the world.

What does this mean for you? In what ways do you already reveal the face of Christ to the world? What concrete opportunities do you have to do more to serve "the least" among us and witness to the Good News of Christ? The Church needs your powerful witness at this amazing time in your life.

Pope Benedict XVI says not to waste your youth; the Church needs you now. If you were to use your God-given abilities only for yourself, imagine how the metaphor about the bushel basket and light would relate to your life. Would the basket be covering the light?

How Are You Needed?

You may have a particular talent that gives joy to others, like a gift for music, art, writing, or mechanics. If so, continue to develop it. Share it with others. Don't hide it under a basket, but take it as far as it will go. It will enhance your life and the lives of many other people.

If you can bake, you can hold a bake sale to raise money for people in need. If you can listen, you can visit a lonely older person who wants to share years of wisdom with you. If you can do simple math calculations and read, you can tutor a younger child. If not you, then who?

Your gifts and talents are needed by the Body of Christ around the world. In chapter 13, "The Church and the World," you learned about Catholic Relief Services (CRS), an international relief and development agency founded by the Catholics bishops of the United States to help people in need all over the globe. Young people have raised money for this worthy cause by sponsoring car washes or running mini-marathons. Catholic schools have spent service days helping to package food for CRS to distribute to people in need half a world away. The world needs your gifts.

The Catholic Campaign for Human Development (CCHD) is another organization sponsored by the bishops of the United States. CCHD seeks to increase the standard of living for people in the United States. Every year CCHD calls for donations that are used for projects in our own country. The Body of Christ needs your gifts.

In your own parish, why not volunteer to share your singing talent in the choir or offer your services as a musician? Does your parish need greeters? altar servers? sacristy help? catechists? ushers? Your parish needs your gifts.

The Catholic Worker movement has homes around the country run by volunteers who provide assistance for men, women, and children in need. Is there a Catholic Worker house in your community?

Your local town or city needs you too. A coach working with younger children learning to play basketball could use your help to run drills and praise the kids for their improvement. Notice how being salt can help other people to shine.

If you can bag a lunch, you can help at a soup kitchen. In one town, the teens from several parishes joined forces to go door to door collecting cans of food for a neighborhood food pantry. Two girls' volleyball teams from rival high schools played a volleyball game to raise money for premature babies in their local hospital. Admission proceeds went to the families of the hospitalized babies. If you investigate your own area, you might find a need that calls you to serve. Your community needs your gifts.

When you consider national and worldwide issues of importance, you can find even more ways to serve. Is there an issue that affects your city or state? Write to your local representatives or your elected officials in the U.S. Congress. Many young people participate in right-to-life

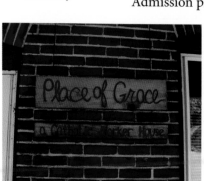

© Used with permission of Place of Grace; La Crosse, WI

Primary Sources

Dorothy Day: Change and Love

Dorothy Day (1897–1980) was one of the founders of the Catholic Worker movement, dedicated to promoting the principles of nonviolence and to helping the poor in a practical way. The first Catholic Worker house and soup kitchen was founded in New York City, and many others have since been established in our country and around the world. This quotation from Dorothy's writings gives us a glimpse into her vision of service:

We can, to a certain extent, change the world; we can work for the oasis, the little cell of joy and peace in a harried world. We can throw the pebble in the pond and be confident that its ever widening circle will reach around the world. We repeat, there is nothing we can do but love, and, dear God, please enlarge our hearts to love each other, to love our neighbor, to love our enemy as our friend. ("Love Is the Measure," in *By Little and By Little*, page 98)

marches each year, traveling to their state capital city or to Washington, DC, to do so. Let your voice be heard on these issues of national importance. Let the world taste a little of your salt! Let your light shine!

> **How do you already use your talents to benefit the Church and the world?**

Article 60: Discipleship in Daily Life

Discipleship is countercultural. Our culture so often says, "Me first!" But in the Church, we serve one another. Our culture so often says, "You are on your own." But in the Church, we are one in Jesus Christ. Our culture so often has many little rules: "Be this! Do this! Wear this! Act like this!" In the Church, we adhere to the Gospel, where Jesus gives us this rule: "Do to others whatever you would have them do to you" (Matthew 7:12).

Let's look at a typical school day to see practical ways you can live as a disciple of Jesus. Notice the opportunities to love others that arise in your own schedule.

Morning

Are you a morning person? For some people morning is the hardest part of the day, and they run late every morning. It is more difficult to be kind when you are tired and stressed because you are running late. Going to bed earlier can decrease your fatigue. Preparing ahead of time can also head off conflicts with your parents or siblings. Try to get things like books and lunch ready the night before. Use any down time, such as waiting for or riding a bus or sitting in traffic, to center yourself and to ask God's blessing on your day. Sometimes choosing love means creating the opportunity to have loving interactions with other people and avoiding situations in which you are not at your best.

School

Most of your days are spent dealing with people at school. The desire for good grades is laudable, but it

As a student, you can live as a disciple by striving to fully utilize the gift of intellect that God has given you and by acting with integrity in all your studies.

can also create temptation. Many students want to go on to specific colleges and universities, which can at times make grades seem more important than learning. Worrying excessively about grades can get you into trouble as a disciple. To keep your grade point average up, you might hear yourself asking, "Can I copy your homework?" Or you might be tempted to ask, "Can you get me the answers for the geometry test?"

© michaeljung/Shutterstock.com

If you experience this temptation, try to put your goals into proper perspective. More important than grades is who you are as a child of God. You are in

Pray It!

The Breastplate of Saint Patrick

Saint Patrick is believed to have composed the lengthy prayer known as "Saint Patrick's Breastplate" as he prepared to confront a pagan king. That's why it is called a "breastplate," or body armor, of prayer. Pray this excerpt from his prayer at various moments during your day:

Christ with me
Christ before me, Christ behind me
Christ in me
Christ beneath me, Christ above me
Christ on my right, Christ on my left
Christ when I lie down
Christ when I sit down
Christ when I arise
Christ in the heart of everyone who thinks of me
Christ in the mouth of everyone who speaks of me
Christ in every eye that sees me
Christ in every ear that hears me.

charge of the person you become. Ask God for help with schoolwork if it becomes challenging. Go to your teachers and parents for extra assistance rather than compromising your integrity.

Thoughts and Feelings

All day long, thoughts and feelings come into our consciousness—or, in some cases, dominate it. It is natural to be distracted by the guy or girl you met last weekend, a problem with a friend, tensions at home, or your least favorite class. Amid these distractions also come discouraging thoughts such as, "I am too fat or skinny, too tall or short, too stupid or smart."

Make a choice. Which thoughts or feelings will you take with you in your life? Will you accept negative thoughts? Will you internalize put-downs or rejections? Or will you discipline yourself by calmly turning your thoughts and feelings in a more positive direction or by praying and hearing the truth about you from God?

Evenings and Weekends

For some of you, the end of the day is a typical time for relaxing. Others may feel exhausted from work or from caring for younger brothers or sisters. All of you probably hear, "Please set the table, wash the dishes, mow the lawn, take the baby, or wash the car." Life in a household means having shared responsibilities and conflicting needs.

Perhaps you want to snap back at your parents when they ask you for help. Let it go, and consciously choose to be cooperative for God's sake. Sacrifice your time for God, and ask for his help if making this choice is difficult.

Take Responsibility for Your Faith Each Day

Being a disciple is up to you. The life of a disciple involves regular participation in the celebration of the Sacraments, with the Eucharist on Sundays being the

most important. Be sure to receive the Sacrament of
Penance and Reconciliation for forgiveness and strength.
Follow the liturgical seasons and pray with them, because
they reflect all aspects of the Christian life.

Take time to pray. Stop by the chapel at school for
a few minutes, or carve out some regular time at home
when you shut out all of the usual distractions. Read
Sacred Scripture, write to God in a journal, pray the
Rosary, thank God for the blessings he has given you, or
meditate on an important word such as *love* or *Jesus* or
peace.

A disciple is one who makes conscious choices to
follow Christ's example of treating others with care and
respect, spending time in prayer, being truthful, and

Faith in Action
The "Little Way" of Saint Thérèse of Lisieux

© Zvonimir Atletic / Shutterstock.com

Saint Thérèse of Lisieux (1873–1897) was born Thérèse Martin in Lisieux, France. She entered a Carmelite monastery when she was only fifteen. This was an unusual decision for such a young woman, but she appealed personally to the Pope for this privilege.

Thérèse believed she was called to love in the little ways of everyday life. She called this way of love her "little way to God." She was convinced that anyone could follow it, as she did, by being considerate of others, by not pouting when disappointed, by volunteering for the job no one else wants. Through her "little way" of love, a teenager showed the rest of the Church one way to take responsibility for our faith.

Thérèse died of tuberculosis at the age of twenty-four. But despite her short life, the example she set through her "little way" led to spiritual greatness. In 1997, during his papacy, Pope Saint John Paul II declared Saint Thérèse of Lisieux a Doctor of the Church in recognition of her spiritual wisdom.

letting God take the lead. And never forget that Christ is with you at all times.

> **What does it mean to take responsibility for your faith?**

Article 61: Empowered by the Holy Spirit

We conclude our study of the Church by looking at the Nicene Creed. First we profess faith in the Father, then in the Son, and then in the Holy Spirit. In the Creed, we profess our belief in the Church as part of the works of the Holy Spirit. The Holy Spirit is central to the life of the Church.

The Holy Spirit in the Church

Throughout this course, we have seen the Holy Spirit work in the Church in many ways. On the day of Pente-

Did You Know?

The Acts of the Apostles

© The Crosiers / Gene Plaisted, OSC

The Acts of the Apostles is sometimes called the Book of the Holy Spirit. It recounts the early days of the Church, the days after Pentecost, when the Apostles seemed to explode out of the upper room with the joyous message of Jesus' life, death, and Resurrection. The Acts of the Apostles recounts their travels, their troubles, and their triumphs in those first days of the Church.

The Acts of the Apostles was written by the Evangelist Luke. It is considered his "second volume," the first volume being his Gospel. Acts documents the Church's gradual expansion beyond the Jewish community to reach people of other places and other cultures. It ends with Saint Paul's imprisonment in Rome. Though this imprisonment almost foretells the unhappy ending of Paul's martyrdom, Luke sees it also as a triumph for the young Church: This little band of disciples, carrying the message of Jesus, has penetrated the very heart of the Roman Empire.

cost, when Jesus poured the Holy Spirit onto the Church, frightened Apostles turned into bold missionaries. Energized by the Holy Spirit, the Apostles then took to the road to spread the Good News of Jesus Christ. The Holy Spirit was at work in the hearts and minds of Saint Paul and the early Apostles, guiding them to proclaim Christ's work of salvation among the Jews and Gentiles and to build up the early Church.

The Holy Spirit enabled the early martyrs to willingly accept their impending death, and he led the bishops at the early Church Councils as they articulated the truths of the faith. The Holy Spirit set the hearts of countless saints on fire with love for God—such as Saint Francis of Assisi's total renunciation of possessions and power, the great wisdom of the rule written by Saint Benedict of Nursia, or Saint Thérèse of Lisieux's "little way" to holiness.

The Holy Spirit enlivens the mind as well as the heart. He was at work in the endeavors of great theologians such as Saint Augustine of Hippo and Saint Thomas Aquinas, who helped others to grow in their understanding of the faith through their writings.

The Holy Spirit worked through men and women in the Church, such as Pope Gregory the Great, and continues to work today through you.

© Bildarchiv Preussischer Kulturbesitz / Art Resource, NY

The Gifts of the Holy Spirit help us to honor God through our abilities and talents. Over the centuries, these gifts have resulted in magnificent expressions of praise to God, such as the grand cathedrals of the Middle Ages, the religious art of the Renaissance masters, and the timeless sacred music of Baroque composers.

The Church's history contains countless accounts of the working of the Holy Spirit in the lives of those who, like the Virgin Mary, said yes to God's invitation to work in their lives, to enable them to bring him greater glory.

Live with the End in Mind

Maybe you have already started looking at life after high school and the options that await you. You might be exploring colleges or trade schools and thinking about what you would like to do in your future. Many teens consider the financial implications of choosing one career over another. Some anticipate being parents and would like a career that is flexible to some extent. But most people don't really think beyond their career, maybe family, and perhaps retirement.

Your destination in life is actually not retirement, of course. Your destination is life in communion with the Trinity for all eternity. What does career planning look like in light of this destination? Here are some questions you might ask yourself:

- How is the Holy Spirit working in my life now? What talents and gifts have I been given?

- How is the Holy Spirit calling me to serve God and neighbor?

- Does fear keep me from pursuing interests because I hear that those interests don't make any money? (Fear does not come from the Holy Spirit, who instead brings faith, hope, and love.)

- Will the colleges I like help me to grow in faith, or will my faith constantly be challenged there? Do these colleges have a Catholic community on campus that I can belong to?

© Orhan Cam / Shutterstock.com

What are you planning to do after high school? You may choose to go to college, get a job, join the military, or do any number of other things. Whatever you are planning, it is important to remember that your ultimate goal is communion with God in Heaven.

- Is the career that interests me one that contributes to the well-being of other people, especially the poor?

Throughout your life you will have many significant decisions to make. With your final destination in mind, invite the Holy Spirit to help you in your decision making.

Start Now

The Holy Spirit is at work within you now, calling you to the Church, to Christ. Instead of drowning out the sound of the Holy Spirit, take time for silence, which can be an opportunity for the Holy Spirit to speak with you. Carve out some silence for him. Exciting possibilities await you!

Chapter Review

1. What does it mean to be salt for the earth and light for the world?

2. How did Pope Benedict XVI describe you as youth today?

3. What rule does Jesus give us about how to live?

4. What are some of the ways you can take responsibility for your faith?

5. Name two ways we have seen the Holy Spirit at work during this course.

6. What is your final destination in life?

Glossary

A

actual grace God's interventions and support for us in the everyday moments of our lives. Actual graces are important for conversion and for continuing growth in holiness. *(page 80)*

Age of Reason The age at which a person can be morally responsible. This is generally regarded to be the age of seven. *(page 218)*

animate To give life to. *(page 28)*

apostolate The Christian person's activity that fulfills the apostolic nature of the whole Church when he or she works to extend the Kingdom of Christ to the entire world. If your school shares the wisdom of its founder, its namesake, or the charism of the religious order that founded it, it is important to learn about this person or order and his or her charism, because as a graduate you will likely want to incorporate this charism into your own apostolate. *(page 119)*

apostolic To be founded on the Twelve Apostles. *(page 109)*

Apostolic Succession The uninterrupted passing on of apostolic preaching and authority from the Apostles directly to all bishops. It is accomplished through the laying on of hands when a bishop is ordained in the Sacrament of Holy Orders as instituted by Christ. The office of bishop is permanent, because at ordination a bishop is marked with an indelible, sacred character. *(page 63)*

aspiration A short prayer meant to be memorized and repeated throughout the day. The word comes from the Latin *aspirare*, "to breathe upon." In this way, we can heed Saint Paul's injunction to pray without ceasing and continually turn our thoughts toward God. *(page 224)*

Assumption of the Blessed Virgin Mary The dogma that recognizes that the body of the Blessed Virgin Mary was taken directly to Heaven after her life on earth had ended. *(page 37)*

B

bishop One who has received the fullness of the Sacrament of Holy Orders and is a successor to the Apostles. *(page 18)*

blasphemy Speaking, acting, or thinking about God, Jesus Christ, the Virgin Mary, or the saints in a way that is irreverent, mocking, or offensive. Blasphemy is a sin against the Second Commandment. *(page 47)*

Body of Christ A term that when capitalized designates Jesus' Body in the Eucharist, or the entire Church, which is also referred to as the Mystical Body of Christ. *(page 29)*

(religious) brother A layman in a religious order who has made permanent vows of poverty, chastity, and obedience. *(page 169)*

C

canonize The act by which the Church officially recognizes a deceased Catholic as a saint. *(page 102)*

catechesis, catechists Catechesis is the process by which Christians of all ages are taught the essentials of Christian doctrine and are formed as disciples of Christ. Catechists instruct others in Christian doctrine and for entry into the Church. *(page 140)*

Catholic Along with One, Holy, and Apostolic, Catholic is one of the four Marks of the Church. *Catholic* means "universal." The Church is Catholic in two senses. She is Catholic because Christ is present in her and has given her the fullness of the means of salvation and also because she reaches throughout the world to all people. *(page 93)*

celibacy The state or condition of those who have chosen or taken vows to remain unmarried in order to devote themselves entirely to the service of the Church and the Kingdom of God. *(page 139)*

charism A special gift or grace of the Holy Spirit given to an individual Christian or community, commonly for the benefit and building up of the entire Church. *(page 34))*

chastity The virtue by which people are able to successfully and healthfully integrate their sexuality into their total person; recognized as one of the fruits of the Holy Spirit. Also one of the vows of religious life. *(page 158)*

Church The term *Church* has three inseparable meanings: (1) the entire People of God throughout the world; (2) the diocese, which is also known as the local Church; (3) the assembly of believers gathered for the celebration of the liturgy, especially the Eucharist. In the Nicene Creed, the Church is recognized as One, Holy, Catholic, and Apostolic—traits that together are referred to as "Marks of the Church." *(page 11)*

College of Bishops The assembly of bishops, headed by the Pope, that holds the teaching authority and responsibility in the Church. *(page 96)*

collegial Characterized by the equal sharing of responsibility and authority among the members of a group who form a college. The bishops of the Church together with the Pope at their head form a college, which has full authority over the Church. *(page 134)*

Communion Refers to receiving the Body and Blood of Christ. In general, your companionship and union with Jesus and other baptized Christians in the Church. This union has its origin and high point in the celebration of the Eucharist. In this sense, the deepest vocation of the Church is Communion. *(page 24)*

consecrated life A state of life recognized by the Church in which a person publicly professes vows of poverty, chastity, and obedience. *(page 76)*

conversion A change of heart, turning away from sin and toward God. *(page 43)*

creed Based on the Latin *credo*, meaning, "I believe," a creed is an official presentation of the faith, usually prepared and presented by a council of the Church and used in the Church's liturgy. Two creeds occupy a special place in the Church's life: the Apostles' Creed and the Nicene Creed. *(page 59)*

D

diocese Also known as a "particular" or "local" Church, the regional community of believers, who commonly gather in parishes, under the leadership of a bishop. At times, a diocese is determined not on the basis of geography but on the basis of language or rite. *(page 11)*

discernment From a Latin word meaning "to separate or to distinguish between," the practice of listening for God's call in our lives and distinguishing between good and bad choices. *(page 138)*

doctrine An official, authoritative teaching of the Church based on the Revelation of God. *(page 37)*

dogma Teachings recognized as central to Church teaching, defined by the Magisterium and considered definitive and authoritative. *(page 64)*

domestic church A name for the first and most fundamental community of faith: the family. *(page 128)*

E

ecclesial Of or relating to a church. *(page 114)*

Ecumenical Council A gathering of the Church's bishops from around the world convened by the Pope or approved by him to address pressing issues in the Church. *(page 37)*

ecumenism The movement to restore unity among all Christians, the unity to which the Church is called by the Holy Spirit. *(page 69)*

episcopal Of or relating to a bishop. *(page 116)*

eremitic Relating to the life of a hermit, characterized by self-denial and solitude. *(page 173)*

evangelical counsels The call to go beyond the minimum rules of life required by God (such as the Ten Commandments and the Precepts of the Church) and strive for spiritual perfection through a life marked by a commitment to chastity, poverty, and obedience. *(page 158)*

evangelization, evangelist The proclamation of the Good News of Jesus Christ through words and witness. An evangelist is one who actively works to spread the Gospel message of salvation. *(page 27)*

excommunication A severe penalty that results from grave sin against Church law. The penalty is either imposed by a Church official or happens automatically as a result of the offense. An excommunicated person is not permitted to celebrate or receive the Sacraments. *(page 65)*

F

Fathers of the Church (Church Fathers) During the early centuries of the Church, those teachers whose writings extended the Tradition of the Apostles and who continue to be important for the Church's teachings. *(page 14)*

fiat Latin for "let it be done." *(page 88)*

foreshadow To represent or prefigure a person before his or her life or an event before it occurs. *(page 14)*

G

Gentile A non-Jewish person. In Sacred Scripture, the Gentiles were the uncircumcised, those who did not honor the God of the Torah. Saint Paul and other evangelists reached out to the Gentiles, baptizing them into the family of God. *(page 24)*

grace The free and undeserved gift that God gives us to empower us to respond to his call and to live as his adopted sons and daughters. Grace restores our loving communion with the Holy Trinity, lost through sin. *(page 18)*

H

Hellenistic Of or relating to Greek history, culture, or art after Alexander the Great. *(page 43)*

heresy The conscious and deliberate rejection of a truth of the faith. *(page 64)*

hermit A person who lives a solitary life in order to commit himself or herself more fully to prayer and in some cases to be completely free for service to others. *(page 168)*

Holy Orders, Sacrament of The Sacrament by which baptized men are ordained for permanent ministry in the Church as bishops, priests, or deacons. *(page 63)*

Holy See This term is a translation of the Latin *sancta sedes*, which literally means "holy seat." The word *see* refers to a diocese or seat of a bishop. The Holy See is the seat of the central administration of the whole Church, under the leadership of the Pope, the Bishop of Rome. *(page 127)*

I

icon From a Greek word meaning "likeness," a sacred image of Christ, Mary, or the saints, especially in the artwork of the Eastern Churches. *(page 104)*

iconostasis A screen or partition with doors and tiers of icons that separates the bema, the raised part of the church with the altar, from the nave, the main part of the church, in Eastern Churches. *(page 104)*

Incarnation From the Latin, meaning "to become flesh," referring to the mystery of Jesus Christ, the Divine Son of God, becoming man. In the Incarnation, Jesus Christ became truly man while remaining truly God. *(page 17)*

indefectibility of the Church The Church's remaining uncorrupted and faithful to Christ's teachings, until the end of human history. *(page 149)*

indulgence The means by which the Church takes away the punishment that a person would receive in Purgatory. *(page 66)*

infallibility The gift given by the Holy Spirit to the Church whereby the pastors of the Church, the Pope and the bishops in union with him, can definitively proclaim a doctrine of faith and morals without error. *(page 36)*

institute An organization devoted to a common cause. Religious orders are a type of religious institute. *(page 168)*

intercession A prayer on behalf of another person or group. *(page 33)*

K

Kingdom of God The culmination or goal of God's plan of salvation, the Kingdom of God is announced by the Gospel and present in Jesus Christ. The Kingdom is the reign or rule of God over the hearts of people and, as a consequence of that, the development of a new social order based on unconditional love. The fullness of God's Kingdom will not be realized until the end of time. Also called the Reign of God or the Kingdom of Heaven. *(page 13)*

L

Latin Church That part of the Catholic Church that follows the disciplines and teachings of the Diocese of Rome, especially the liturgical traditions. It is called the Latin Church because Latin has been the official language since the fourth century. The majority of the world's Catholics belong to the Latin Church. *(page 103)*

laypeople (laity) All members of the Church with the exception of those who are ordained as bishops, priests, or deacons. The laity share in Christ's role as priest, prophet, and king, witnessing to God's love and power in the world. *(page 119)*

Liturgical Year The Church's annual cycle of feasts and seasons that celebrate the events and mysteries of Christ's birth, life, death, Resurrection, and Ascension, and forms the context for the Church's worship. *(page 199)*

liturgy The Church's official, public, communal prayer. It is God's work, in which the People of God participate. The Church's most important liturgy is the Eucharist, or the Mass. *(page 11)*

M

Marks of the Church The four essential features or characteristics of the Church: One, Holy, Catholic (universal), and Apostolic. *(page 55)*

martyr A person who suffers death because of his or her beliefs. The Church has canonized many Christian martyrs as saints. *(page 48)*

ministry Based on a word for "service," a way of caring for and serving others and helping the Church to fulfill her mission. Ministry refers to the work of sanctification performed by those in Holy Orders through the preaching of God's Word and the celebration of the Sacraments. It also refers to the work of the laity in living out their baptismal call to mission through lay ministries, such as that of lector or catechist. *(page 93)*

monk A male member of a religious community who lives a life of prayer and work according to a specific rule of life, such as the rule of Saint Benedict. *(page 169)*

mysterium The hidden reality of God's plan of salvation. *(page 193)*

mystical Having a spiritual meaning or reality that is neither apparent to the senses nor obvious to the intelligence; the visible sign of the hidden reality of salvation. *(page 187)*

N

Nicene Creed The formal statement or profession of Christian belief originally formulated at the Council of Nicaea in 325 and amplified at the Council of Constantinople in 381. *(page 59)*

O

Original Sin From the Latin *origo*, meaning "beginning" or "birth." The term has two meanings: (1) the sin of the first human beings, who disobeyed God's command by choosing to follow their own will and thus lost their original holiness and became subject to death, (2) the fallen state of human nature that affects every person born into the world, except Jesus and Mary. *(page 87)*

P

Paschal Mystery The work of salvation accomplished by Jesus Christ mainly through his Passion, death, Resurrection, and Ascension. *(page 199)*

Pentecost The fiftieth day following Easter, which commemorates the descent of the Holy Spirit on the early Apostles and disciples. *(page 22)*

petition A prayer form in which one asks God for help and forgiveness. *(page 33)*

presbytery, presbyterate The name given to priests as a group, especially in a diocese; based on the Greek word *presbyter*, which means "elder." *(page 135)*

province A grouping of two or more dioceses with an archbishop as its head. *(page 132)*

Purgatory A state of final purification or cleansing, which one may need to enter following death and before entering Heaven. *(page 83)*

R

(religious) brother A layman in a religious order who has made permanent vows of poverty, chastity, and obedience. *(page 169)*

(religious) sister A laywoman in a religious order who has made permanent vows of poverty, chastity, and obedience. *(page 169)*

S

sacramental grace The gifts proper to each of the Seven Sacraments. *(page 80)*

sacramentum The visible sign of the hidden reality of salvation. *(page 193)*

Sacred Chrism Perfumed olive oil consecrated by the bishop that is used for anointing in the Sacraments of Baptism, Confirmation, and Holy Orders. *(page 218)*

Sacred Tradition *Tradition* comes from the Latin *tradere*, meaning "to hand on." Sacred Tradition refers to the process of passing on the Gospel message. It began with the oral communication of the Gospel by the Apostles, was written down in Sacred Scripture, and is interpreted by the Magisterium under the guidance of the Holy Spirit. *(page 30)*

sanctify To make holy; sanctification is the process of responding to God's grace and becoming closer to God. *(page 28)*

sanctifying grace The grace that heals our human nature wounded by sin and restores us to friendship with God by giving us a share in the divine life of the Trinity. It is a supernatural gift of God, infused into our souls by the Holy Spirit, that continues the work of making us holy. *(page 80)*

schism A major break that causes division. A schism in the Church is caused by the refusal to submit to the Pope or to be in communion with the Church's members. *(page 64)*

secular Relating to worldly concerns rather than religion. *(page 173)*

T

theologian One who engages in the academic discipline of theology, or "the study of God," in an effort to understand, interpret, and order our experience of God and Christian faith. *(page 71)*

Theology of the Body The name given to Pope Saint John Paul II's teachings on the human body and sexuality delivered during his papacy via 129 short lectures between September 1979 and November 1984. *(page 186)*

Theotokos A Greek title for Mary meaning "God bearer." *(page 89)*

Transubstantiation In the Sacrament of the Eucharist, this is the name given to the action of changing the bread and wine into the Body and Blood of Jesus Christ. *(page 183)*

Trinitarian Of or relating to the Trinity or the doctrine of the Trinity. *(page 41)*

Trinity From the Latin *trinus*, meaning "threefold," referring to the central mystery of the Christian faith that God exists as a communion of three distinct and interrelated divine Persons: Father, Son, and Holy Spirit. The doctrine of the Trinity is a mystery that is inaccessible to human reason alone and is known through Divine Revelation only. *(page 22)*

V

Vatican Council II The Ecumenical or general Council of the Roman Catholic Church that Pope Saint John XXIII (1958–1963) convened as Pope in 1962 and that continued under Pope Venerable Paul VI (1963–1978) until 1965. *(page 56)*

Vicar of Christ A title for the Pope, identifying his role as Christ's human representative on earth. *(page 58)*

virtue A habitual and firm disposition to do good. *(page 29)*

vocation A call from God to all members of the Church to embrace a life of holiness. Specifically, it refers to a call to live the holy life as an ordained minister, as a vowed religious (sister or brother), or in a Christian marriage. Single life that involves a personal consecration or commitment to a permanent, celibate gift of self to God and one's neighbor is also a vocational state. *(page 76)*

vow A free and conscious commitment made to other persons (as in Marriage), to the Church, or to God. *(page 139)*

Index

P

Pachomius, 169
Palestine, 184
Parable of the Weeds, 77–78
parents, 167–168, 217–218
parishes, 11, 128, 136, 227–228
Paschal Mystery, 55–56, 86–87, 199
Passion, 55, 153–154
Pastoral Constitution on the Church in the Modern World, 147, 149, 204–205
Patrick, 236
Paul (Saul)
 apostolic authority of, 109–111
 background, 43
 Baptism, 29
 Body of Christ, 183, 185
 bride/bridegroom imagery, 185
 calling of, 217
 charisms, 34
 Church of Rome authority, 96
 conversion of, 43
 discipleship, 18
 diversity within unity, 56, 101–102
 Eucharist as unity symbol, 62
 Holy Spirit and lifestyle choices, 32
 Holy Spirit and prayer, 33
 intercessory prayers on feast of, 118
 laying on of hands, 116
 leadership charisms, 36
 martyrdom of, 49, 129, 239
 missionary travels of, 41, 42
 prayer instruction, 171, 224–225
 at Stephen's martyrdom, 19
 teaching audiences and methods, 43–44
 temple imagery, 186
Paulist Fathers, 174
Paul VI, 56, 70, 139, 142–143, 151
peace, 98, 100, 105, 184
Penance and Reconciliation, 97, 136, 137, 222–223, 238
Pentecost, 22, 23, 24–29, 239–240
People of God, 18, 97–101, 105, 179–181, 200
perfection, 24, 76, 79, 158, 167
persecution, 39, 46–50, 131. *See also* martyrdom

Peter
 Apostolic mission and leadership, 24–25, 111–112, 117
 bishops ordained by, 114
 calling of, 216
 Church of Rome authority due to, 96
 intercessory prayers on feast of, 118
 leadership appointments, 10, 19, 57, 72, 96, 108, 117
 martyrdom of, 48–49, 129
 power of Christ claims, 111
 successors to, 128–129
petition prayers, 182
Piety, 34, 35
pilgrimages, 105
Pius IX, 203
Pius XII, 37, 151, 174
politics, 166, 205–206, 207, 208, 234–235
Polycarp of Smyrna, 47
Pontifical Biblical Commission, 126
Pontifical Council for Promoting Christian Unity, 71
poor people, 110, 170, 206, 234. *See also* poverty
Popes
 assemblies headed by, 38, 96
 authority of, 69, 96, 108, 151
 charisms of, 37
 Church structure and origins of, 18–20
 leadership roles and descriptions, 58, 117–118, 126, 128–130, 132
 obedience to, 160–161
 praying for, 129
 seat of, 96
 sin and, 149
 as unity symbol, 57–58, 130
Posadas, Las, 105
poverty, 23, 76, 158–159, 168. See also poor people
praise, prayers of, 33
prayer(s)
 aspirations, 224
 bedtime, 162
 for Body of Christ, 193
 for Christian unity, 71
 for Church hierarchy, 129
 for deacons, 142

Acknowledgments

The scriptural quotations in this book are from the *New American Bible, revised edition* © 2010, 1991, 1986, and 1970 by the Confraternity of Christian Doctrine, Washington, D.C. All Rights Reserved. No part of this work may be reproduced or transmitted in any form or by any means, electronic or mechanical, including photocopying, recording, or by any information storage and retrieval system, without permission in writing from the copyright owner.

The excerpts marked *Catechism* and *CCC* are from the English translation of the *Catechism of the Catholic Church* for use in the United States of America, second edition. Copyright © 1994 by the United States Catholic Conference, Inc.— Libreria Editrice Vaticana (LEV). English translation of the *Catechism of the Catholic Church: Modifications from the Editio Typica* copyright © 1997 by the United States Catholic Conference, Inc.—LEV.

The excerpts on pages 16, 99, and 101 are from *Declaration on the Relation of the Church to Non-Christian Religions* (*Nostra Aetate*, 1965), numbers 4, 4, and 2, respectively, at *www.vatican.va/archivehist_councils /ii_vatican_council/documents/vat-ii_decl_19651028_nostra-aetate_ en.html*. Copyright © LEV.

The Pentecost Sequence prayer on page 27 is from *Lectionary for Mass for Use in the Dioceses of the United States of America*, second typical edition, by the United States Conference of Catholic Bishops (USCCB) (New Jersey: Catholic Book Publishing Company, 1998), volume I, page 483. Copyright © 2001, 1998, 1992, 1986 Confraternity of Christian Doctrine (CCD), Washington, D.C. Used with permission of the CCD, Washington, D.C. No portion of this text may be reproduced by any means without permission in writing from the copyright owner.

The information about the Sisters of the Holy Spirit and Mary Immaculate on page 36 is from the Healy-Murphy Center website, at *www.healymurphy.org/index.cfm?fuseaction=about_History*.

The excerpt on page 37 is from "Homily of His Holiness Benedict XVI," during the 23rd World Youth Day 2008, at *www.vatican.va/holy_father /benedict_xvi/ homilies/2008/documents/hf_ben-xvi_hom_20080720_ xxiii-wyd_en.html*. Copyright © 2008 LEV.

The excerpt on page 40 and the quotations on pages 208 , 209, and 210 are from *Redemptoris Missio: On the Permanent Validity of the Church's Missionary Mandate*, numbers 92, 33, 33, and 63, respectively, at *www.vatican.va/holy_father/john_paul_ii/encyclicals/documents/hf_jp-ii_ enc_07121990_redemptoris-missio_ en.html*. Copyright © LEV.

The words and prayers from the Mass on pages 52, 59, 60 and 86 are from the English translation of *The Roman Missal* © 2010, International Commission on English in the Liturgy Corporation (ICEL) (Washington, DC: USCCB, 2011), pages 527, 528, 527, 649, and 645, respectively. Copyright © 2011 USCCB. All rights reserved. Used with permission of the ICEL. Published with the approval of the Committee on Divine Worship, USCCB.

The excerpt on page 56 and the quotations on pages 63 (photo caption) and 194 are from *Dogmatic Constitution on the Church* (*Lumen Gentium*, 1964), numbers 13, 23, and 48, at *www.vatican.va/archive/hist_ councils/ii_vatican_council/documents/ vat-ii_const_19641121_lumen- gentium_en.html*. Copyright © LEV.

The quotations on pages 58 and 63 are from *Ut Unum Sint: On Commitment to Ecumenism*, numbers 88 and 84, at *www.vatican.va /holy_father/john_paul_ii/encyclicals/documents/hf_jp-ii_enc_25051995 _ut-unum-sint_en.html*. Copyright © LEV.

The excerpt on page 61 is from "Young Adults and Prayer at Taizé," at *www. taize.fr/en_article3148.html*.

The quotations on page 69 from *Decree on Ecumenism* (*Unitatis Redintegratio*, 1964), numbers 3 and 22; the quotation on page 99 from *Declaration on the Relation of the Church to Non-Christian Religions* (*Nostra Aetate*, 1965), number 4; and the quotations on pages 149 , 204, and 204–205 from *Pastoral Constitution on the Church in the Modern World* (*Gaudium et Spes*, 1965), numbers 43, 4, and 58, are from *Vatican Council II: Constitutions, Decrees, Declarations*, Austin Flannery, general editor (Northport, NY: Costello Publishing Company, 1996), pages 502, 520, 573, 213, 234, and 165, respectively. Copyright © 1996 by Reverend Austin Flannery, OP.

The quotation by Pope John Paul II on page 57 is from "One Passes through Taizé as One Passes Close to a Spring of Water," at *www.taize.fr /en_article6718.html*.

The quotation by Pope Benedict XVI on page 57 is from "Celebration of the 70th Anniversary of Taizé-Echoes," at *www.taize.fr /en_article11166.html*.

The prayer on page 71 is from "Resources for the Week of Prayer for Christian Unity, and Throughout the Year 2009," Prayer for Day

7, at *www.vatican.va/roman_curia/pontifical_councils/chrstuni/weeks-prayer-doc/rc_pc_chrstuni_doc_20080630_ week-prayer-2009_en.html*. Copyright © LEV.

The excerpt on page 84 is from "Reflection by Cardinal José Saraiva Martins," number 2, at *www.vatican.va/roman_curia/congregationscsaints/documents/rc_con_csaints_doc_20030315_martins-saints_en.html*. Copyright © LEV.

The excerpt on page 94 is from *Catechetical Lectures 18.23*, at *www.newadvent.org/fathers/310118.htm*.

The excerpt on page 95 is from "Exposition of the Apostles' Creed," by Thomas Aquinas, as quoted in *The Catholicity of the Church*, by Avery Dulles (Oxford: Oxford University Press, 1985), page 181.

The quotation from Saint Irenaeus on page 96 is from *Against Heresies*, Book III, Chapter 3, number 2, at *www.newadvent.org/fathers/013303.htm*.

The prayer on page 100 is from "Day of Prayer for Peace in the World, January 24, 2002," at *www.vatican.va/news_services/liturgy/documents/ns_lit_doc_20020124_ assisi-impegno_it.html*. Copyright © LEV.

The words of Saint Josephine Bakhita on page 103 are found on the National Black Catholic Congress website, at *congress.org/black-catholics/black-saints-saintjosephine-bakhita.asp*.

The excerpt from Saint Clement on page 114 is quoted from "To the Corinthians," numbers 42 and 44, in *The Apostolic Fathers*, volume one, English translation by Kirsopp Lake (Cambridge, MA: Harvard University Press, 1912), pages 79, 81, and 85, respectively.

The prayer on page 118 is from the English translation of the Intercessions from *The Liturgy of the Hours*, © 1973, 1974, 1975 ICEL, prepared by the ICEL (New York: Catholic Book Publishing Company, 1975), volume III page 1502. Copyright © 1976 by the Catholic Book Publishing Company, New York. Used with permission of the ICEL.

The quotations from the letters of Ignatius of Antioch on page 135 are from *The Apostolic Fathers*, edited and translated by Bart D. Ehrman (Cambridge, MA: Harvard University Press, 2003), pages 247, 225, and 247, respectively. Copyright © 2003 by the President and Fellows of Harvard College.

The statistics on page 142 are from "A Portrait of the Permanent Diaconate: A Study for the U.S. Conference of Catholic Bishops 2012–2013," by the Center for Applied Research in the Apostolate, Georgetown University, Washington, D.C., 2013.

The prayer for deacons on page 142 and the excerpt on celibacy on page 160 are from the English translation of *Rites of Ordination of a Bishop, of Priests, and of Deacons,* Second Typical Edition © 2000, 2002, ICEL, numbers 277 and 267, respectively (Washington, DC: USCCB, 2003). Copyright © 2003 USCCB. All rights reserved. Used with permission of the ICEL. Published with the approval of the Committee on Divine Worship, USCCB.

The list of activities on page 143 is adapted from *The Sacred Order of Deacons (Sacrum Diaconatus Ordinem),* number 26, at *www.vatican.va /holy_father/paul_vi/motu_proprio/documents/hf_p-vi_motuproprio _19670618_sacrum-diaconatus_en.html.* Copyright © LEV.

The theological inquiry quotation and the excerpt on page 147 are from *Pastoral Constitution on the Church in the Modern World (Gaudium et Spes,* 1965), numbers 62 and 1, at *www.vatican.va/archive/histcouncils /ii_vatican_council/documents/vat-ii_cons_19651207_gaudium-et-spesen .html.* Copyright © LEV.

The contemplation and study quotation on page 147–148 is from *Dogmatic Constitution on Divine Revelation (Dei Verbum,* 1965), number 8, at *www.vatican.va/archive/ hist_councils/ii_vatican_council/documents /vat-ii_const_19651118_dei-verbum_en.html.* Copyright © LEV.

The quotation from the First Vatican Council on page 149 is quoted from "The Bishop of Rome Is Peter's Successor," at *www.vatican.vaholy _father/john_paul_ii/ audiences/alpha/data/aud19930127en.html.* Copyright © LEV.

The quotation from the Council of Chalcedon on page 152 is quoted from *Christ, the Eternal King (Sempiternus Rex Christus), Encyclical of Pope Pius XII on the Council of Chalcedon,* number 23, at *www.vatican .va/holy_father/pius_xii/encyclicals/documents/hf_p-xii_enc_08091951 _sempiternus-rex-christus_en.html.* Copyright © LEV.

The prayer on page 155 is from the English translation of *The Roman Missal* © 1973, ICEL (New York: Catholic Book Publishing, 1985), page 152. Illustrations and arrangement © 1985–1974 Catholic Book Publishing Company Used with permission of the ICEL. Published with the approval of the Committee on Divine Worship, USCCB.

The prayer honoring Saint Gianna Molla on page 167 is from *www.saintgianna.org/ prayersofgianna.htm.* Used with permission of the Society of Saint Gianna Beretta Molla.

The story on page 172 is from *The Desert Fathers: Sayings of the Early Christian Monks,* translated by Benedicta Ward (London: Penguin Books, 2003), page 165. Copyright © 2003 by Benedicta Ward.

The excerpt by Pope Francis on page 218 is from "Homily of Pope Francis: Celebration of Palm Sunday of the Passion of Our Lord," number 3, at *www.vatican.va/holy_father/francesco/homilies/2013 /documents/papa-francesco_20130324_palme_en.html*. Copyright © 2013 LEV.

The excerpt and quotation on page 232 are from "Meeting with Youth: Address of His Holiness Benedict XVI," number 7, during an apostolic journey to Brazil, at *www.vatican.va/holy_father/benedict_xvi /speeches/2007/may/documents/hf_ben-xvi_spe_20070510_youth-brazil _en.html*. Copyright © 2007 by LEV.

The excerpt on page 234 is from "Love Is the Measure," by Dorothy Day, originally published in *The Catholic Worker*, June 1946, and reprinted in *By Little and By Little: The Selected Writings of Dorothy Day*, edited by Robert Ellsberg (New York: Alfred A. Knopf, 1983), page 98. Copyright © 1983 by Robert Ellsberg and Tamar Hennessy.

To view copyright terms and conditions for Internet materials cited here, log on to the home pages for the referenced websites.

During this book's preparation, all citations, facts, figures, names, addresses, telephone numbers, Internet URLs, and other pieces of information cited within were verified for accuracy. The authors and Saint Mary's Press staff have made every attempt to reference current and valid sources, but we cannot guarantee the content of any source, and we are not responsible for any changes that may have occurred since our verification. If you find an error in, or have a question or concern about, any of the information or sources listed within, please contact Saint Mary's Press.

Endnotes Cited in Quotations from the *Catechism of the Catholic Church*, Second Edition

Chapter 3
1. *Martyrium Polycarpi* 14, 2–3: J. P. Migne, ed., Patrologia Graeca (Paris, 1857–1866) 5, 1040; Sources Chrétiennes (Paris: 1942–) 10, 228.
2. Saint Ignatius of Antioch, *Ad Rom.* 6, 1–2: Sources Chrétiennes (Paris: 1942–) 10, 114.
3. Tertullian, *Apol.* 50, 13: J. P. Migne, ed., Patrologia Latina (Paris: 1841–1855) 1, 603.

Chapter 5
1. Cf. *Matthew* 13:24–30.

Chapter 7
1. *Dei Verbum* 8 § 1.

Chapter 14

1. *Dei Verbum* 25; cf. *Philippians* 3:8 and Saint Jerome, *Commentariorum in Isaiam libri xviii* prol.: J. P. Migne, ed., Patrologia Latina Supplement (Paris, 1841–1855) 24, 17b.